AF758471

Police Abuse and Reform in America

Other books in the Contemporary Debates series:

Consumer Rights and Protections
Media Bias
American Foreign Policy
Women's Equality in America
Human Trafficking
Political Control of America's Courts
American National Debt
Energy Resources
Vaccination
Sexual Assault and Harassment in America
LGBTQ Life in America
Public and Private Education in America
Guns in America
Race Relations in America
Voting in America

Police Abuse and Reform in America

Examining the Facts

James J. Nolan, Howard Ryan, and Mackenzie Freeman

BLOOMSBURY ACADEMIC
NEW YORK • LONDON • OXFORD • NEW DELHI • SYDNEY

BLOOMSBURY ACADEMIC
Bloomsbury Publishing Inc, 1385 Broadway, New York, NY 10018, USA
Bloomsbury Publishing Plc, 50 Bedford Square, London, WC1B 3DP, UK
Bloomsbury Publishing Ireland, 29 Earlsfort Terrace, Dublin 2, D02 AY28, Ireland

BLOOMSBURY, BLOOMSBURY ACADEMIC and the Diana logo are trademarks of Bloomsbury Publishing Plc

First published in the United States of America 2025

Copyright © Bloomsbury Publishing Inc, 2025

For legal purposes the Acknowledgments on p. xv constitute an extension of this copyright page.

Cover image: Megan Jelinger/SOPA Images/LightRocket via Getty Images

All rights reserved. No part of this publication may be: i) reproduced or transmitted in any form, electronic or mechanical, including photocopying, recording or by means of any information storage or retrieval system without prior permission in writing from the publishers; or ii) used or reproduced in any way for the training, development or operation of artificial intelligence (AI) technologies, including generative AI technologies. The rights holders expressly reserve this publication from the text and data mining exception as per Article 4(3) of the Digital Single Market Directive (EU) 2019/790.

Bloomsbury Publishing Inc does not have any control over, or responsibility for, any third-party websites referred to or in this book. All internet addresses given in this book were correct at the time of going to press. The author and publisher regret any inconvenience caused if addresses have changed or sites have ceased to exist, but can accept no responsibility for any such changes.

A catalog record for this book is available from the Library of Congress.

ISBN: HB: 978-1-4408-8134-3
ePDF: 979-8-2161-8299-3
eBook: 978-1-4408-8135-0

Series: Contemporary Debates

Typeset by Newgen KnowledgeWorks Pvt. Ltd., Chennai, India
Printed and bound in the United States of America

For product safety related questions contact productsafety@bloomsbury.com.

To find out more about our authors and books visit www.bloomsbury.com and sign up for our newsletters.

This book is dedicated to
Barbara Ann Folger Nolan
April 4, 1930–June 22, 2024.
A matriarch of blue bloods.

Contents

How to Use This Book

Police Abuse and Reform in America: Examining the Facts is the next volume in ABC-CLIO's new Contemporary Debates reference series. Each title in this series, which is intended for use by high-school and undergraduate students as well as members of the general public, examines the veracity of controversial claims or beliefs surrounding a major political and cultural issue in the United States. The purpose of the series is to give readers a clear and unbiased understanding of current issues by informing them about falsehoods, half-truths, and misconceptions—and confirming the factual validity of other assertions—that have gained traction in America's political and cultural discourse. Ultimately, this series has been crafted to give readers the tools for a fuller understanding of controversial issues, policies, and laws that occupy center stage in American life and politics.

Each volume in this series identifies thirty to forty questions swirling about the larger topic under discussion. These questions are examined in individualized entries, which are in turn arranged in broad subject chapters that cover certain aspects of the issue being examined, for example, history of concern about the issue, potential economic or social impact, findings of latest scholarly research, and so on.

Each chapter features approximately two to ten individual entries. Each entry begins by stating an important or well-known **Question** about the issue being studied—for example, "Can excessive and deadly force in American policing be explained by rising violence against officers?" or "Can evidence-based policing, which guided the Obama task force, produce a systemic remedy to police abuse?"

The entry then provides a concise and objective one- or two-paragraph **Answer** to the featured question, followed by a more comprehensive, detailed explanation of **The Facts**. This latter portion of each entry uses quantifiable, evidence-based information from respected sources to fully address each question and provide readers with the information they need to be informed citizens. Importantly, entries will also acknowledge instances in which conflicting data exist or data are incomplete. Finally, each entry concludes with a **Further Reading** section, providing users with information on other important or influential resources.

The ultimate purpose of every book in the Contemporary Debates series is to reject "false equivalence," in which demonstrably false beliefs or statements are given the same exposure and credence as the facts; to puncture myths that diminish our understanding of important policies and positions; to provide needed context for misleading statements and claims; and to confirm the factual accuracy of other assertions. In other words, volumes in this series are being crafted to clear the air surrounding some of the most contentious and misunderstood issues of our time—not just add another layer of obfuscation and uncertainty to the debate.

Preface

Howard Ryan, Mackenzie Freeman, and I have taken a critical look at the institution of American policing, while paying particular attention to the issues of abuse and reform. I know firsthand what it is like to be a police officer, and how hard it is to listen to the criticisms from outside the profession. In my experience, most police officers want to do the right things. They are committed to reducing crime and violence in communities. They want to find solutions, but as law enforcement officers, their options are limited.

I know this because my professional career began as a police officer in Wilmington, Delaware. In thirteen years at that department, I worked in a variety of assignments including uniformed patrol division and the drug, organized crime, and vice unit. This was in the 1980s and 1990s during the heaviest fighting in the war on drugs. As frontline law enforcement officers, we did our best to disrupt illegal drug markets and get guns off the streets. This involved many hours of surveillance, early morning and late evening drug raids, long and tedious wiretap investigations, hundreds of undercover drug buys, and thousands of arrests for selling and possessing drugs.

The Delaware state legislature was caught up in the fervor of the drug war too. It had passed trafficking and mandatory minimum sentencing statutes intending to deter people from illegal drugs. This was great for cops, because it made it easier for us to convert arrestees into confidential informants. When we made arrests, we would tack on multiple felony charges, making it hard for arrestees not to snitch. Then we would let the offenders plead to one or two felonies, instead of going to court for six or seven, if they helped us make undercover buys and arrest more people. None of these strategies changed things in communities, but they did help officers achieve status in the department as good cops. Good cops were aggressive law enforcers. Locking up "bad guys" was simply the right thing to do. And we were rewarded for doing it.

In the 1990s, I was selected to attend the prestigious FBI National Academy. I was also promoted to sergeant and then lieutenant. In addition, I was appointed to lead the department's "Weed and Seed" strategy. Operation Weed and Seed was a US Department of Justice-funded multiagency approach to violent crime (USDOJ 2004). The idea was to have law enforcement agencies and prosecutors weed out "criminals" from designated neighborhoods, so that seeds of prevention, intervention, treatment, and revitalization might grow. Wilmington was one of the first sixteen sites in the nation selected for the Weed and Seed strategy. My unit's task was to work with communities to prepare for seeding. As the police supervisor for the project, it was my first experience thinking about police abuse and reform differently.

Before Weed and Seed, I believed the root cause of crime was the criminal who must be arrested and locked away, both as a deterrent and to keep good people safe. When aggressive law enforcement didn't work, I blamed liberal prosecutors, judges, and corrections officials for letting dangerous people go free. Further, I saw emerging technologies as the way to improve the efficacy of policing. However, while sitting in kitchens and talking with residents in the so-called dangerous Weed and Seed neighborhoods, my perceptions changed. The conditions in these local places made many of the criminal behaviors logical. This is why crime rates were high, not because more criminals happened to live there.

During the Weed and Seed project, my unit worked together with residents to change these conditions. For example, we stood together on the drug corners three or four nights a week to disrupt drug sales. We also opened three police mini-stations in community centers on the city's West Side so that residents could talk with us about their problems without calling 911. We worked with residents at these community centers to access city and state resources and to connect with neighbors willing to help resolve neighborhood problems peacefully. We played basketball and softball with the young people at these centers and really got to know all the residents in the neighborhood very well.

However, the task of helping communities solve chronic problems by strengthening relationships and easing access to resources was beyond what the police department was willing to do. There were simply too few police resources committed to the project. And it was difficult to compete for more because the metrics that count in this regard—the number of lockups, and guns and drugs seized— was not what the community wanted or needed. Instead, they wanted help in solving many of the chronic problems that made life in these neighborhoods intolerable. These conditions were the breeding ground for crime and violence, and the police were in the best position to help alleviate them.

It wasn't long before the officers assigned with me to the Weed and Seed unit could see the writing on the wall. For police officers in a law enforcement profession, Weed and Seed was no way to get ahead. The project died a slow death in the department. It could not sustain momentum because it did not align with law enforcement priorities. After spending millions of dollars and countless hours working with residents in communities, nothing improved. Drug dealing continued and the neighborhoods remained unsafe.

Inside the department, Weed and Seed and similar "community policing" initiatives were considered a joke by many officers. It was not "real" police work. The real cops were on SWAT and working in plain clothes, making undercover drug buys, kicking in doors, and jumping out on street corners to disrupt open-air drug markets. They were making tons of lockups, seizing vehicles and other assets. This was exciting work that benefited the police way more than it did the community. The "real police" were also disrupting the social fabric of communities by sending informants into tight-knit groups to betray families and friends. From inside the department, community policing was only valuable if it helped officers make connections with residents who might eventually inform on people involved in crime. This was a dilemma for officers who wanted a successful police career—and to be recognized by peers as a good cop—and yet saw aggressive law enforcement as counterproductive and discriminatory.

Most police officers I worked with at the Wilmington Police Department thought like I did before the Weed and Seed project. We were the thin blue line protecting good people from bad. It is simply too hard to see the fallacy of this from inside the profession, especially when physically and emotionally disconnected from the community.

Howard, Mackenzie, and I admire the women and men who serve as police officers. In this book, our critique is of the American police institution and not the people who wear the badge. This is important because reforms that make policing more effective and safer for all concerned will never happen without the cops.

James J. Nolan

Further Reading

United States Department of Justice (USDOJ). 2004. *The Weed and Seed Strategy.* Washington, DC. https://www.ojp.gov/pdffiles1/207498.pdf. Accessed September 19, 2024.

Acknowledgments

We would like to thank Kevin Hillstrom for the invitation to write this book and for guiding us through the process. We would also like to thank our friends and families for their ongoing love and support, while we scrambled to meet publication deadlines. In addition, we appreciate the ongoing support from our colleagues at West Virginia University, especially at the Center for Research on Violence, the Higher Education in Prison Initiative (HEPI), the WVU ADVANCE Center, and the Department of Sociology and Anthropology. Furthermore, none of this would have been possible had it not been for support years ago from the Community Oriented Policing Services, United States Department of Justice, for developing the concepts and tools for situational policing. Finally, we acknowledge the inspiration we receive from many police officers, active or retired, who remind us why this work is so important.

Introduction

On January 7, 2023, Memphis police stopped Tyre Nichols, a 29-year-old black man, for a traffic violation. During the stop, officers aggressively removed Nichols from the car. They used pepper spray and a Taser on him. Nichols broke free and ran toward his home just a short distance away. The officers pursued and caught Nichols. They then beat him brutally, causing serious injuries to the head and back. Following the assault, Nichols was hospitalized in critical condition. He died three days later. Police body cameras and a camera affixed to a nearby utility pole captured the initial traffic stop and the gruesome beating. The five officers involved in the arrest, all black, were released from the Memphis Police Department and charged with attempted murder (Stein, Cardia, and Reneau 2023). This incident in Memphis occurred less than three years after the horrific murder of George Floyd by Minneapolis police officers.

In the decade leading up to the tragic incidents in Memphis and Minneapolis, cell phone and body cam videos distributed on social media exposed many similar cases of deadly force by the police against unarmed black men and women. These highly publicized incidents of bigotry and excessive force in the practice of American policing generated widespread protest and repeated calls for police reform. However, what emerged from all these tragic events, and the civil unrest that followed, was not a unified vision for progress or a commitment to reform the police. Instead, it produced two competing views: one to *defund* or *abolish* the police, and the other to *defend* and *reform* them.

In this book on police abuse and reform, we examine the facts about police violence in the United States. We present the arguments surrounding the issues, including challenges to both the abolitionists and the conventional reformers. To set the stage for the chapters that follow, we want to first make five basic points:

1. Facts rarely speak for themselves. Instead, we each provide meaning to them. In any debate, both sides of an issue claim to own the facts. However, facts themselves rarely, if ever, carry some objective truth. Instead, each one of us interprets facts through lenses distorted by our worldviews. For example, consider the fact that each year in the United States, the police shoot and kill about one thousand people. In addition, consider the related fact that the annual number of people gunned down by the police is higher than the number of US soldiers killed annually in Iraq during the most violent years of the war. Both facts tell us something about police violence; yet, there is little agreement on what they mean. To those who call to defund or abolish the police, this level of deadly force is evidence that police violence is excessive, unnecessary, counterproductive, and discriminatory. On the other hand, those who defend the police see these same facts as a lawful and necessary response to violent crime.

In this simple example, one can see the difficulty in clearing things up with facts. The meanings we attribute to them are conditioned by cultural, contextual, social, and ideological differences. Therefore, it is unlikely that everyone presented with the same set of facts will see things the same way.

2. "Doing right" in policing is a matter of perspective. The concern about "doing right" has been a major focus in philosophy for more than three thousand years, and it has renewed relevance in today's discussion of police abuse and reform. Essentially, there are two main ways to think about doing right in policing. The *deontological* view assumes there is a duty to follow a law or policy. The term *deontology* is derived from the Greek words *deon* for duty and *logos* for logic or science. The police generally accept the morality of laws and organizational policies, so following them means doing right. On the other hand, the *consequentialist* view sets moral *outcomes* as the benchmark for righteous behavior. From this perspective, doing right in policing means achieving moral outcomes, such as equity, justice, and safety for all people. These two contrasting perspectives are key to understanding what it means to do right in the practice of American policing today.

To provide an example, consider the threefold way the term *police abuse* is conceptualized by coauthor Howard Ryan (2022: 26). Abuse involves (1) excessive and deadly force; (2) over-arrest and its linkage to mass incarceration; and (3) racism. A deontological assessment of excessive and deadly force seeks to answer the question, "Did the officer follow the law (e.g., was it constitutional)?" By contrast, a consequentialist assessment asks whether, for example, the use of force was excessive or the officer's actions discriminatory, giving rise to the further question, "Could this have been handled differently?"

Let's apply this same deontological/consequentialist difference to Ryan's second area of abuse, which is over-arrest and its linkage to mass incarceration. For the deontologist, the arrest is almost always morally correct if the officer's behavior is within the bounds of law and department policy. For the consequentialist, however, all options should be considered, and better outcomes may be achieved without an arrest.

Ryan's third area of abuse, racism, can also be assessed through our philosophical dichotomy. We can assess a wide array of police interventions—arrests, stop and frisks, citations, warnings—from either a deontological or consequentialist standard. In all such instances, the deontologist asks whether the officer is following the law, whereas the consequentialist asks about outcomes, including racial disparities or other harms accruing from police practice.

Conventional police reform too often fails to achieve its goals, such as reducing discrimination and excessive force, because it operates within deontological assumptions. That is, it assumes that following the law meets the standard for effective police service and public safety. On the other hand, the consequentialist may shift the focus of policing to the building of strong and safe community outcomes.

3. The thesis of the "bad-apple" cop is problematic but popular. When horrific acts of police violence occur, it is very easy to see the offenders as the sole source of the problem. This is the "bad-apple" thesis. It generally sets in motion measures for police accountability and transparency that ensure bad-apple, bigoted cops are identified, punished, fired, and prevented from joining other departments. Doing this gives the appearance that the problems in policing are solved. However, this view obscures the much more serious structural violence and discrimination that occurs in policing.

Structural violence refers to the patterns of domination and inequality produced and maintained by the police and the criminal justice system. We rarely acknowledge the collective harm from routine police practices or what is sometimes called structural violence. This is because policing as we have come to know it—as social control through law enforcement—is misrecognized as "natural" and, therefore, unchangeable. This is also why aggressive law enforcement that targets poor and minoritized neighborhoods is justified as an appropriate *response* to violence rather than a contributing *cause* of it. (In this book, we use the term *minoritized* rather than *minority* to recognize the fact that adults in underrepresented groups, such as black and brown communities, are often treated as children by authorities—i.e., minoritized—in need of control

[Kendi 2016].) When violence in pursuit of social control is experienced as excessive and unjust, it breaks the social bonds that keep communities safe. In part, this is why the bad-apple cop thesis is problematic and how its popularity works to keep things the same.

4. A sociological perspective can provide a greater range of options for reform. In this book, we examine the issues of police abuse and reform through a sociological lens. Because each of us attributes meaning to facts based on our own ideological, contextual, and cultural views, a sociological framework for a discussion of police abuse and reform is important. It can help us better understand the sources of police violence and discrimination and its impact in local places and society as a whole. It also helps us to see why reforms over the past one hundred years or more have not worked—and really cannot work.

For our purposes, social structures refer to social institutions. In each institution there exist sets of policies and procedures that pattern interactions over time and shape behavior in specific ways (Messerschmidt 1997). Social structures and structured practice coproduce each other. Social structures determine practice, and structured practice reproduces the institutional structure. The symbiotic relationship between institutional structures and structured practices is what maintains consistently high rates of crime and police violence.

One way to think about structure and structured practice in policing is to recognize how similar they are to structure and structured practice on a sports field, such as football or soccer (Bourdieu [1977]2013). The game is structured. There are boundaries and positions on the field. The game provides the logic for action. It also identifies the things that count as distinctive and worthy of high status. As we describe in the book, the current game in American policing is crime control and social order through "law enforcement." The police game is generally viewed as a contest of good versus evil, in which stories of heroism abound and the model police officer is an aggressive law enforcer.

To succeed in this game, officers develop a worldview and disposition that helps them succeed on the field. This often puts the police at odds with the community. The battle lines are the "thin blue lines" the police draw between good and evil, order and disorder, and us and them. In this environment, relationships between police and community have become extremely strained and often violent. The efforts to reform the American police have ignored the game entirely and only look for new ways to play it.

5. A sociological perspective helps us find alternative ways to mitigate crime and promote public safety. Most people would agree that the role of the police is to advance public safety. Many would likewise contend that the role of the criminal justice and prison system—for which police are the primary gateway—is to protect our safety and security by punishing those who break the law and thereby serving as a deterrent as well. Yet, things are not as simple as they seem. If a society pursues public safety only, or primarily, through arresting and jailing lawbreakers, then we can wind up with problems such as mass incarceration. The United States has one of the world's highest rates of incarceration.

It may be *impossible* for the police alone to "protect" us. For one thing, the police are not in our homes when crimes occur. According to the FBI, this is where more than half of all violent crimes happen. Or, perhaps the rigorous enforcement of laws makes conditions in neighborhoods and communities more conducive to crime and violence, not less, as is discussed in Chapter 9. Aggressive enforcement of laws can pit the community against the police in ways that create high levels of frustration and conflict, the conditions most associated with crime and violence.

Fortunately, we have other ways to advance public safety. One way, which is taken up in Chapter 5 through a study of the 1960s, is through social programs that address some of the "roots of crime" by promoting full employment, ensuring robust social and health services, and working to end racial and other kinds of inequities. Another "non-criminalizing" way to support public safety is by rethinking and reimagining the police themselves, as we discuss in Chapter 9.

This book consists of nine chapters. Chapter 1 sets forth a sociological perspective that informs the chapters, questions, and facts examined throughout the book. The major focus in Chapter 1 is the police mandate. The American police mandate for crime control and social order through law enforcement provides the logic for police practice. It also shapes the officer's professional outlook, guides police action, and predisposes communities to certain outcomes. This police mandate is problematic, as it makes policing more abusive. In Chapters 2 and 3, we examine the police abuse triad: over-arrest, excessive force, and discrimination. We review official sources of information on police abuse and some of the popular explanations for it. In Chapters 4 through 8, we examine the history of police reform in the United States from its origins in the early colonies leading up to the present day. Each chapter explores a particular era of reform. In Chapter 9, we review America's long experience and struggle with police reform and speculate on its future. We look closely at some of the most sacred ideas held about policing in American society.

To solve the current problems in American policing, a transformation must occur. While the nature of that transformation continues to be debated, an effective pathway likely requires the profession to retain the goal of building safe, strong communities, but looking for new collaborative ways to achieve it.

Further Reading

Bourdieu, Pierre. [1977] 2013. *Outline of a Theory of Practice*. Cambridge: Cambridge University Press.

Kendi, Ibram X. 2016. *Stamped from the Beginning: The Definitive History of Racist Ideas in America*. New York: Bold Type Books.

Messerschmidt, James W. 1997. *Crime as Structured Action: Gender, Race, Class, and Crime in the Making*. Thousand Oaks, CA: Sage.

Nolan, James J., Frank Crispino, and Timothy Parsons. 2021. *Policing in an Age of Reform: An Agenda for Research and Practice*. London: Palgrave Macmillan.

Ryan, Howard. 2022. "Police Abolitionism: A Marxist Critique." *Social Justice* 49, no. 1/2: 25–54.

Stein, Robin, Alexander Cardia, and Natalie Reneau. 2023. "71 Commands in 13 Minutes: Officers Gave Tyre Nichols Impossible Orders." *New York Times*. January 29: 3.

1

The American Police Mandate: A Game, Playbook, and Scorecard

Most people today recognize there are problems in American policing, but there is little agreement on what to do about it. The over-enforcement of relatively minor laws, excessive violence in the use of force in police-citizen encounters, and the discriminatory nature of both enforcement and violence are some of the reasons why so many people call for reform.

Of the reform measures to date, most tend to focus on surveillance to identify, expose, punish, train, replace, or rehabilitate "bad-apple" cops. This is because the problem of police violence and discrimination is mostly cast as the result of overly aggressive, bigoted cops who slip through the screening process and direct their hostilities in poor black and brown communities. Therefore, reformers call for improved and more transparent accountability measures within police organizations.

In addition to the reforms promising better surveillance and greater accountability and transparency, there have been hundreds of legal reforms limiting some of the more problematic police practices, including chokeholds and no-knock warrants, while also instituting civilian review boards, strengthening police decertification processes, and setting minimal training standards (Crampton 2021). Furthermore, there have been new programs developed to divert certain noncriminal calls, such as mental health crises, to trained professionals who are better equipped to respond (Marshall Project 2022). Finally, there have been special training facilities constructed, such as Cop City in Atlanta, to provide a better place for antibias and de-escalation training (Lartey 2023).

Despite the public attention to police violence and discrimination in recent years and the widespread collective and political action to curb it, many still argue that nothing has changed (Equal Justice Initiative 2019). The fact that the country is still divided over the efficacy and legitimacy of police, especially following so many comprehensive reforms, points to a more complex and fundamental concern. What are the American police supposed to do? And what are they expected to accomplish by doing it? This may sound odd, because we often hear slogans such as "protect and serve," and we are presented with images such as the "thin blue line," all emphasizing that the role of the police in American society is to protect us. However, this level of abstraction can lead to widespread disagreements about what the police are supposed to do and what they are expected to achieve by doing it.

In this book, when we talk about what the police are organized to do, we mean the police mandate. In the sections that follow, we explore in some detail the American police mandate and consider ways to understand and refine it. For our purposes, an institutional mandate refers to the services and functions that "the institution's existence makes available to society" (Bittner 1970: 46). The term *mandate* has been used to refer to the license bestowed on an occupation to carry out certain functions in society that others may not (Manning 1997). For example, attorneys have a legal right to represent clients in a court of law. Medical doctors have a license to prescribe medication and perform surgery. Social workers have a legal right to remove children from their biological parents under certain conditions, such as when the children are neglected or abused. Schoolteachers are authorized by law to teach our children and evaluate their academic progress. And psychologists have a license to provide counseling services or to conduct psychological testing. Criminologists Manning and Van Maanen (1978: 7) describe the occupational mandate as follows:

> The right to perform an occupation may include the permission to pick up garbage or to cut open human bodies and transfer organs from one to another. It also involves, however, a series of tasks and associated attitudes and other values that set apart a specialized occupational group from all the others.

In this book, we describe the professional police mandate as having three parts: a game, a playbook, and a scorecard. The *game* refers to the structure and logic of action on a social field. The idea that human behavior tends to conform to a game's logic was introduced by French sociologist Pierre Bourdieu ([1977]2013). Consider how the structure and logic of the games of football and baseball affect the behavior of players on the field. This is why the players act, think, and communicate so differently. Where it is logical to violently tackle a player with the ball to prevent a score on a football field, this same behavior would get a player ejected (or maybe even arrested) on a baseball field. The different games produce in players a very different disposition and way of seeing things (Goodwin 1994). However, even though the structure and logic of these two games are different, the fact that action on the field and the disposition of the players is guided by the structure and logic of the various games is what is important for understanding the roots of police violence and abuse. It is also important to see what is necessary for effective reform to occur.

The *playbook* refers to the diverse strategies and technologies used on the field to score points in furtherance of the game's purpose and in accord with its logic. In the world of sports, a change in the coaching staff often introduces new playbooks. In this way, changing playbooks may be considered a type of reform as it introduces new strategies, technologies, and accountability in hopes of producing better outcomes. This is the kind of reform that is pervasive in American policing. New technology playbooks provide hope that the chronic problems on the field and their adverse outcomes can be alleviated without having to consider changing the game.

Finally, the *scorecard* provides the metrics for team and individual success. The scorecard guides action on the field by outlining what counts as distinctive and worthy of reward and recognition. The scorecard on the field of policing focuses on *outputs*—that is, arrests, citations, the seizure of illegal drugs and guns—rather than community *outcomes*. Rarely are the police recognized for creating the conditions in communities that are preventive or healing, and where crime and violence or other social problems are less likely to thrive.

What makes institutions so difficult to change is that, over time, they appear natural and immutable rather than socially constructed and changeable. This is why the problems of violence and discrimination in American policing are blamed on bad apples rather than the institution itself. Any attempt to change the game draws the familiar criticism, "that's not what the police are supposed to do"—as if there is something in nature that the police are *supposed* to do.

In this chapter, we explore the American police mandate, including the game, playbook, and scorecard. Then we examine this mandate's contribution to the problems of violence and discrimination in our current times. Finally, we look at some of the most popular practices used by the American police to carry out its mandate.

Further Reading

Bittner, Egon. 1970. *The Functions of Police in Modern Society: A Review of Background Factors, Current Practices, and Possible Role Models*. Chevy Chase, MD: National Institute of Mental Health, Center for Studies of Crime and Delinquency.

Bourdieu, Pierre. [1977] 2013. *Outline of a Theory of Practice*. New York: Cambridge University Press.
Crampton, Liz. 2021. "States Passed 243 Policing Bills—and Left Activists Wanting." *Politico*. May 26.
Equal Justice Initiative. 2019. "Five Years after Ferguson, Policing Reform Is Abandoned." August 12. Accessed August 11, 2024. https://eji.org/news/five-years-after-ferguson-policing-reform-abandoned/.
Goodwin, Charles. 1994. "Professional Vision." *American Anthropologist* 96, no. 3: 606–33.
Lartey, Jamiles. 2023. "What the Fight over Atlanta's 'Cop City' Reveals about Policing of Protests." June 24. The Marshall Project. https://www.themarshallproject.org/2023/06/24/atlanta-cop-city-protest-police.
Manning, Peter K. 1997. *Police Work: The Social Organization of Policing*, 2nd ed. Long Grove, IL: Waveland Press.
Manning, Peter K., and John Van Maanen, eds. 1978. *Policing: A View from the Street*. Santa Monica, CA: Goodyear Publishing Company.
Marshall Project and NPR's Embedded Podcast Series. 2022. "Changing the Police." https://www.themarshallproject.org/2022/07/14/we-spent-a-year-following-a-troubled-police-force-listen-to-what-we-learned-about-reform.

Q1: Is there an official mandate in American policing?

Answer: Yes. The police in the United States have a professional mandate for crime control and social order through law enforcement. In American society today, the terms police and law enforcement are used interchangeably as synonyms. This has not always been the case, and it reflects reforms that took place at the beginning of the twentieth century (Bittner 1970; Carte and Carte 1975).

The Facts: The development of policing in the United States initially followed the English system. In the early colonies, a night watch maintained street lamps, stayed on the lookout for fires, looked for suspicious people lurking around, and performed a number of other broad public safety and public health tasks (Uchida 2005). As the population in urban centers grew and the economy became more complex, the need emerged for more formalized police organizations. The survival of the emerging political economy demanded more systematic social control. A particularly sinister form of this social control had long been occurring in the Southern states. This is where the earliest forms of law enforcement took shape as slave patrols (Williams and Murphy 1990). Initially, their purpose was to enforce compliance with slave laws by chasing down runaway slaves, prevent slave revolts through organized terror, and administer discipline for violating plantation rules (Platt 1982; Reichel 1992). After the civil war, slave patrols evolved into the early Southern police departments with a revised purpose to control freed slaves and enforce Jim Crow segregation laws.

In the early part of the nineteenth century, urban centers in the United States were experiencing rapid population growth. In New York City, for example, the population grew by 350 percent in just forty years. This was mostly due to European immigration, particularly from Ireland and Germany (Uchida 2005). These new arrivals had come to America in search of employment and better lives. However, they were perceived as threats by native-born US citizens, mostly because they were competing for limited job opportunities. The new ethnic tensions—combined with the pervasive, deep-rooted racial animus—proved to be an incendiary mix. Mass rioting emerged in New York and many other cities. In Philadelphia, for example, 15,000 residents were involved in a riot on Broad Street in 1834, after firefighters returning to their station could not get past an Irish funeral procession (25).

The social and economic disorder occurring in mid-nineteenth-century America necessitated a new type of policing. Cities like New York, Philadelphia, Boston, Buffalo, and Detroit established local, centralized, bureaucratic police departments influenced by the model used by Sir Robert Peel in London (Uchida 2005). The mandate for the new American police was the maintenance of social and political order. A point of departure from the Peel model was that the police in American cities received their legitimacy from local political bosses rather than from a centralized government. Therefore, the police were political operatives. As such, they provided a range of social services, which included running soup lines, providing temporary lodging in station houses for those emigrating to the United States, assisting political leaders in finding work for new immigrants, and returning runaway children to homes or orphanages.

During this era, police officers were selected because of their ethnic background and political affiliation. Officers lived in the neighborhoods they patrolled and consulted with local political leaders about police priorities and progress (Kelling and Moore 1988). In addition, the police in this era were well paid: in the late 1800s, the average officer salary was twice that of a worker in manufacturing. But police job security was poor: on election day, there would be mass turnover in the department if the incumbent lost the election (Walker 1977).

In this era of rapid social and economic change, the new police mandate for social control produced a specific *game* with a logic of practice aimed at maintaining order and providing service to the public—albeit for the greater purpose of maintaining political power (see discussion of game analogy in this chapter's introductory text). The police were selected from the neighborhoods they served. Therefore, they could help solve problems in ways that were personalized and grounded in intimate knowledge of the issues. The *playbooks* for this game were developed by police leaders in collaboration with political bosses, which reflected the dominant racial, ethnic, economic, and political interests of the community. The department or precinct's *scorecard* reflected what political leaders wanted in terms of serving their interests and the established order. This included interfering with elections, helping local community members thrive, and maintaining social control via nightstick justice in furtherance of the racial, ethnic, economic, and political hierarchy. In addition, an officer's scorecard would also include things like nonenforcement or lax enforcement of certain laws, such as those related to liquor prohibition (Kelling and Moore 1988).

By the early twentieth century, most police reformers sought to uncouple the police from politics. They took aim at political and economic corruption, brutality, and sheer incompetence of the police in carrying out its social control mandate under local political umbrellas. The key reform-minded figures from inside the police profession included August Vollmer, chief of the Berkeley, California, police department; his student O. W. Wilson, who much later was appointed police commissioner of Chicago; and J. Edgar Hoover, the director of the FBI. These reformers viewed the source of the problem in American policing *as* politics, and they sought to remove this alliance through professional standards and the law.

Unchaining the police from political control happened through civil service laws; policies granting lifetime tenure to police chiefs, ensuring they could be removed only for cause; and by ending requirements that police officers come from the areas they served. For example, in Philadelphia it was illegal for police officers to live in the same neighborhoods they worked. In this way, officers could be protected from the pressure to serve local interests, especially those conflicting with a new law enforcement mandate, to which we now turn.

This professional law enforcement mandate created a new game with new playbooks and scorecards. The logic of the professional policing game was to control crime by enforcing the law. This change in the policing game narrowed the function of the police to a very circumscribed set of behaviors and functions. It was at this time, beginning in the late 1920s, that police agencies became law enforcement agencies (Kelling and Moore 1988). Under this new mandate, anything that deviated from the enforcement of laws—such as settling neighborhood disputes or domestic arguments—was pejoratively labeled "social work," as it no longer fit the logic of the new game. The "thin blue line" emerged with the law enforcement mandate: it symbolized the police as the line between order and chaos, good and evil.

Playbooks (such as policy manuals) and scorecards were revised in accordance with this new game. What counted most, and what became the focus of police scorecards, was crime control, which was viewed as social control of "the dangerous classes." Emerging technologies were added to law enforcement playbooks. Foot patrols were replaced by motor vehicles. Public calls for assistance were addressed by telephone and later by 911 centers with automated dispatch.

The shift from political control to crime control required new metrics for police scorecards. Vollmer, in conjunction with the newly formed International Association of Chiefs of Police (IACP), worked to implement the Uniform Crime Reporting (UCR) program, both as a means for evaluating police agency effectiveness and to debunk claims of crime waves and ineffective policing. Soon, UCR became a primary scorecard for police agencies. The metrics included the volume of reported crimes, numbers and types of arrests, and crime clearance rates.

The quality and quantity of arrests, and the seizures of illegal guns and drugs, were what counted most in the law enforcement game. In addition, the new game rewarded officers who developed good working relationships with top brass in the department, such as those heading detective divisions or other specialized units. The ability to assemble large numbers of confidential informants was also valued in this law enforcement game. The informants would be on tap to help solve various crimes, particularly those that occurred in neighborhoods that were at odds with the police. Finally, in this new law enforcement game, status as a good law enforcer was recognized and rewarded through promotions or by transfers to special units where officers were likely to work lots of overtime.

On the field of policing, a police officer personality emerged that was purposely impersonal and oriented to solving crimes rather than tending to the emotional needs of victims and communities (Kelling and Moore 1988). The aim of the police when engaged with citizens was to take control. A no-nonsense disposition on the streets was desirable in the law enforcement game. Any disagreement or argument was treated as "contempt of cop" (Manning 2022: 301). The citizen's role also changed under this new mandate. Citizens were expected to simply defer to the professional judgment of officers on issues related to crime control (ibid.).

In the 1960s, the professional law enforcement model ran into trouble. Crime rates began to rise along with the size of police departments. Rising crime led to growing fear in many neighborhoods. Although law enforcement agencies promised impartiality, officers did much of their enforcement in black neighborhoods. The civil rights and anti-Vietnam war movements challenged the legitimacy of the police in this period. Many citizens disapproved of the aggressive tactics being used by police against protesters. This combination of factors ignited widespread interest, once again, in police reform.

In 1967, President Lyndon Johnson's Commission on Law Enforcement and Administration of Justice convened to deal with American police reform. However, instead of changing what the police do to make communities safe, it reinforced the professional mandate by identifying police as the law enforcement component of the criminal justice system (President's Commission 1968).

Beginning in the late 1970s and extending into the present time, there have been attempts to reform the police in ways that appear more effective in controlling crime and disorder. Moreover, these new methods promise to reduce or eliminate police violence and discrimination, which have been endemic with the crime-control-via-law-enforcement mandate. It has been the ineffectiveness of the police in preventing crime, administering justice, and reducing violence and discrimination that has resulted in their loss of legitimacy.

Some scholars referred to the emerging practices of community and problem-oriented policing in the 1980s and 1990s as the dawn of a new era in policing. However, this never really materialized. Instead, the language of community policing was rhetoric and the crime-control-via-law-enforcement mandate continued unimpeded (Manning 1997). Although it is widely recognized that the police do much more than simply enforce the law, their primary professional identity is law enforcement. The game, playbooks, and scorecards still support this fact. Since police agencies have no explicit goals other than crime control and social order through law enforcement, they rely on measuring police *outputs*—arrests, tickets, citations, illegal drug and gun seizures—rather than community *outcomes* (Monkkonen 1981; Manning 2022).

The game and scorecard in American policing have remained unchanged for more than one hundred years. What has changed are playbooks that incorporate new technologies, techniques, and accountability structures by *retrofitting* them to the old law enforcement machine. This is the nature of American police reform today. It adds new technologies and evidence-based strategies to playbooks. It also seeks to improve police-community relations. However, it does not change the law enforcement game or its scorecard. We demonstrate with the following case example of the police department in Wilmington, Delaware.

The Wilmington Police Department (WPD) is a modern, accredited law enforcement agency. It receives periodic reviews by the Commission on Accreditation for Law Enforcement Agencies (CALEA). CALEA is a well-recognized accrediting organization in contemporary policing. It refers to police agencies as law enforcement agencies. The mandate for crime control and social order via law enforcement is reflected in the department's own description, its mission, and in its playbook and scorecards.

The WPD website provides a description of the department and its mission (Wilmington Police Department n.d.). The section "About the Department" states, in pertinent part,

> The Wilmington Police Department is responsible for providing *law enforcement services* to Delaware's largest city. The agency traces its roots in public safety and service to the year 1739, and presently includes 312 sworn police officers in addition to civilian support staff. The department has been accredited by the Commission on Accreditation for Law Enforcement Agencies (CALEA) since 1994 and is committed to providing professional law enforcement and investigative services. (emphasis added)

Similarly, the department mission statement describes the game as the provision of law enforcement services:

> The mission of the Wilmington Department of Police is to work in a true partnership with our fellow citizens, and *to raise the level of public safety through law enforcement* and thereby reduce the fear and incidence of crime. This mission will be fostered by every member of the department. (emphasis added)

The organizational structure of WPD is hierarchical and bureaucratic. The WPD summarizes its playbook as follows: "In recent years, the Wilmington Police Department has adopted a range of research-based, proven crime reduction strategies that form the foundation of our plan to enhance public safety in Delaware's largest city." Its strategies, the WPD explains, include:

- Community Policing (with each and every member of the agency serving as a community policing officer);
- CompStat Methodology (applying business management principles to policing to ensure greater levels of focus and accountability);

- District Integrity (assigning the same officers to the same neighborhood each time they report for duty);
- Intelligence-Led Policing (leveraging the department's Real Time Crime Center to help gather and disseminate intelligence to all personnel);
- Group Violence Intervention (blending law enforcement and social service provision into a holistic crime prevention strategy); and
- The integration of NIBIN firearm and ballistic tracing and analysis and the launch of an embedded Crime Gun Intelligence Center in partnership with the Federal Bureau of Alcohol, Tobacco, Firearms and Explosives (ATF).

The law enforcement game is expressed in the WPD scorecards. There is one for the department and one for the officers. The department's scorecard is publicized in its end-of-year report (Wilmington Police Department 2023). The report includes the numbers of crime complaints, victim service calls, foot patrols, and community meetings. It also includes crime data for murders, rapes, robberies, aggravated assaults, burglaries, thefts, auto thefts, shooting incidents, and shooting victims. In addition, the department scorecard includes multiyear crime clearance rates for murder and gun arrests.

The police officer scorecard reflects what counts for distinction and deserving of high praise in the department. The following is a list of commendations and awards for exceptional police service in Wilmington (Wilmington Police Department 2024).

- *Class B Commendation*—While on or off duty and without being dispatched apprehends a person for felony theft, theft of automobile, drug law violations OR 3 separate arrests for delivery or possession with the intent to deliver illegal drugs in a 3 month period.
- *Class A Commendation*—While on or off duty and without being dispatched makes an arrest for first degree assault, burglary, drug trafficking (5 arrests in a year) OR when an officer goes above or beyond the call of duty to arrest a person wanted for a serious crime.
- *Merit Award*—When an employee performs a special service to promote or improve the efficiency or effectiveness of the department internally or externally OR an officer saves a life via first aid.
- *Outstanding Service Award*—When an employee has been awarded Class A commendations 3 times in a 12-month period, affects a rescue of a trapped or endangered person at hazard to his (*sic*) own personal safety OR any incident not included above where a division commander feels an outstanding police service has occurred.

- *Distinguished Service Award*—When an employee on or off duty and without being dispatched arrests a person in the commission or flight from a homicide, rape, robbery, burglary (1st degree), any other serious felony.
- *Medal of Honor*—When an officer, in an act of uncommon valor, saves the life of a fellow officer or citizen OR when an officer, whose life is severely threatened in the line of duty, acts above and beyond the call of duty to make an apprehension.

WPD clearly embraces the professional mandate for crime control and social order via law enforcement. CALEA, the accrediting agency that reviews policies and procedures in the department, refers to WPD as a "law enforcement" agency (CALEA n.d.). The WPD sets up a *game* that has officers looking for criminals to arrest. The department and officer *scorecards* center almost exclusively on criminal apprehensions. They count what the police do—number and type of criminal apprehensions, amount of illegal guns and drugs seized, the number of calls for service, the number of victim services delivered—rather than what the department achieves by doing these things. The WPD *playbook* is mostly concerned with fighting crime and gives little attention to the conditions that give rise to crime in the first place.

In the following sections of this chapter, we further explore the American police mandate to see the extent to which the police are successful in carrying out their mandate. We also consider how this mandate might contribute to the contemporary problems of police abuse in the United States and why it is so difficult to change.

Further Reading

Bittner, Egon. 1970. *The Functions of Police in Modern Society: A Review of Background Factors, Current Practices, and Possible Role Models*. Chevy Chase, MD: National Institute of Mental Health, Center for Studies of Crime and Delinquency.

Carte, Gene E., and Elaine H. Carte. 1975. *Police Reform in the United States: The Era of August Vollmer*. Berkeley: University of California Press.

Commission on Accreditation for Law Enforcement Agencies (CALEA). n.d. "CALEA Accreditation." Accessed October 24, 2024. https://www.wilmingtonde.gov/government/public-safety/wilmington-police-department/calea-accreditation.

Kelling, George L., and Mark H. Moore. 1988. "The Evolving Strategy of Policing." *Perspectives on Policing* 4 (November). https://www.ojp.gov/pdffiles1/nij/114213.pdf.

Manning, Peter K. 1978. "The Police: Mandate, Strategies, and Appearances." In Peter K. Manning and John Van Maanen, eds., *Policing: A View from the Street*, 7–32. Santa Monica, CA: Goodyear Publishing.
Manning, Peter K. 1997. *Police Work: The Social Organization of Policing*, 2nd ed. Long Grove, IL: Waveland Press.
Manning, Peter K. 2022. "Goffman on Police Work: A Pragmatic Dance in Action." In Michael H. Jacobsen and Greg Smith, eds., *The Routledge International Handbook of Goffman Studies*. New York: Routledge.
Monkkonen, Eric H. 1981. *Police in Urban America, 1860–1920*. London: Cambridge University Press.
Platt, Tony. 1982. "Crime and Punishment in the United States: Immediate and Long-Term Reforms from a Marxist Perspective." *Crime and Social Justice* 18: 38–45.
President's Commission on Law Enforcement and Administration of Justice. 1968. *The Challenge of Crime in a Free Society*. New York: Dutton.
Reichel, Philip L. 1992. "The Misplaced Emphasis on Urbanization in Police Development." *Policing and Society* 3, no. 1: 1–12.
Uchida, Craig, D. 2005. "The Development of the American Police: An Historical Overview." In Roger D. Dunham and Geoffrey P. Alpert, eds., *Critical Issues in Policing*, 5th ed. Long Grove, IL: Waveland Press.
Walker, Samuel. 1977. *A Critical History of Police Reform: The Emergence of Professionalism*. Lanham, MD: Lexington Books.
Williams, Hubert, and Patrick V. Murphy. 1990. "The Evolving Strategy of Police: A Minority View." *Perspectives on Policing*. Washington, DC: National Institute of Justice.
Wilmington Police Department. 2023. "End of Year Report, 2023." Wilmington, DE. https://www.wilmingtonde.gov/government/public-safety/wilmington-police-department/wpd-year-end-report.
Wilmington Police Department. n. d. "Awards and Commendations, Written Directive: 6.55." Wilmington, DE. Accessed May 14, 2024. https://www.wilmingtonde.gov/home/showpublisheddocument/12308/638515408401370000.
Wilmington Police Department. n. d. "About the Department" and "Mission Statement." Wilmington, DE. Accessed October 24, 2024. https://www.wilmingtonde.gov/government/city-departments/department-of-police.

Q2: Are the police effective in carrying out their mandate?

Answer: It depends on how you look at it. On one hand, the American police make many arrests and issue many citations. This is an indicator of success in carrying out the professional law enforcement mandate. On the other hand, these arrests are not very effective in preventing or solving crimes, particularly in communities most in need of help.

The Facts: It is a fact that the police are successful in carrying out their mandate by making criminal arrests. However, the fact that arrests are prioritized over more holistic place-based prevention strategies seriously limits their effectiveness in terms of controlling crime (Weisburd 2008).

The game that emerges from the police mandate prioritizes criminal apprehensions as the *raison d'etre* (reason for being) of the profession. (See this chapter's introductory text for more on our game analogy.) When this is internalized in officers, it becomes common sense that arresting people is the way to make communities safer. Although the police do much more than arrest people, the officers' scorecards still prioritize criminal apprehensions and the seizure of illegal guns and drugs. The law enforcement identity that emerges from the police mandate is reinforced by popular media, public officials, and policing scholars. What we mean by this is that popular TV shows like *Law & Order*, commissions like President Obama's 21st Century Policing Task Force (President's Task Force 2015), and the plethora of research outlined in the scholarly evidence-based playbook all depict the police profession as "law enforcement" (Lum and Koper 2017).

The evidence-based police research reinforces the current police mandate by giving the appearance that the solution to crime control and police abuse is in the playbook and not the game and scorecard. The game's logic is expressed in the scorecard. The scorecard prioritizes law enforcement outputs over community outcomes. This produces in officers a law enforcement identity, disposition, and worldview. The most effective strategies in the evidence-based playbooks, such as building community while solving problems, do not fit well with the logic of the law enforcement game and its scorecard (Nolan and Hinkle 2021).

This is generally how it works. The police make lots of arrests in the attempt to control crime in what they deem are crime-prone populations. For example, between 2011 and 2021, the police in the United States made 82,855,769 total arrests. The number of arrests is not the number of separate people arrested. In fact, many people are arrested multiple times. Instead, it is simply the number of times *someone* was arrested for criminal—not traffic—violations. Sixty-five percent of these arrests fit into a category we call *social control*. Social control refers to arrests for crimes against society or against the public order. Therefore, the arrest is not the successful end of an investigation for a crime against a person or against property. Instead, it is a way to control behavior that offends the mainstream public, such as vagrancy, liquor, drugs, gun, and curfew violations. This practice, which readily becomes what we call *over-arrest*, is discussed more fully in Chapter 2 as part of "over-enforcement."

So yes, the police do make lots of arrests. In doing so they score points on their scorecards. However, such law enforcement activity—especially when driven by police scorecard priorities, rather than priorities of affected communities—may not necessarily serve the safety needs of communities.

Further Reading

Lum, Cynthia, and Christopher Koper. 2017. *The Playbook: Plays for Law Enforcement Officers to Help Prevent Crime and Increase Citizen Trust and Confidence*. Fairfax, VA: The Center for Evidence Based Crime Policy. https://cebcp.org/wp-content/evidence-based-policing/PLAYBOOK.pdf.

Nolan, James J., and Joshua C. Hinkle. 2021. "Changing the Game: A Sociological Perspective on Police Reform." In James J. Nolan, Frank Crispino, and Timothy Parsons, eds., *Policing in an Age of Reform: An Agenda for Research and Practice*, 61–83. London: Palgrave Macmillan.

President's Task Force on 21st Century Policing. 2015. *Final Report of the President's Task Force on 21st Century Policing*. Washington, DC: Community Oriented Policing Services.

Weisburd, David. 2008. "Place-Based Policing." *Ideas in American Policing* 9. Washington, DC: The Police Foundation.

Q3: How does the police mandate contribute to the problem of abuse in policing today?

Answer: The popular depiction of abuse in American policing is the bigoted, bad-apple cop roughing up unarmed, defenseless black and brown suspects. However, the reality is much more complex. The logic of *law enforcement* practice, as part of the police mandate discussed earlier, with its scorecard that prioritizes catching criminals over creating safe environments, has black, white, male, and female officers all doing the same harmful and counterproductive things. Enforcing laws as an end in itself in a society steeped in racial and economic inequality is the source of systemic violence and discrimination in American policing today.

The Facts: A sociological framing of the roots of abuse in American policing expands our gaze beyond the bigoted, bad-apple cops. This is certainly not to say that bigoted, bad-apple cops do not exist—they do. However, it is probably more accurate and helpful to view the endemic violence and discrimination in American policing as the result of *conformity* to the law and police policy rather than as *deviance* from it (Nolan and Hinkle 2021).

The professional mandate for crime control and social order through law enforcement produces a game on the social field. This game contains a logic for action that is reinforced by a scorecard that prioritizes arrests and the seizure of illegal drugs and guns over the conditions that make communities safe. A law enforcement identity emerges on this field that affects the way officers see things, and therefore, interact with the public. Linguist Charles Goodwin (1994) calls this ability to see objects of interest in a particular way a *professional vision*. By this he means that seeing is not a transparent psychological process, as if everyone who looks at a certain thing or event sees it the same way. He writes, "All vision is perspectival and lodged within endogenous communities of practice" (606). He gives the example of a farmer and archaeologist looking at the same patch of dirt. Where the farmer sees in the dirt the ability to support certain types of crops, the archaeologist sees "stains, features, and artifacts that provide evidence of human activity at this spot" (606). In this same way, police officers—socialized as law enforcement officers with a professional mandate to maintain order and control crime—develop a disposition and worldview that affects the way they see things.

Officers learn to see *bad neighborhoods* and distinguish them from the good ones. They learn to see *criminals* and distinguish them from noncriminals and potential criminals. From a great distance and in the dark of night, officers can see drug transactions on street corners. They learn to spot criminality in the way a person looks or the way they are dressed or their gait while walking down the street. They learn to spot *lookouts*, that is, those who are positioned to warn others of a police presence in the area. They can see signs of weapons and drugs under heavy clothing. And from what they see with their professional vision, they purportedly know if a person is up to no good. This professional vision helps officers score points and become successful in the game of law enforcement. However, since this professional law enforcement vision is fraught with error, many of those at the receiving end of police action are left frustrated and angry. This is particularly true in neighborhoods that get the most focus of law enforcement attention.

In their book, *Murder Town USA* (2023), sociologist Yasser Payne and his colleagues provide an example. Using participatory action research methods in the majority-black town of Wilmington, Delaware, the authors studied urban street life and the social institutions that shape it, including the police. Most of the street-identified black men and women in the study thought the police could not care less about the hardships associated with poverty and racial inequality. Instead, they believed the police consistently saw them as "up to no good." It was the duty of police to "hold them accountable" (125). Further, the respondents reported feeling "unfairly targeted, stopped, harassed, frisked, arrested … for minor crimes they did not commit" (121). Some felt disrespected by the police. Police officers' commands for compliance during interactions were translated by most participants in the study as a demand to "bow down" or be docile in their presence (121). This is one of the paradoxes of the law enforcement game. What the police believe is the best way to ensure their own personal safety—demand compliance to commands—creates conditions that are more hostile and, therefore, more dangerous for everyone involved. One of the participants in the study put it this way:

> I've never seen a cop protect. … I never seen it. Cops do a lot of stuff they don't gotta do. … They so forceful, … they know they got that badge and that gun and that taser gun. … They got the whole unit behind them. Take that off and see me in the streets! (qtd. in ibid.: 121)

The general attitude of those interviewed about the police was very negative. Seventy-five percent of the respondents interviewed disagreed with the statement, "Police do their jobs well." More than half of the respondents agreed with the statement, "Police sometimes allow crime to occur without stopping it." And 80 percent agreed with the statement, "The police give people a hard time for no reason" (122).

Often, the neighborhoods and communities most affected by structural disadvantage—such as concentrated poverty and access to quality education, professional employment, and intergenerational wealth—experience elevated rates of crime, violence, and other social problems. Street violence in these communities is often viewed from within as a rational adaptation to structured disadvantage. The police as law enforcers unwittingly contribute to making conditions worse. For example, the wide police declarations of wars on drugs and crime in urban neighborhoods has decimated families and communities and blocked pathways to more conventional economic opportunities, the accumulation of intergenerational wealth, and reductions in the conditions associated with health inequities (Cohen et al. 2022).

What we mean by claiming the police unwittingly reproduce conditions for crime and violence refers not simply to the implications of arrests and the stigma of criminal justice involvement. Instead, it also refers to the implications of aggressive law enforcement action on the well-being of places (National Academies 2018). This means a few different things. For one, when police action in particular neighborhoods is viewed as unjust, there is a tendency for residents to view the whole institution as unjust. This increases the risk for violence by the police and against them (Worden and McLean 2017; Tyler 2006). It also means that the racial and ethnic disparities in the outcomes of law enforcement practice increase tensions in the structurally disadvantaged communities (Ekins 2016; Lytle 2014). In addition, the law enforcement mandate has officers enforcing unpopular laws, such as those that prohibit marijuana use, drinking alcohol in public, playing music too loudly on porches and stoops, or hanging out late on street corners. This too creates tensions between police and community, and can result in residents feeling threatened and less safe when the police are around (Hinkle and Weisburd 2008). Finally, the aggressive law enforcement outputs that count most on police officer scorecards work against the neighborhood conditions that prevent crime, that is, social cohesion and trust among residents and trust in the police institution to help (Nolan, DeKeseredy, and Brownstein 2022; Nolan and Hinkle 2021).

To summarize, the roots of police violence and discrimination can be traced to the police mandate itself. The mandate produces a game with a logic for coercive law enforcement practice. Police playbooks emphasize crimefighting, while scorecards prioritize arrests, citations, and the seizure of illegal guns and drugs. This mandate fosters in officers a disposition and worldview that puts them at odds with the community. Officers remain highly suspicious of strangers, hypervigilant of danger, fixated on sorting good people from bad, and indifferent to the long-term harms to individuals and communities resulting from aggressive law enforcement. In Chapter 9, we explore an alternative to this law enforcement mandate, one focused on making places safer for the community and the police.

Further Reading

Cohen Aliza, Sheila P. Vakharia, Julie Netherland, and Kassandra Frederique. 2022. "How the War on Drugs Impacts Social Determinants of Health beyond the Criminal Legal System." *Annals of Medicine* 54: 2024–38.

Ekins, Emily. 2016. *Policing in America: Understanding Public Attitudes toward the Police*. Washington, DC: Cato Institute. https://www.cato.org.

Goodwin, Charles. 1994. "Professional Vision." *American Anthropologist* 96, no.3: 606–33.

Hinkle, Joshua. C., and David Weisburd. 2008. "The Irony of Broken Windows Policing: A Micro-place Study of the Relationship between Disorder, Focused Police Crackdowns and Fear of Crime." *Journal of Criminal Justice* 36, no. 6: 503–12.

Lytle, Daniel J. 2014. "The Effects of Suspect Characteristics: A Meta-analysis." *Journal of Criminal Justice* 42, no. 6: 589–97.

National Academies of Sciences, Engineering, and Medicine. 2018. *Proactive Policing: Effects on Crime and Communities*. Washington, DC: National Academies Press.

Nolan, James J., Walter S. DeKeseredy, and Henry H. Brownstein. 2022. "Police Ethics in Rural Contexts: A Left Realist Consequentialist View." *International Journal of Rural Criminology* 7, no. 1: 1–25.

Nolan, James J., and Joshua C. Hinkle. 2021. "Changing the Game: A Sociological Perspective on Police Reform." In James J. Nolan, Frank Crispino, and Timothy Parsons, eds., *Policing in an Age of Reform: An Agenda for Research and Practice*, 61–83. London: Palgrave Macmillan.

Payne, Yasser Arafat, Brooklynn K. Hitchens, and Darryl L. Chambers. 2023. *Murder Town, USA: Homicide, Structural Violence, and Activism in Wilmington*. New Brunswick, NJ: Rutgers University Press.

Tyler, Tom R. 2006. *Why People Obey the Law*. Princeton, NJ: Princeton University Press.

Worden, Robert E., and Sarah J. McLean. 2017. *Mirage of Police Reform: Procedural Justice and Police Legitimacy*. Oakland: University of California Press.

Q4: Is it possible to change the American police mandate?

Answer. Yes, but it is difficult to do. Throughout the history of American policing, many reforms have occurred. We document the significant ones later in this book. However, the parts of the mandate we call the game and scorecard have rarely changed. Instead, it is mostly the playbooks that have changed. New playbooks have included more formalized accountability measures, evidence-based law enforcement and community relations strategies, and advanced technologies and databases. The reason the game (crime control and social order via law enforcement) and scorecard (law enforcement outputs such as arrests, citations, and seizure of illegal guns and drugs) have not changed is primarily because policing *as* law enforcement is misrecognized as natural and immutable, rather than socially constructed and changeable. We explain this further in the Facts section, then dedicate several chapters later in the book to a more thorough examination of the variety of reforms that have occurred in recent history.

The Facts: To explain *police abuse* and to explore varieties of *police reform*, we introduced a sociological perspective—that is, the professional mandate (Manning 1997). Further, we described the mandate as being operationalized in the game, playbook, and scorecard. This formulation is heavily influenced by the work of French sociologist Pierre Bourdieu ([1977]2013). We think it provides a helpful way to examine the roots of police abuse and to examine the types of reforms that have occurred in American policing over the years. However, we do not think our framing helps to answer the question, "Why is it so hard to change the police institution?" Let's now consider this.

This chapter's conception of the American policing model with its game, scorecard, and playbook is James Nolan's adaptation of Pierre Bourdieu's theory of practice (Nolan and Hinkle 2021; Bourdieu [1977]2013; see also Grenfell 2008). Bourdieu's concepts of field and capital are equivalent to Nolan's game and scorecard. Nolan then added a *playbook* to represent the different strategies for playing a particular game. Nolan's game (or Bourdieu's field) refers to the policies, practices, and organizational hierarchies and positions that create a logic for action. Nolan's scorecard (or Bourdieu's capital) refers to the things that count as important in the game and that, therefore, are rewarded economically—such as through promotion in rank—and symbolically, such as through official commendations and award ribbons. Bourdieu also adds a third conceptual tool, *habitus*, which can help us understand how the game is continually reproduced. Whereas the game and scorecard exist outside of people, habitus exists within them.

Through a process of socialization, the logic of the game and the value of its rewards through the scorecard are internalized. Like a "fish in water," the players misrecognize the game as the natural way things should be (Maton 2008: 57). The players develop a "feel for the game," and its logic becomes *common sense* (ibid.: 54). The common sense of the law enforcement game is, in large part, the reason why it is so difficult to change.

This may be easier to see if we think of things that were once common sense, such as enslaving black people or holding women in subordinate positions to men. These past forms of common sense were fought through generations, although some of their legacies remain. People in positions of power did benefit from these discriminatory practices, but they were reproduced generation after generation because the logic of slavery and male superiority had become common sense (habitus).

In a similar way, the common sense of the law enforcement game is rarely examined. This is certainly true inside the police profession, but it is true outside as well. Policy leaders, such as the Obama policing task force (Chapter 7), and thought leaders, such as the National Academies of Science and evidence-based policing scholars (Chapter 7), regularly refer to the police profession as law enforcement, and never put this driving paradigm into question. In addition, federal funding streams, which set the direction for police research along with police-related curricula at top-ranked academic programs, equally accept without question the law enforcement game and the common sense it produces. The game's common sense is further reinforced through the popular media, which depict the police as crimefighters—not community builders. Finally, the common sense of the law enforcement game becomes internalized in most of us. Many of us are comfortable with the notion that the police can keep us safe—when safe communities instead require proactive community engagement, police-community collaboration, along with robust economic and health safety nets.

Whether the current system's overwhelming focus on the enforcement of laws is effective or harmful itself deserves greater scrutiny than it now receives. It is not simply that police leaders or other stakeholders receive some benefit for keeping things the same—although many certainly do. Rather, it is because of habitus—a common sense that is internalized in police officers, many other stakeholders, and in the public at large—that the law enforcement game is reproduced over the years, while the validity of its underlying assumptions is rarely examined.

In addition to the impediments to reform from inside the police institution, there are forces from outside that also present change. Outside the police institution, the field-as-is is upheld by experts, such as academics and evidence-based researchers who support the law enforcement game but look for better ways to do it. Political leaders, state and federal government officials, and the courts also reinforce the field. Through grant funding, program development, professional training, and court-ordered oversight, they aim to make policing less violent and less discriminatory while keeping the field intact.

In the following chapter, we examine the impact of the law enforcement mandate on police abuse. Later, we show the limitations of this approach and how it could change.

Further Reading

Bourdieu, Pierre. [1977] 2013. *Outline of a Theory of Practice.* Cambridge: Cambridge University Press.

Grenfell, Michael, ed. 2008. *Pierre Bourdieu: Key Concepts*. Durham: Acumen.

Manning, Peter K. 1997. *Police Work: The Social Organization of Policing*, 2nd ed. Long Grove, IL: Waveland Press.

Maton, Karl. 2008. "Habitus." In Michael Grenfell, ed., *Pierre Bourdieu: Key Concepts*, 49–66. Durham: Acumen.

Nolan, James J., and Joshua C. Hinkle. 2021. "Changing the Game: A Sociological Perspective on Police Reform." In James J. Nolan, Frank Crispino, and Timothy Parsons, eds., *Policing in an Age of Reform: An Agenda for Research and Practice*, 61–83. London: Palgrave Macmillan.

2

The American Police Abuse Triad: Over-Enforcement, Excessive Force, and Discrimination

The following passage was written by sociologist Egon Bittner (1970: 10) more than fifty years ago:

> It was not assumed initially that the police would enforce laws in the broad sense, but that they would concentrate on the control of individuals and collective tendencies toward transgression and disorder issuing from what were referred to as the "dangerous classes."

It recognizes a fact about American policing that is still true today. Crime control is mostly social control of the "dangerous classes." *Social control* generally means both the socialization process for acquiring self-control and the application of external social sanctions to ensure conformity to social norms (Akers 1998). In a more specific way, however, social control means the organized ways in which a society responds to "behavior and people it regards as deviant, problematic, worrying, threatening, troublesome or undesirable in some way or another" (Cohen 1985: 1). *Informal* social control includes rewards and sanctions administered by families, neighborhoods, schools, and communities. *Formal* social control is administered by the government or other institutions that regulate human behavior. The American police are generally referred to as agents of formal social control (Currie, DeKeseredy, and Maclean 1990).

The term *police abuse* generally refers to an officer's use of force in violation of the law or department policy. But this narrow definition fails to capture the more pervasive and harmful police behaviors that clog the criminal justice system, stigmatize impoverished communities, block education and career opportunities, lead to mass incarceration, destroy trust, make communities less safe, and put both the community and police in greater danger. Therefore, we define police abuse as three interrelated behaviors: over-enforcement, excessive force, and discrimination.

Over-enforcement means an overreliance on coercive police action as the primary way the police provide formal social control. This often involves the routine enforcement of relatively minor infractions in neighborhoods. It includes arrests for loitering, disorderly conduct, vagrancy, panhandling, and curfew and alcohol violations. These types of offenses are categorized by the FBI as "crimes against society" (FBI 2019). We refer to such enforcement as *social control arrests*. And we make a distinction between social control arrests and the arrests the police make for crimes such as murder, robbery, rape, assault, burglary, and theft. Over-enforcement also includes the regular police practice of temporarily detaining, questioning, and sometimes searching people on the street without the "reasonable suspicion" that federal judge Shira Scheindlin found, in a landmark ruling (*Floyd v. City of New York* 2013), was too often missing when New York City police stopped and frisked citizens (see also Jones-Brown, Gill, and Trone 2010).

Excessive force refers to both the overuse and unnecessary level of violence used by the police for crime and social control. This includes the regular use of nonlethal force, such as physical restraints and the use of Tasers, stun guns, chemical agents, and batons. It also includes the use of deadly force when the law prohibits it or when it could have been avoided. It is the mandate for crime and social control through law enforcement that creates a logic and disposition for excessive force. The use of force by police is often rationalized as being in accord with police policies and legal frameworks. Such rationales can wind up serving as a foundation for the law enforcement game. In later chapters, we discuss police reforms that make violence less necessary.

Discrimination refers to behaviors that result in harm or disadvantage to members of particular social groups, such as by gender, race, ethnicity, religion, or sexual orientation. Discrimination against black and brown people is the most prevalent type of discrimination in today's American policing, and thus our framework focuses on discrimination's racial and ethnic manifestations (Davis 2018).

All forms of police abuse in this triad affect individuals and communities, either directly, indirectly, or both. Over-enforcement and excessive force arising from normalized institutional practices have disparate impacts on economically disadvantaged black and brown communities. This includes rates of serious physical injury or death. It also includes less direct harms, such as criminal labels that are memorialized in law enforcement databases and in news stories easily accessible on social media (Ferguson 2017). These can limit the range of available opportunities after criminal justice system involvement. In addition, the debt incurred from fines, fees, and medical expenses from over-enforcement and excessive force can significantly impact the poor. The discriminatory nature of over-enforcement and excessive force fracture families and communities. They reduce trust, generate fear and anger, and are directly linked to mass incarceration (Alexander 2012). This creates the conditions in local places where crime, violence, and related social problems continue to thrive. Finally, the police abuse triad is generative in producing collateral consequences limiting access to pathways out of poverty throughout a lifetime.

Further Reading

Akers, Ronald L. 1998. *Social Learning and Social Structure: A General Theory of Crime and Deviance.* Boston: Northeastern University Press.

Alexander, Michelle. 2012. *The New Jim Crow: Mass Incarceration in the Age of Colorblindness.* New York: New Press.

Bittner, Egon. 1970. *The Functions of Police in Modern Society: A Review of Background Factors, Current Practices, and Possible Role Models.* Washington, DC: National Institute of Mental Health, Center for Studies in Crime and Delinquency.

Cohen, Stanley. 1985. *Visions of Social Control: Crime, Punishment and Classification.* Cambridge, UK: Polity Press.

Currie, Dawn H., Walter S. DeKeseredy, and Brian D. MacLean. 1990. "Reconstituting Social Order and Social Control." *Journal of Human Justice* 2, no. 1: 29–54.

Davis, Angela J., ed. 2018. *Policing the Black Man: Arrest, Prosecution, and Imprisonment.* New York: Vintage.

Federal Bureau of Investigation (FBI), Uniform Crime Reporting Program. 2019. *National Incident-Based Reporting System (NIBRS), 2018.* https://ucr.fbi.gov/nibrs/2018/resource-pages/crimes_against_persons_property_and_society-2018.pdf.

Ferguson, Andrew G. 2017. *The Rise of Big Data Policing.* New York: New York University Press.

Floyd v. City of New York, 959 F. Supp. 2d 540 (U.S. Southern District of New York), 2013.

Jones-Brown, Delores, Jaspreet Gill, and Jennifer Trone. 2010. "Stop, Question & Frisk Policing Practices in New York City: A Primer." March. Center on Race, Crime and Justice, John Jay College of Criminal Justice. https://www.rooseveltho use.hunter.cuny.edu/devdev/wp-content/uploads/2013/11/PRIMER_electronic_version.pdf.

Q5: Is over-enforcement pervasive in American policing?

Answer: Yes. In 2022, the American police arrested 6,196,771 people. More than 66 percent of these arrests were social control arrests. In fact, the police made nearly eight times more arrests for drug-abuse violations than they did for burglary and four times more arrests for disorderly conduct than for robbery (FBI n.d.). The hyper-focus on arrests does not mean the police are solving crimes. That same year, 87 percent of burglaries, 76 percent of robberies, 58 percent of assaults, 51 percent of homicides, 85 percent of vandalisms, 90 percent of frauds, 91 percent of motor vehicle thefts, and 76 percent of arsons were unsolved. The excessive use of enforcement for the purpose of social control—especially to the point it becomes counterproductive—is what we mean by over-enforcement.

The Facts: Between 2013 and 2022, the American police made 83,015,031 criminal arrests. This number is equivalent to 41 percent of every citizen in the United States between the ages of eighteen and sixty-five (U.S. Census Bureau n.d.). More than 66 percent of these were social control arrests. This includes arrests for offenses such as disorderly conduct, failure to obey the command of a police officer, drunkenness, drug abuse, vagrancy, and other offenses the FBI defines as crimes against society. This large number of arrests was not related to the police solving more serious crimes, such as murder, rape, robbery, burglary, and theft. Instead, they serve a different purpose. Making arrests has become its own end. Abysmal crime clearance rates no longer matter, as long as officers are making arrests. A good police officer is a good law enforcer and the objective measure of an officer's success in the profession is usually the quantity and quality of law enforcement outputs, such as arrests, citations, and the seizure of guns and drugs.

Table 2.1 provides specific examples from four cities whose violent crime rate is consistently higher than the national average. For each city, the table shows the total number of arrests, the percentage of arrests for social control offenses, the number of arrests as a percentage of the population between the ages of eighteen and sixty-five, and the percentage of unsolved homicides, violent crimes, and property crimes over an eleven-year period. The point of these examples is to show the importance of enforcement, especially for the purpose of social control. The police arrest so many people that the number is equivalent to a significant percentage of entire adult population. And even

Table 2.1 The Nature, Extent, and Effect of Arrests in Four Urban Police Departments, 2011–21

	St. Louis, MO	Atlanta, GA	Baltimore, MD	Wilmington, DE
Total arrests	181,087	148,528	286,543	38,802
Percentage of arrests as social control	59%	61%	67%	44%
Number of arrests as percentage of population 18–65	96%	41%	78%	85%
Unsolved homicides	54%	28%	58%	63%
Unsolved violent crimes	60%	59%	70%	58%
Unsolved property crimes	89%	87%	94%	87%

Source: Data obtained from the FBI Crime Data Explorer and US Census 2023.

though the police make this large number of arrests, the majority of serious crimes remained unsolved.

The police in all four cities made a huge number of criminal arrests between 2011 and 2021. Many were for social control. In St. Louis, for example, the number of criminal arrests is equivalent to 96 percent of the entire population between the ages of eighteen and sixty-five. In Atlanta, the number of arrests was equivalent to 41 percent of residents in this age group. In Baltimore and Wilmington, it was 78 percent and 85 percent, respectively. With all the enforcement in these cities, there was still a significant percentage of unsolved homicides, violent crimes, and property crimes. More than half of the homicides in this eleven-year period remained unsolved in St. Louis, Baltimore, and Wilmington. In all four cities, more than half of violent crimes and more than 85 percent of property crimes remained unsolved.

The police sometimes argue that social control arrests are necessary to reduce the more serious violent crimes. This thesis was tested following the recent spate of highly publicized police killings of unarmed black men and women. The civil unrest that followed led many police departments to intentionally decrease hyper-enforcement of public order offenses (Cheng and Long 2022). Some refer to this as *de-policing* or the Ferguson or Minneapolis Effect (Cassell 2020). Law professor Paul Cassell (2020) explains this simply as the redeployment of officers from law enforcement activities to managing protests. He writes, “even after the protests began to wane, police have pulled back from some kinds of *proactive policing*—that is, self-initiated policing methods designed to reduce crime by using preventive strategies, such as street stops or anti-gun patrols" (97). Proactive policing means to control crime by increasing social control enforcement. De-policing means to slow it down.

Criminologists Richard Rosenfeld and Joel Wallman (2019) examined the relationship between a decrease in social control enforcement and homicide rates between 2010 and 2015 in fifty-three large cities. They found no evidence to support a claim that decreasing enforcement of these offenses affects homicide rates. However, in the 1990s, researchers did report a small but statistically significant effect of social control arrests on homicide and robbery in New York City (Rosenfeld, Fornango, and Rengifo 2007). Still others have found that over-enforcement can exacerbate problems. For example, aggressive law enforcement for drug crimes can create power vacuums causing more violence and a spiral of retaliatory violence. This is especially true where the drugs are controlled by street gangs and the arrests destabilize the power dynamics (Ratcliffe and Taniguchi 2008).

Legal scholars and police practitioners sometimes argue that over-enforcement can be remedied by strict adherence to the US Constitution (Hardy 2023). Constitutional policing, as it is called, tries to refocus police on the principles and legal frameworks that authorize law enforcement practices. However, this overlooks the fact that hyper-enforcement by police is often justified by the courts on constitutional grounds. To make this point clearer, consider the case of Gail Atwater (Frase 2003).

In 1997, Gail Atwater was driving her pickup truck in Lago Vista, Texas, with her three-year-old son and five-year-old daughter in the front seat. None of them was wearing a seatbelt. A police officer observed the violation and pulled Atwater over. The officer yelled something to the effect of "we've met before" and "you're going to jail" (Frase 2003: 336). The officer had previously stopped Atwater and misremembered it as a seatbelt violation. He thought of this as a second offense. The officer called for a backup and asked Ms. Atwater for her license and insurance card. She told the officer that she did not have the documents, because her purse had been stolen the previous day. The officer responded that he had "heard that story two-hundred times before" (336). Ms. Atwater was handcuffed and placed in the back of the police car. She was transported to police headquarters where she was booked and spent time in a jail cell before a magistrate set bail at $310. She ultimately pleaded no contest to the misdemeanor seatbelt violation and paid a $50 fine (Frase 2003).

The Fourth Amendment guarantees the right to be free from "unreasonable searches and seizures." A full custodial arrest is a seizure that, therefore, must be reasonable. Over-arrest in American policing assumes it is reasonable to take a person into custody—suffering the indignities of handcuffing, full body search, booking, and a period of incarceration pending arraignment and bail hearing—even for a minor offense punishable by only a fine. The US Supreme Court agreed in *Atwater v. City of Lago Vista* (1999). The court decided that a person's Fourth Amendment rights are not violated when he or she is arrested for minor offenses such as driving without a seatbelt. The court concluded that a custodial arrest for a misdemeanor that is punishable only by a fine does not constitute an unreasonable seizure under the Fourth Amendment. This case, and others like it, give constitutional legitimacy to over-enforcement as a fundamental practice in American policing (Natapoff 2018).

Further Reading

Cassell, Paul G. 2020. "Explaining the Recent Homicide Spikes in U.S. Cities: The 'Minneapolis Effect' and the Decline in Proactive Policing." *Federal Sentencing Reporter* 33, no. 1/2: 83–127.

Cheng, Cheng, and Wei Long. 2022. "The Effect of Highly Publicized Police Killings on Policing: Evidence from Large U.S. Cities." *Journal of Public Economics* 206: 1–18.

Federal Bureau of Investigation (FBI). 2019. Crime Data Explorer. Accessed 2023. https://cde.ucr.cjis.gov/LATEST/webapp/#/pages/explorer/crime/arrest.

Frase, Richard. 2003. "What Were They Thinking? Fourth Amendment Unreasonableness in *Atwater v. City of Lago Vista*." *Fordham Law Review* 71: 329–421.

Hardy, Michael A., ed. 2023. *Constitutional Policing: Striving for a More Perfect Union.* Chicago: American Bar Association.

Natapoff, Alexandra. 2018. *Punishment without Crime: How Our Massive Misdemeanor System Traps the Innocent and Makes America More Unequal.* New York: Basic Books.

Ratcliffe, Jerry H., and Travis A. Taniguchi. 2008. "Is Crime Higher around Drug Gang Street Corners? Two Spatial Approaches to the Relationship between Gang Set Spaces and Local Crime Levels." *Crime Patterns and Analysis* 1, no. 1: 23–46.

Rosenfeld, Richard, Robert Fornango, and Andres F. Rengifo. 2007. "The Impact of Order-Maintenance Policing on New York City Homicide and Robbery Rates: 1988–2001." *Criminology* 45, no. 2: 355–84.

Rosenfeld, Richard, and Joel Wallman. 2019. "Did De-policing Cause the Increase in Homicide Rates?" *Criminology & Public Policy* 18, no. 1: 51–75.

U.S. Census Bureau. n. d. Accessed 2023. https://www.census.gov/quickfacts/fact/table/US/PST045222.

Q6: Is excessive force pervasive in American policing?

Answer: Yes, excessive force is pervasive in American policing. It occurs only as a small percentage of the total number of police-community interactions, but it is still a large number in absolute terms. In a single year, the American police threaten or use nonlethal force about one million times, according to the Bureau of Justice Statistics (BJS 2022). Moreover, the police shoot and kill more than one thousand people per year. This rate of deadly violence is higher than the rate of US military and Department of Defense (DOD) civilians killed during the combined wars in Iraq and Afghanistan (DOD 2024). It is also the highest rate of deadly police violence of any developed country in the world (Jones and Sawyer 2020).

The Facts: According to the BJS, only a small percentage of official police-community interactions involve the use of force. In 2020, BJS estimated that 53 million people in the United States over the age of sixteen reported they had had official contact with a police officer. Of these contacts, more than 25 million were police-initiated traffic and pedestrian stops (BJS 2022). The data revealed significant racial disparities in pedestrian stops, as well as in the searches and arrests once stopped (Tapp and Davis 2022).

During police stops, officers threatened or used nonlethal force about one million times in 2020 (Tapp and Davis 2022). That same year, US police officers shot and killed about a thousand people, and that number appears to be rising (authors' analysis of *Washington Post* n.d.). Figure 2.1 presents the number of people shot and killed by the police each year from 2015 through 2023. To put this US pattern in perspective, the combined fatal police shootings for England and Wales for 2022 and 2023 was three (Inquest n.d.). The rate of fatal police shootings in the United States is more than three times that of Canada and Australia, and it is fifteen times higher than that in the Netherlands and New Zealand (Jones and Sawyer 2020).

Let us take a closer look at some of these fatal police shootings. Sixty-one percent of people shot and killed by the police had a gun on them at the time of the incident. Seventeen percent were armed with a knife. Twelve percent of those killed were identified as being unarmed or it could not be determined if they had a weapon. (To arrive at this percentage, we combined the categories *unarmed*, *undetermined*, and *unknown*. The total number of people killed by police while unarmed between 2015 and 2023 was 528. The number listed as undetermined was 395, and unknown, 144.) Nearly 4 percent of the police killings involved

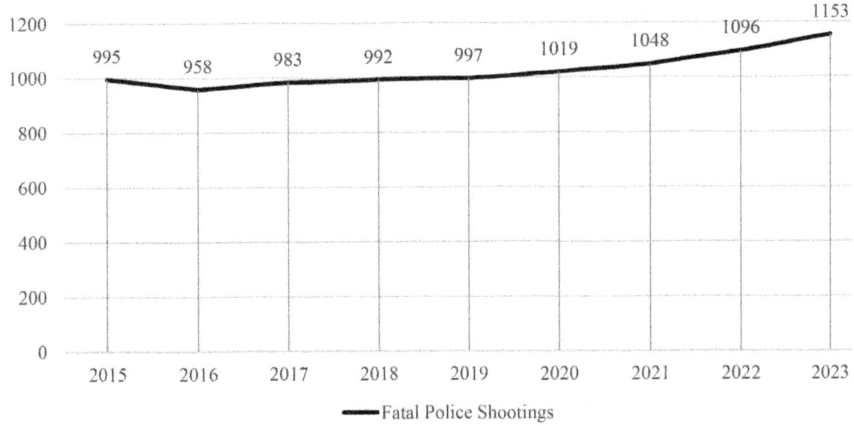

Figure 2.1 Number of people shot and killed by police, 2015–23.

Source: Data from Washington Post Fatal Police Shootings Database, https://www.washingtonpost.com/graphics/investigations/police-shootings-database/.

a vehicle as the suspect's deadly weapon. In another 3 percent of the cases, the suspect was in possession of a toy or replica gun.

In almost all situations in which the police use deadly violence, officers are on the scene as professional law enforcers—that is, not social workers, mental health professionals, family members, or as members of a community. In Chapter 1, we describe the police officer disposition and worldview that emerges from the law enforcement mandate. Officers are hypervigilant for danger and on high alert for deadly weapons that could be used against them or the public. They are oriented to pursue criminal offenders at all costs, demand compliance, and to never back down. So, a good question to ask might be, "How many of the more than one thousand per-year police killings could be prevented given a different police-officer mindset?"

The answer to this question is difficult to determine, partly because officials do not often ask how police killings can be prevented. As you review the following accounts of real events, we encourage you to make your own judgments. Had the officers involved had a different mindset, was their deadly use of force preventable?

Armed with a gun. On January 9, 2020, 47-year-old Claude Washington Fain was shot and killed by police in Philadelphia. Officers had approached Fain's apartment to serve a warrant for his arrest. When they arrived, Fain fired shots at officers and was killed in an exchange of gunfire with members of a police SWAT team (Cohen 2020).

Armed with a knife. On January 4, 2020, 25-year-old Tyree Davis was shot and killed by Chicago police. The police had been called to a local dollar store where Davis was alleged to be shoplifting. When police arrived, Davis—who had previously been diagnosed with bipolar disorder and schizophrenia—ran from the store. When officers caught him, they tasered him multiple times. When he continued to move toward the officers and failed to drop a knife, the officers shot him multiple times (Cohen 2020).

Armed with a toy gun. On November 12, 2014, twelve-year-old Tamir Rice was shot and killed by Cleveland police. Rice had been playing with a toy gun at Cudell Park. Someone in the park called 911 to report a person with a pistol who was "probably a juvenile" and that the gun was "probably fake." Cleveland police arrived and, within two seconds of opening the passenger door of the police vehicle, fired two shots, striking Rice in the abdomen (DOJ 2020).

On August 7, 2015, thirty-year-old Aaron Marchese was shot and killed by Fresno police. The police were called to the area for a report of a man with a gun. An officer ordered Marchese to show his hands. Instead, Marchese simply walked away. After a short distance, Marchese turned and pulled what appeared to be a gun out of his pants. The police officer opened fire, killing him. Marchese had suffered from mental illness most of his life. At the time of the killing, he was in possession of a toy gun. His family said he would often pretend broomsticks were weapons and point them at cars ("Suspect" 2015).

Armed with a blunt object. On April 29, 2015, 22-year-old Erick Emmanuel Sanchez was shot and killed by El Paso, Texas, police. The police had responded to a report of a residential burglary around 9:00 p.m. When they arrived, they found Sanchez inside the home. He armed himself with a blunt metal object and threatened to kill the officers. One officer used a Taser to stop Sanchez, but it had no effect. When Sanchez charged at officers with the metal object in hand, they shot and killed him (Martinez 2015). The victim's mother told a different story. She alleged that she was outside her home talking to the police. Erick Sanchez was inside the house trying to stop his mother from talking to the police. He referred to them as "dogs" and told them to leave. In response the police forced their way into her home and attacked Sanchez (Kree and Cross 2019). One of the officers was eventually charged with manslaughter but was found not guilty.

Unarmed. On November 19, 2015, 29-year-old Nathaniel Pickett was stopped by a San Bernardino County, California, sheriff's deputy outside of a motel for questioning. Pickett asked the deputy if he had done anything wrong. The deputy told Pickett there was no problem, but he continued questioning Pickett about his arrest history, whether he was originally from the area, and where he intended to go next. Pickett, a former engineering student, asked the deputy if he was free to go to his room. He told the deputy that if he had no probable cause to arrest him, then he had the right to walk away. The deputy grabbed Pickett, said "stop resisting," and threatened to use a Taser on him. Pickett tried to run to his room but tripped and fell. The deputy punched Pickett fifteen to twenty times before pulling his service weapon. Then he pressed the barrel against Pickett's chest and fired two shots (Thompson 2021).

Undetermined. On October 22, 2015, a Kentucky State Police officer shot and killed Stephen Brock. Neighbors called the police because they observed him walking up and down the narrow drive to his trailer home armed with a gun, yelling, and cursing. Afraid, and aware that Brock suffered from mental illness, they called 911. When police arrived, Brock was hiding behind a bush threatening to shoot. Police fired three rounds from an M16 assault rifle, killing Brock, who, they then discovered, was unarmed.

Vehicle as a deadly weapon. On January 20, 2018, seventeen-year-old John Albers was shot and killed by Overland Park, Kansas police. Albers was home alone when someone called police to conduct a welfare check at his residence. Albers had been depressed and the caller suspected he was contemplating suicide. When the police arrived, they approached the house. As they stood outside, the garage door opened and Albers began slowly backing out, driving the family minivan. One of the officers jumped behind the van, aiming his weapon and yelling for Albers to stop. As Albers continued, the officer jumped to the right of the van and fired twice, hitting the teenager. Albers was unable to control the vehicle. As it sped in reverse, the officer fired eleven more shots at the minivan. Six of the bullets struck Albers in the head, neck, shoulder, and lower lip (Ortiz 2021).

In each of these eight incidents, officers were cleared of wrongdoing—either by the police department, attorney general's office, or the courts—because, when they fired their weapons, they claimed to fear for their own lives or the lives of others. However, some of these deadly force cases appear to be connected to the law enforcement mindset. In the Tamir Rice case, officers responded to a call about a person ("probably a juvenile") armed with a gun ("probably fake"). It is likely that the killing of this twelve-year-old boy could have been prevented if officers had taken more time to engage with him from a distance and under cover. Similarly, the killing of Nathaniel Pickett might have been prevented if officers had let Pickett go to his room rather than force him to remain in a stop and interrogation without reasonable suspicion or probable cause. Likewise, the Sanchez killing might have been prevented had the officers not reacted to his verbal threats or insults with force (tasering). In the John Albers killing, the police commanded the juvenile to stop as he was backing his parent's vehicle out of the garage. Albers was suspected of being suicidal, and it is likely he did not hear the officer's command to stop. The officer perceived the failure to immediately stop the car as a justifiable threat to his life. This error in judgment was probably related to the officer's disposition and worldview related to the law enforcement mandate. Perhaps a different perspective would have prevented this fatal police shooting from occurring.

These scenarios may be helpful in thinking about the number of fatal police shootings that occur throughout the United States. Table 2.2, which relies on the Washington Post's fatal police shootings database, drills deeper into this national phenomenon with a state-level analysis, listing the number of fatal police shootings by weapon type (or lack thereof) from 2015 to 2023. The total number of killings by state are provided as well as a computed rate based on the size of the state population.

Most police killings occurred in California, Texas, Florida, and Georgia. But the states with the highest rates of fatal police shootings (per 100,000 in the population) are New Mexico, Alaska, Oklahoma, Colorado, and Arizona, in that order. Most people shot and killed by the police were armed with a deadly weapon. However, more than half of the fatal police shootings in California, New Jersey, Vermont, Hawaii, and Massachusetts involved suspects with *no* gun. In nearly 20 percent of the fatal police shootings in Kentucky, Louisiana, and Mississippi the suspects were listed as unarmed or undetermined. Rhode Island, Delaware, and Hawaii had the highest percentage of fatal police shootings involving vehicles as weapons. In about 20 percent of all fatal police shootings, the victim was alleged to have been suffering from some form of mental illness. In shooting incidents in which the suspects were armed with a toy or replica weapon, the rate of suspected mental illness is nearly 40 percent.

The police are considered justified in using deadly force when they fear for their own lives or the lives of others. As we show later in this chapter, the standard set by the US Supreme Court in evaluating the police use of deadly force is the reasonable police officer standard. This is problematic because police officers are socialized to be on high alert for danger. This is why toy guns look like real threats, vehicles look like deadly weapons, and a person with no weapon can look to trained police officers as armed and dangerous. Thus, we need to raise the question as to whether justified fatal police shootings could be prevented with a change in the police mindset as they respond to emergency situations involving troubled people.

One problem in examining and addressing excessive force in American policing is a lack of data. There is a lack of reliable information on police violence in the United States from official government sources (Zimring 2017: chap. 2). To fill the void, organizations like the *Washington Post* have stepped in. The

Table 2.2 Police Killings by State and Suspect Weapon, 2015–23

State	Suspect's Weapon						Total Police Killings
	Gun	Knife	Replica/ Toy Gun	Blunt Object	Unarmed/ Undetermined	Vehicle	
AK	43	6	3	1	4	0	57
AL	125	11	4	4	21	5	170
AR	77	20	3	2	13	7	122
AZ	237	68	15	11	54	10	395
CA	570	314	81	69	167	46	1,247
CO	227	42	7	2	38	14	330
CT	14	7	1	0	4	1	27
DC	15	2	3	0	3	2	25
DE	11	1	1	0	2	3	18
FL	363	102	13	12	58	20	568
GA	226	47	9	7	37	17	343
HI	17	10	2	0	4	4	37
IA	32	8	3	1	7	3	54
ID	48	15	2	0	9	3	77
IL	125	29	5	6	16	2	183
IN	121	27	7	4	14	7	180
KS	55	10	2	1	11	5	84
KY	97	18	1	4	27	9	156
LA	109	19	3	3	32	7	173
MA	23	22	5	1	3	2	56
MD	67	24	4	1	11	5	112
ME	23	5	2	0	6	2	38
MI	106	22	4	6	19	6	163
MN	52	24	2	3	12	1	94
MO	165	25	2	3	25	9	229
MS	78	11	3	1	23	4	120
MT	35	7	3	1	8	2	56
NC	186	39	8	3	22	6	264
ND	10	2	0	0	7	0	19
NE	28	8	0	0	6	2	44
NH	15	4	2	0	5	0	26
NJ	41	28	7	4	14	5	99
NM	128	23	5	6	22	4	188

(*Continued*)

Table 2.2 (*Continued*)

State	Suspect's Weapon: Gun	Knife	Replica/ Toy Gun	Blunt Object	Unarmed/ Undetermined	Vehicle	Total Police Killings
NV	94	27	5	2	12	8	148
NY	88	53	8	5	11	3	168
OH	161	37	13	3	28	9	251
OK	141	47	2	8	28	10	236
OR	79	30	9	5	20	2	145
PA	116	30	6	2	21	11	186
RI	4	0	1	0	0	2	7
SC	105	19	0	1	17	2	144
SD	20	4	0	2	4	1	31
TN	158	39	5	4	30	14	250
TX	550	120	18	20	100	25	833
UT	64	22	5	4	15	4	114
VA	106	26	4	6	20	2	164
VT	5	2	3	0	3	1	14
WA	125	60	4	3	29	13	234
WI	92	29	5	0	11	4	141
WV	58	9	4	4	10	1	86
WY	18	5	1	0	4	1	29
TOTAL	5,453	1,559	305	225	1,067	326	8,935

Source: James Nolan's analysis of the *Washington Post* Fatal Police Shooting Database, https://www.washingtonpost.com/graphics/investigations/police-shootings-database/.

analysis we presented earlier on fatal police shootings could not have been done otherwise. Still, national data on police less-than-lethal violence have been difficult to obtain. In fact, the FBI just began collecting it (FBI 2019).

In 2021, 8,815 (out of 18,514) police agencies in the United States participated in the FBI's new program. These agencies employ 65 percent of all police officers in the nation. The number of participating police agencies in this new data collection program is significant. However, based on early reports, the FBI indicates that less than 2 percent of these police agencies reported using a level of force that resulted in death or serious injury. And this was mostly explained by the citizen's failure to comply with verbal commands or other types of passive resistance. (The limited data available can be accessed via the FBI's Crime Data Explorer [FBI n.d.].) These early reports implied that over 98 percent of the agencies had refrained from using injurious or deadly levels of force in 2021. The accuracy of these reports is at least questionable, given the nature and extent of police violence in the news and in the *Washington Post* fatal police shooting database, which lists more than 3,500 separate jurisdictions with police-involved killings between 2015 and 2023.

Although this new federal data collection appears to contain comprehensive information about the use of force in American policing, the FBI releases very little of it to the public. Therefore, in the following sections, we examine the public data that are available on police use of force in three cities—Phoenix, New Orleans, and Cincinnati—and then speculate on what questions might be asked and answered with reliable national data.

Phoenix, Arizona. In 2022, the population of Phoenix was 1,644, 409. Forty-two percent of the population is Hispanic or Latino, 41 percent white, and 7 percent black (US Census Bureau n.d.). In 2023, the Phoenix police department had a total of 2,567 sworn officers. Sixty-nine percent were white, 21 percent Hispanic, and 5 percent black.

Between January 1, 2015, and December 31, 2023, Phoenix police officers shot and killed 106 people. This is much higher than any other city in the United States. Only the Los Angeles Police Department killed more people during this time. Thirty-two of those killed by Phoenix police were white, thirty-two were Hispanic, eighteen were black, four Native American, and twenty unknown races. About 66 percent of the people shot and killed by Phoenix police were armed with a gun. Eighteen percent were armed with a knife or blunt instrument, 15 percent were either unarmed/undetermined or they had a toy gun (authors' analysis of *Washington Post* n.d.).

In addition, between January 1, 2021, and December 31, 2022, the Phoenix police pointed their guns at citizens 3,457 times. Figure 2.2 compares the monthly totals during these two years. This type of force—pointing a gun at a person—was consistently higher in 2022 compared to 2021 and may reflect a general trend toward more police violence in Phoenix.

However, this is not the only way the police in Phoenix use force against citizens. Between January 1, 2018 and July 3, 2023, the Phoenix police used several other types of force to apprehend suspects, including deploying police dogs (198 times), the use of electrical weapons like Tasers (706 times), deadly force (111 times), direct impact munitions—that is, foam bullets with chemical irritants (691 times), hard empty hand control, that is, physical strikes (1,389 times), soft empty hand control and restraining devices (1,230 times), and tripping or tackling (680 times). Table 2.3 shows these use-of-force incidents by the officer's and suspect's weapons (or lack thereof). This can give some

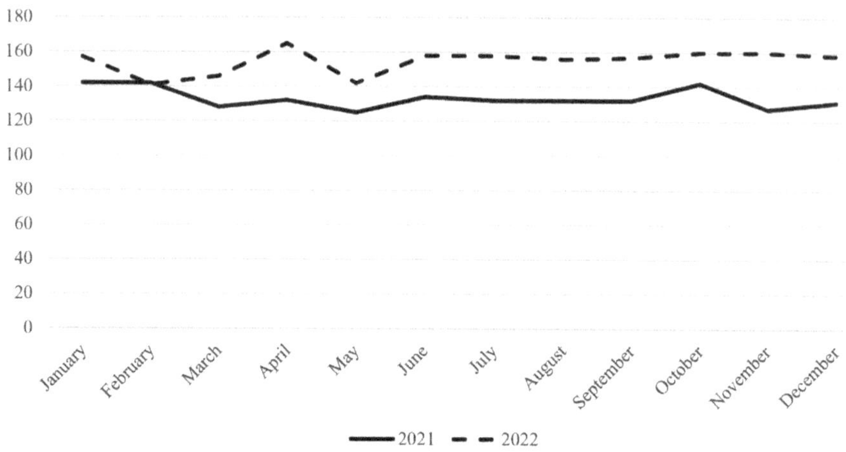

Figure 2.2 Phoenix Police Department monthly counts of times officers point their guns at citizens, 2021–2.

Source: Data from Phoenix Police Department Open Data, https://www.phoenixopendata.com/dataset/pgp/resource/67d5f435-36ea-414c-98e5-a652a7f31c4e.

indication of the nature of the incident in which force was used. Of the 230 times the Phoenix police faced a gun-toting suspect, officers countered with deadly force only 65 times (28 percent). The rest of the time they used a variety of less-than-lethal weapons, including the use of canines (11), Taser (18), foam bullets (47), and empty hand strike (54). On the other hand, the Phoenix police used deadly force in thirteen incidents in which the suspect was unarmed.

New Orleans, Louisiana. The population of the city of New Orleans is 369,749. Fifty-eight percent of residents are black, 33 percent white, 3 percent Asian, and 5 percent Hispanic. There are 1,238 sworn officers in the New Orleans police department (NOPD). Sixty-five percent are black and 30 percent are white. Between 2021 and 2022, the NOPD documented 853 use-of-force incidents. About 51 percent of these incidents involve physical force on the part of officers attempting to make an arrest. Other types of force include the display of weapon at a citizen (14 percent) and the deployment of a chemical agent (6 percent) or canine (2 percent). The justifications for the use of force in these incidents is listed in Table 2.4. Ninety-six (96) percent of use-of-force cases were justified by NOPD officials. Two percent were not justified. One percent is still pending investigation, and 1 percent was determined to be unfounded.

Cincinnati, Ohio. The population of Cincinnati, Ohio, is 309,513. Forty-nine percent of the population is white and non-Hispanic, 40 percent is black, 4 percent is Hispanic, 2 percent is Asian, and 5 percent is mixed race. About 28 percent of the officers in the department are black.

Table 2.3 Use of Force by Officer and Suspect Weapon Type, January 1, 2018–July 3, 2023

Officer Weapon	Suspect Weapon						
	(1) Blunt Instrument	(2) Bodily Force	(3) Cutting Instrument	(4) Gun	(5) None	(6) Other	(7) Total
Canines	3	2	10	11	158	14	198
Carotid	2	0	3	2	29	3	39
Conducted Electrical Weapons (Taser)	52	145	90	18	360	41	706
Deadly Physical Force	3	0	16	65	13	14	111
Direct Impact Munitions—Foam Round with Irritant	39	32	110	47	429	34	691
Hard Empty Hand Control	39	475	44	54	721	56	1,389
Impact Weapons	0	2	2	5	7	3	19
Irritants	0	3	8	1	34	6	52
None	0	0	0	0	1	0	1
Other	0	0	1	0	10	0	11
Soft Empty Hand Techniques and Restraining Devices	14	148	22	14	1,000	32	1,230
Tripping/Tackling	5	117	10	13	526	9	680
Total	157	924	316	230	3,288	212	5,127

Source: James Nolan's analysis of Phoenix Police Department Use of Force Data, January 1, 2018–July 3, 2023, https://www.phoenixopendata.com/dataset/ouof/resource/15e44940-0fde-4922-943a-93b717ebfb7a.

The Cincinnati Police Department (CPD) defines the use of force as the means of compelling compliance or overcoming resistance to an officer's command(s) to protect life or property or to take a person into custody. Between 2015 and 2023, the Cincinnati police shot and killed six people, five were black and one was white (authors' analysis of *Washington Post* n.d.). In addition to the use of deadly force, the Cincinnati police capture data on less-than-lethal force used by officers to compel compliance. This includes the use of chemical irritants, physical force that injures a prisoner, physical force on a noncompliant arrestee,

Table 2.4 New Orleans Police Department: Justifications for Use of Force, 2021–2

Justification for Use of Force	Number
Battery on Police Officer	54
Building Clearing	1
Escape	20
Escorting/Handcuffed	1
Felony Vehicle Stop	1
Flight from an Officer	146
Other	46
Other-Create Distance	1
Other-Resisting	1
Refuse Verbal Commands	184
Resisting Lawful Arrest	220
Resisting Officer w/Weapon	20
Resisting Officer w/Weapon | Refuse Verbal Commands	1
Room Clearing—Making Sure No One Is Hiding during Police Search of a Building or Home	5
Tactical Deployments	36
Weapon Exhibited	116
Total	853

Source: Data from City of New Orleans, Open Data, https://portal-nolagis.opendata.arcgis.com/.

and the use of a Taser, beanbag or foam round. Figure 2.3 summarizes the use of force used by CPD from 2005 to 2021. The trend in using force by the police has declined since 2005. The most common type of force used by CPD is the nonlethal weapon, that is, Taser/beanbag/pepper ball round. Next is physical force causing injury to prisoners, then physical force to subdue a suspect or arrestee, and, finally, the use of a chemical irritant by police.

The Phoenix data point to a possible connection between pointing firearms at citizens and the use of deadly force. This might be important information to consider in a national data collection. In addition, the New Orleans data show the circumstances in which violence is most often used. NOPD officers, for example, used force against civilians 184 times for refusing to obey their commands. Is this when the police are most likely to harm citizens? If national data were to capture the reasons why the police used force against a member of the public, the type of force used, and the injuries sustained, perhaps effective policies and practices could be implemented. The Cincinnati data raise many questions that could potentially be answered about police violence involving

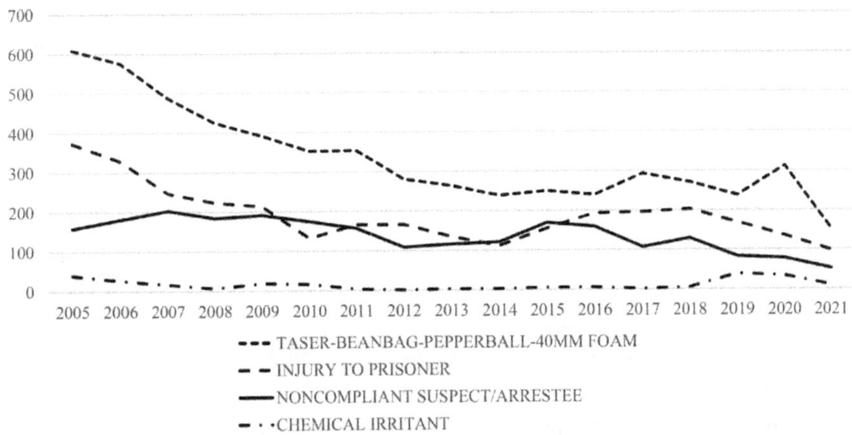

Figure 2.3 Use of force by Cincinnati Police, 2005–21.
Source: Data from City of Cincinnati, Ohio Open Data, https://data.cincinnati-oh.gov/Safety/PDI-Police-Data-Initiative-Use-of-Force/8us8-wi2w.

using canines and less-than-lethal weapons, such as Tasers and beanbag rounds, with a national data collection that included this information.

In summary, the American police use deadly violence more than any other developed nation in the world. The use of force by the police against the public is a small percentage of their total interactions but still a large number. The importance of the issue of police violence cannot be overstated, and the collection and availability of accurate data at a national level could be a useful tool in developing policies and practices that address the problem more effectively than past efforts.

Further Reading

Bureau of Justice Statistics (BJS). 2022. *Police-Public Contact Survey* (PPCS). https://bjs.ojp.gov/data-collection/police-public-contact-survey-ppcs.

Center for Disease Control and Prevention (CDC). National Violent Death Reporting System (NVDRS). Accessed August 11, 2024. https://www.cdc.gov/violenceprevention/datasources/nvdrs/index.html.

City of New Orleans, Louisiana Open Data, New Orleans Police Department. Accessed August 11, 2024. https://data.nola.gov/Public-Safety-and-Preparedness/NOPD-Use-of-Force-Incidents/9mnw-mbde.

City of Phoenix, Arizona Open Data, Phoenix Police Department. Accessed August 11, 2024. https://www.phoenixopendata.com/dataset/pgp.

Cohen, Li. 2020. "Police in the U.S. Killed 164 Black People in the First 8 Months of 2020. These Are Their Names." CBS News, September 10.

DOJ Press Release. 2020. https://www.justice.gov/opa/pr/justice-department-announces-closing-investigation-2014-officer-involved-shooting-cleveland, December 29. Accessed January 10, 2025.

Federal Bureau of Investigation (FBI). n. d. Crime Data Explorer. https://cde.ucr.cjis.gov/LATEST/webapp/#/pages/le/uof.

Federal Bureau of Investigation (FBI). 2019. National Use of Force Data Collection. https://www.fbi.gov/how-we-can-help-you/more-fbi-services-and-information/ucr/use-of-force.

Inquest. n.d. "Fatal Police Shootings." Accessed February 8, 2025. https://www.inquest.org.uk/fatal-police-shootings.

Jones, Alex, and Wendy Sawyer. 2020. "Not Just 'a Few Bad Apples': U.S. Police Kill Civilians at Much Higher Rates than Other Countries." Prison Policy Initiative. June 5. https://www.prisonpolicy.org/blog/2020/06/05/policekillings.

Kree, Justin, and David Cross. 2019. "El Paso Police Officer Found Not Guilty of Manslaughter in Shooting Death of Man in 2015." KFOX 14, October 11. Accessed January 10, 2025. https://kfoxtv.com/news/local/jury-hears-testimony-from-mother-of-man-shot-killed-by-el-paso-police-officer.

Martinez, Aaron. 2015. "El Paso Police Shot and Killed Burglary Suspect Wednesday Night." *El Paso Times*, April 30. Accessed January 10, 2025. https://www.nbcnews.com/news/us-news/family-kansas-teen-fatally-shot-police-during-wellness-check-blasts-n1265881.

Ortiz, Eric. 2021. "Family of Kansas Teen Fatally Shot by Police During Wellness Check Blasts Investigation." NBC News, April 30.

"Suspect with Replica Gun Killed in Fresno County Officer-Involved Shooting." ABC News. August 7, 2015.

Tapp, Susannah N., and Elizabeth J. Davis. 2022. *Contacts between Police and the Public.* Washington, DC: Bureau of Justice Statistics. https://bjs.ojp.gov/sites/g/files/xyckuh236/files/media/document/cbpp20.pdf.

Thompson, Cheryl W. 2021. "Fatal Police Shootings of Unarmed Black People Reveal Troubling Patterns." NPR, January 25.

US Census Bureau. Accessed February 8, 2025. https://www.census.gov/quickfacts/fact/table/US/PST045222.

US Department of Defense (DOD). 2024. "Casualty Status." Press Release. https://www.defense.gov/casualty.pdf.

US Department of Justice (DOJ). 2020. "Justice Department Announces Closing of Investigation into 2014 Officer Involved Shooting in Cleveland, Ohio." Press Release, December 29. https://www.justice.gov/opa/pr/justice-department-announces-closing-investigation-2014-officer-involved-shooting-cleveland.

Washington Post Police Shootings Database. Accessed February 8, 2025. https://www.washingtonpost.com/graphics/investigations/police-shootings-database/.

Zimring, Franklin E. 2017. *When Police Kill.* Cambridge, MA: Harvard University Press.

Q7: Is discrimination pervasive in American policing?

Answer: Yes. Racial disparities are present in every state and in all aspects of policing, including stops, citations, arrests, searches, and the use of force.

The Facts: In this section, we examine facts about the nature and extent of discrimination in American policing. We begin with official arrest data collected by the FBI. We then look at national data on fatal police shootings collected by the *Washington Post* (*Washington Post* n.d.). Finally, we examine a few local examples, including data from two cities and one mostly rural state.

One way to examine discrimination in American policing is to look at disparities in the rates at which people are arrested and subjected to the use of force by race. To do this, we use census population figures as benchmarks. Researchers sometimes argue against benchmarks using census data because it does not adequately weight the conditions that put certain groups at higher risk for arrests, stops, frisks, and the use of force (Smith et al. 2019: 2). One way to adjust is to weight census populations by the proportion of crime-suspect descriptions in a community (Ridgeway 2007). We disagree on conceptual and statistical grounds, however. Conceptually, we want to examine *systemic* discrimination NOT police officer or police agency bias. As an institution, the American police are an integral part of the same social system that produces disparities in crime-suspect descriptions. The census population denominator allows us to compute per person rates in a state or city in the same way public health officials assess the risk of disease by group (Howlader et al. 2021) or criminologists study the risk of victimization by race, sex, and age (Akiyama et al. 2015).

We compute a racial disparity index by Equation 1:

Equation 1. Racial Disparity Index ("I")

$$I = \frac{\frac{a}{b}}{\frac{c}{d}}, \text{ where}$$

a = the number of people arrested or subjected to use of force who are identified as black
b = the black population
c = the number of people arrested or subjected to the use of force who are identified as white
d = the white population

A racial disparity index of 1 means there is no difference between the groups. An index of 1.8 means the rate is 1.8 times higher for black people than white. This can also be expressed as 80 percent higher. Note that a racial disparity index greater than 1 does not mean more black people are arrested or shot than whites. This is not usually the case. Instead, it means that the number of black people arrested or shot as a percentage of the black population is higher than the number of white people arrested or shot as a percentage of the white population.

We begin by using the racial disparity index to examine arrests and police killings nationally and with a breakdown by state (as shown in Table 2.5). The total arrest category (column 1) includes crimes against persons and property, such as murder, rape, robbery, assault, burglary, theft, and motor vehicle theft. It also includes crimes against society, such as drug and alcohol violations, disorderly conduct, loitering, and vagrancy. In every state, the arrest rate is higher for black citizens than for whites. This is particularly true for social-control arrests like drug and marijuana arrests (columns 2 and 3). We know from national self-report studies of drug and marijuana use that black and white teens and adults at various ages admit to using drugs and marijuana at about the same rate (Center for Behavioral Health Statistics 2021). However, the racial disparity indexes for both drug and marijuana arrests show that black residents are arrested at much higher rates than whites. In Delaware, for example, black residents are arrested for possession of marijuana at a rate 4.5 times higher than white residents—or 350 percent higher.

The rate at which black Americans are shot and killed by the police, as reflected in the *Washington Post* police shooting database, aligns with the findings from the Centers for Disease Control and Prevention (CDC) that death rates from law enforcement actions were 88 percent higher for blacks than whites (CDC 2021). The statewide comparisons reflect variation in rates of discrimination in police killings. In Washington, DC, the racial disparity index for police shootings is 11, or eleven times higher for black Americans compared to whites. In California, which has the highest number of people shot and killed by the police among all states, the racial disparity index is 6.5, meaning 6.5 times higher for black Americans or a 550 percent higher rate. In Mississippi, a state where police shot and killed 111 people, the racial disparity index is 1.3, or 30 percent higher for blacks than whites. A racial disparity of zero, such as in Vermont and South Dakota, indicates that such states saw no blacks killed by the police in this period.

Next, we examine the public data on arrests and the use of force in two urban police agencies—those of Phoenix and Cincinnati. Then, we examine traffic stops, citations, and searches in West Virginia, a mostly rural state.

Table 2.5 Black Racial Disparity Index for Total Arrests, Drug Arrests, Marijuana Arrests (2017–21) and Fatal Police Shootings (2015–22)

	(1) Total Arrests – Black Racial Disparity	(2) Total Drug Arrests – Black Racial Disparity	(3) Total Marijuana Arrests – Black Racial Disparity	(4) Total Shot and Killed by Police 2015–22	(5) Killed by Police – Black Racial Disparity
AK	2.6	2.1	1.9	54	1.8
AL	1.7	1.6	4.5	161	1.2
AR	2.4	1.9	2.8	117	2.4
AZ	2.6	2.3	3.0	385	3.2
CA	2.2	1.5	1.9	1,205	6.5
CO	2.6	2.1	1.8	308	3.3
CT	3.0	3.5	4.1	23	3.1
DC	12.0	12.0	13.9	26	11.0
DE	2.7	3.2	4.5	19	2.9
FL	2.1	1.5	2.8	540	3.0
GA	1.9	1.8	3.3	322	1.8
HI	1.7	1.2	1.3	41	5.8
IA	5.9	6.0	8.2	50	5.1
ID	3.5	3.5	4.3	70	2.1
IL	9.5	7.0	5.3	171	8.3
IN	3.8	2.9	4.3	158	3.4
KS	3.2	3.8	5.3	82	2.8
KY	2.2	2.7	8.5	150	2.3
LA	2.5	2.4	3.6	167	3.0
MA	2.2	2.5	3.2	57	3.7
MD	2.0	2.2	2.1	112	3.3
ME	3.6	4.4	2.7	34	1.7
MI	3.2	2.8	3.4	144	3.7
MN	4.7	3.3	4.7	93	4.3
MO	3.1	2.2	3.0	221	4.3
MS	1.9	1.6	3.2	111	1.3
MT	5.4	6.2	7.3	55	4.1
NC	2.6	2.5	3.9	243	1.9
ND	4.0	4.8	6.2	18	2.8
NE	4.0	3.8	3.3	42	3.3
NH	2.9	3.1	3.6	23	0.0

(*Continued*)

Table 2.5 (*Continued*)

	(1) Total Arrests – Black Racial Disparity	(2) Total Drug Arrests – Black Racial Disparity	(3) Total Marijuana Arrests – Black Racial Disparity	(4) Total Shot and Killed by Police 2015–22	(5) Killed by Police – Black Racial Disparity
NJ	3.4	3.4	3.5	97	7.3
NM	2.3	2.1	2.7	179	4.3
NV	3.1	2.8	3.5	138	2.7
NY	1.9	1.9	2.1	152	4.2
OH	3.1	3.3	4.3	240	4.3
OK	2.9	2.7	4.1	233	2.9
OR	3.4	2.1	1.7	139	4.2
PA	2.8	3.1	3.2	174	4.6
RI	2.9	3.5	3.6	6	9.4
SC	1.9	2.3	1.7	133	1.5
SD	5.1	5.4	6.6	29	0.0
TN	1.9	1.9	3.5	235	1.8
TX	2.1	2.0	2.6	782	3.5
UT	4.4	4.9	5.6	102	8.6
VA	2.4	2.6	3.6	155	2.6
VT	4.8	8.2	4.8	13	0.0
WA	3.1	2.4	2.1	229	5.5
WI	4.1	4.1	4.8	129	5.8
WV	3.5	4.9	7.5	80	3.8
WY	10.1	5.2	5.7	29	11.0
US Total	2.2	2.1	3.5	8,476	2.9

Source: Data from FBI, arrest data by state 2017–21, and *Washington Post* Police Shootings Database, https://www.washingtonpost.com/graphics/investigations/police-shootings-database/.

Between 2018 and 2024, the Phoenix police arrested 221,540 people on a variety of criminal charges (Phoenix Police Department n.d.). More than half of these arrests were for drug abuse or other crimes against society. Black arrest rates for all crimes were more than three times higher than rates for whites and Hispanics. Hispanics and whites were arrested at about the same rate. The black and Hispanic population are at a much higher risk than whites for the use of force by police, as Table 2.6 shows. Columns 1 through 4 show the number of people in each racial group subjected to police use of force. In columns 6, 7, and

Table 2.6 Use of Force by Phoenix Police Officers by Race

		Race of Person Subjected to Force				**Total**			
		(1) White	(2) Black	(3) Hispanic	(4) Other	(5)	(6) White, Non-Hispanic Population	(7) Hispanic Population	(8) Black Population
Officer Race	White	1,207	924	1,499	284	3,914	674,208	690,651	115,109
	Black	75	93	143	28	339	White Per Person Rate	Hispanic Per Person Rate	Black Per Person Rate
	Hispanic	452	372	698	121	1,643	0.0028	0.0037	0.0131
	Other	150	124	212	36	522		Hispanic Disparity Index	Black Disparity Index
	Total	1,884	1,513	2,552	469	6,418		1.32	4.67

Source: Data from Phoenix Police Department Use of Force Data 2018–23 and US Census 2023.

8, we compute the per person rate of police violence by racial or ethnic group of the person arrested (i.e., the number of arrests divided by the group population).

Between 2018 and 2023, the Phoenix police used physical force more often against Hispanics than any other group (40 percent). The next most frequent group was white, non-Hispanic (29 percent), then black, non-Hispanic (24 percent). Sixty-one percent of the officers using violent force were white (3,914), 26 percent Hispanic (1,643), and 5 percent black. The highest rate of police violence is against the black population (0.0131), then Hispanic (0.0037), then white (0.0028). The rate of police violence against the black population in Phoenix is 4.7 times higher than it is for white and 3.7 times higher than for Hispanic.

The analysis points to disparate risk for arrests and the use of force by race and ethnicity of the offender. The black population in Phoenix has the highest risk for being subjected to coercive force by police officers than either the white or Hispanic populations. Of all those arrested, Hispanics have the highest rate of force used against them by white, black, and Hispanic officers.

Let's now look at Cincinnati. Between 2013 and 2022, the Cincinnati police arrested 38,548 people on criminal charges. Black Americans make up 40 percent of the city's population but 75 percent of the arrests (FBI n.d.; US Census Bureau n.d.). The racial disparity in total arrests is four times higher for blacks than for whites. As shown in Table 2.7, between 2005 and 2021, the Cincinnati police used force to make arrests 11,590 times. The use of force was disproportionately directed at the black population of Cincinnati. The overall racial disparity in the use of force is nearly four times higher for blacks than for whites. The Cincinnati Police Department joins data on the use of three nonlethal weapons—Tasers, beanbags, and foam rounds—into a singular figure. Eighty percent of the Taser/beanbag/foam round targets in the period examined were black. The rate of such targeting against blacks was nearly five times that for whites. Similarly, blacks experienced nearly three times the rate of police chemical irritant spraying, and rate of prisoner injury, as compared to whites.

Turning to West Virginia, in 2006 the West Virginia legislature passed the Racial Profiling Data Collection Act (W. Va Code Section 17-G-2–3), which required "all law enforcement officers to begin gathering information on all traffic stops beginning in January 1, 2007" (Haas, Turley, and Sterling 2009: 1). Each time a police officer stopped the operator of a motor vehicle for a violation of any statute or ordinance, officers were required to complete the West Virginia Motor Vehicle Stop Form (WVMVSF). This comprehensive data collection would last only from April 2007 to September 2008. During that time, West Virgina police stopped 301,479 vehicles. The researchers used a disparity ratio to compare the

Table 2.7 Use of Force by Cincinnati Police: Type of Force by Race of Subject, 2005–21

	Black	Hispanic	Other[a]	Unknown	White	Total	Racial Disparity
Chemical Irritant	158	1	2	8	71	240	2.9
Injury to Prisoner	2,181	21	10	0	1,028	3,240	2.7
Noncompliant Suspect or Arrestee	1,770	14	15	4	569	2,372	3.9
Nonlethal weapon: Taser/ beanbag/foam round	4,482	36	38	27	1,155	5,738	4.9
Total	8,591	72	65	39	2823	11,590	3.9

[a] Other includes Asian, Hawaiian, and mixed race.

Source: Data from City of Cincinnati, Ohio, Open Data,https://data.cincinnati-oh.gov/Safety/PDI-Police-Data-Initiative-Use-of-Force/8us8-wi2w.

treatment of black and Hispanic drivers with white drivers. This included stops, searches, and citations. The analysis also considered contraband "hit rates"—or frequency for which drugs, guns, or other contraband were discovered during police searches—by race and ethnicity.

Statewide, the study found that black and Hispanic drivers were stopped 1.64 and 1.48 times more frequently than white drivers. Once stopped, black and Hispanic drivers were searched more than two times more often than white drivers, but also had much lower contraband hit rates. In addition, black and Hispanic drivers received summonses more frequently than white drivers.

The data for our analysis of discrimination in arrests come from the FBI's National Incident-Based Reporting System (NIBRS). It provides a complete list of arrests in the state of West Virginia, including the age, race, and sex of those arrested. We calculated the per person crime rates using 2023 population data for West Virginia obtained from the US Bureau of Census. Using Equation 1, provided earlier, we computed the risk of one or more arrests for the average person in each age, sex, and race group and examined it in a lifetime frame according to methods produced by mathematician Yoshio Akiyama and others (2015). The results of this analysis are presented in Figure 2.4.

Blacks constitute only 4 percent of West Virginia's population, but they have the highest risk of arrest over the lifetime. For example, the average black male (BM) has more than a 94 percent chance of being arrested by the police in his lifetime (top line). "Lifetime," for this purpose, refers to ages ten through eighty. The second

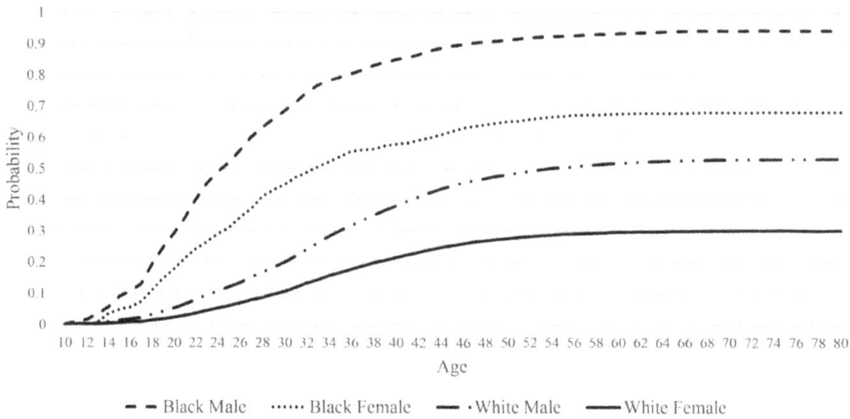

Figure 2.4 Lifetime risk of arrest by age, race, and sex in West Virginia.
Source: James Nolan's calculations using FBI NIBRS arrest data and U.S. Bureau of Census population data for 2023.

highest risk for arrest is the average black female (BF) who has a 68 percent chance of at least one arrest by age eighty. The average white male (WM) has the third highest lifetime risk at just over 50 percent. The lowest risk of arrest is the average white female (WF), whose cumulative risk of arrest over a lifetime is 30 percent.

Following the trend line from age ten, the risk increases earlier and faster for BM and BF than it does for WM and WF. By age eighteen, the BM has a 20 percent chance of having been arrested, whereas the accumulated risk for WM is 3 percent. At age eighteen, BF has a 15 percent chance of having been arrested whereas the risk for WF is 1 percent. The trajectory advances like this over the lifetime, leveling out for all four groups by around the age of fifty.

This analysis of West Virginia arrest data shows the generative nature of systemic discrimination. This does not require personal biases on the part of police officers. Instead, it demonstrates how institutional practices, such as those in American policing, disadvantage groups by race and sex over a lifetime. In summary, the national and local data on the American police abuse triad indicate that over-enforcement, excessive force, and discrimination are pervasive. In the next chapter, we examine some of the issues behind American police abuse.

Further Reading

Akiyama, Yoshio, James J. Nolan, Karen Weiss, and Stacia Gilliard-Matthews. 2015. "Lifetime Likelihood Computations with NIBRS." *Justice Research and Policy* 16, no. 2: 129–46.

Center for Behavioral Health Statistics and Quality. 2021. *Racial/Ethnic Differences in Substance Use, Substance Use Disorders, and Substance Use Treatment Utilization among People Aged 12 or Older (2015–2019)*. Rockville, MD: Substance Abuse and Mental Health Services Administration. https://www.samhsa.gov/data/.

Center for Disease Control and Prevention (CDC). n.d. National Violent Death Reporting System (NVDRS). Accessed 2024. https://www.cdc.gov/violenceprevention/datasources/nvdrs/index.html.

Haas, Stephen M., Erica Turley, and Monicka Sterling. 2009. *West Virginia Traffic Stop Study Final Report*. West Virginia Criminal Justice Statistical Analysis Center, Division of Criminal Justice Services. February. https://das.wv.gov/JCS/ORSP/SAC/Publications/Documents/WVSAC_Traffic_NEWOverviewofStatewideFindings2009.pdf.

Howlader, N., A. M. Noone, M. Krapcho, et al., eds. 2021. "SEER Cancer Statistics Review, 1975–2018." April. Bethesda, MD: National Cancer Institute. https://seer.cancer.gov/csr/1975_2018/.

Phoenix Police Department Open Data. n.d. Accessed 2024. https://www.phoenixopendata.com/dataset/arrests.

Ridgeway, Greg. 2007. "Analysis of Racial Disparities in the New York Police Department's Stop, Question, and Frisk Practices." Santa Monica, CA: Rand Corporation. https://www.rand.org/content/dam/rand/pubs/technical_reports/2007/RAND_TR534.pdf.

Smith, Michael, Rob Tiller, Robin S. Engel, and Jennifer Calnon Cherkauskas. 2019. *A Multi-Method Investigation of Officer Decision-Making and Force Used or Avoided in Arrest Situations: Tulsa, Oklahoma Police Department Administrative Data Analysis Report*. University of Texas San Antonio. https://hcap.utsa.edu/documents/criminal-justice/final-tulsa-data-analysis-report.pdf.

US Census Bureau. n.d. Accessed 2024. https://www.census.gov/en.html.

Washington Post Police Shooting Database. n.d. Accessed 2024. https://www.washingtonpost.com/graphics/investigations/police-shootings-database/.

3

Behind American Police Abuse

In Chapter 2, we presented facts about the American police abuse triad: over-enforcement, excessive force, and discrimination. Although we contend that all three manifestations of abuse can be traced to the police mandate, there is some debate whether these are actually abuse at all. For example, in the 1980s and 1990s, the hyper-enforcement of minor infractions was introduced, in line with a "broken windows" theory that such would prevent more serious crimes (Wilson and Kelling 1982). The argument went like this: when physical and social disorder in neighborhoods arises at alarming rates, the informal controls—such as families watching out for other families—go into decline. When the police prioritize "fixing" broken windows—that is, the enforcement of minor public-order crimes such as littering, painting graffiti, or acting disorderly on street corners—they signal to communities that they take these minor offenses seriously. However, aggressive enforcement of minor laws and infractions can become counterproductive. In this chapter, we examine whether hyper-enforcement is sometimes necessary to help communities stay safe. We also attempt to show how the frequency or intensity of enforcement becomes over-enforcement.

Similarly, what constitutes "excessive" force by police is also contested. Excessive force is sometimes defined as the "unnecessary, unwarranted, and disproportional" use of violence by officers (Pinizzotto et al. 2012: 286). In a US Department of Justice-funded study of deadly force by police officers (Binder and Scharf 1983), researchers suggest there are two things to consider when deciding whether deadly force is necessary and warranted. The first is the distinction between a *reasonable* decision and the *correct* decision. A correct decision to shoot or refrain from shooting is based on the outcome, while a reasonable decision is based on the information available to an officer at the time a decision to shoot or refrain from shooting was made. To illustrate the difference, the authors of the study presented the following scenario.

> Suppose an officer on a burglary call directs a suspect to stop in a dark alley behind the house. The suspect stops and turns around suddenly, reaches into a breast pocket and withdraws something that looks very much like a gun. The officer shoots and kills the suspect. Assuming the literal accuracy of the preceding description, the decision to shoot would be considered reasonable. If the item withdrawn was indeed a gun, the decision to shoot would also be correct. But suppose it was a cigarette lighter … the decision here would obviously be incorrect. (ibid.: 18)

By either standard, correct or reasonable, scholars who analyze the use of deadly force by police limit their purview to the *individual* interactions of citizens and police. In the process, they ignore the *institutional* factors that should be included in the "deadly mix" identified by psychologist Anthony Pinizzotto and others (1992, 2006). This deadly mix should include the attitudes and assumptions of officers as they anticipate the encounter, make initial contact and engage with an offender, and make the final decision to shoot or use other forms of deadly force (Fridell and Binder 1992).

American police officers' wide inclination toward the use of force may be connected to the hypervigilance engendered by the law enforcement mandate. The police are trained to interpret suspects' cues to detect danger, held to be critical for police survival (Pinizzotto, Davis, and Miller 1992). Perhaps, then, the increase in fatal police shootings of civilians since 2015 is connected to a heightened sense of danger from a similar rise in violence against the police. This type of analysis might help determine whether deadly violence by the police over the past decade is excessive, or whether it is appropriate.

In addition, many people argue that discrimination in policing is the result of an officer's implicit biases. The latter refers to the automatic associations among police officers that lead to racial disparities in the enforcement of laws and in the use of force. If implicit bias is the cause of racial discrimination in policing, we might see differences in the way black and white officers arrest and use force in black and brown communities. We explore this in Q10.

The debate over what constitutes over-enforcement and excessive force sometimes turns to legal, policy, or ethical frameworks, but this is tricky. There is so much nuance involved in the circumstances in which the police use force that there is little certainty regarding how a court will decide and whether the decision will set a harmful precedent. Policy frameworks help us decide if the police followed the rules, but not whether the enforcement or force could have been avoided by acting in more beneficial ways. Ethical frameworks can be equally problematic, because there is not one ethical standard. In this chapter, we look at how legal, policy, and ethical frameworks can be applied in specific situations.

Finally, many people contend that the reason over-enforcement, excessive force, and discrimination are problems in American policing is that bad-apple cops are shielded behind a blue wall of silence. We examine the laws that protect good and bad-apple cops alike and consider whether this is really the problem.

Further Reading

Binder, Arnold, and Peter Scharf. 1983. *Final Report on the Use of Deadly Force by Police Officers*. Washington, DC: National Institute of Justice, September.

Fridell, Lorie A., and Arnold Binder. 1992. "Police Officer Decisionmaking in Potentially Violent Confrontations." *Journal of Criminal Justice* 20, no. 5: 385–99.

Pinizzotto, Anthony, Edward F. Davis, and Charles E Miller. 1992. *Killed in the Line of Duty: A Study of Selected Felonious Killings of Law Enforcement Officers*. Washington, DC: US Department of Justice, Federal Bureau of Investigation.

Pinizzotto, Anthony, Edward F. Davis, and Charles E. Miller. 2006. *Violent Encounters: A Study of Felonious Assaults on Our Nation's Law Enforcement Officers*. Washington, DC: U.S. Department of Justice, Federal Bureau of Investigation.

Pinizzotto, Anthony, Edward F. Davis, Shannon B. Bohrer, and Benjamin J. Infanti. 2012. "Law Enforcement Restraint in the Use of Deadly Force within the Context of 'The Deadly Mix.'" *International Journal of Police Science and Management* 14, no. 4: 285–98.

Wilson, James Q., and George Kelling. 1982. "Broken Windows: The Police and Neighborhood Safety." *Atlantic Monthly*: 29–38.

Q8: Is hyper-enforcement necessary, and at what point does it become over-enforcement?

Answer: The research suggests that hyper-enforcement of minor public-order offenses can help neighborhoods in the short term. However, its prolonged use as a routine practice is counterproductive (Hinkle and Weisburd 2008). Hyper-enforcement can stigmatize neighborhoods and residents, introduce bias, contribute to mass incarceration, and reduce trust in the police and criminal justice system. When this happens, it is over-enforcement. Whether the enforcement of laws is appropriate or overused can be evaluated by the extent to which it makes communities stronger and safer. In other words, law enforcement—as one of many methods for making communities safe—is better understood as a means to an end rather than an end in itself.

The Facts: To begin our discussion of over-enforcement as a type of police abuse, we ask the reader to consider the following questions. Is hyper-enforcement of laws in neighborhoods ever appropriate? And if so, who decides?

With its law enforcement mandate, the American police have staked a claim of primary responsibility for crime and social control in public spaces. Therefore, the decision whether to enforce public-order offenses in local neighborhoods is left almost entirely to the discretion of the police. This may be one reason why some of the more problematic hyper-enforcement initiatives under the name *broken-windows policing* have failed. They are almost always initiated by the police rather than in collaboration with the residents of a community. And they are not strategic. Rather, they cast everyone in public spaces in neighborhoods struggling with crime and disorder as potential criminals. As outsiders in this disciplinarian role, the police find themselves as the common enemy of many residents of the neighborhood. This does not mean that residents in the community do not want the police to disrupt open-air drug sales, panhandling, and other forms of social disorder. However, the broad-brush approach officers take in intensified enforcement campaigns pits the police against the community in ways that become counterproductive. This is why we call it "over-enforcement."

Broken-windows policing, as we are describing, follows the logic that if a window in a building is broken and left unrepaired, more windows will soon be broken (Wilson and Kelling 1982). The research that emerged from the broken-windows thesis found that increasing physical and social disorder in local places increased fear (Hinkle and Weisburd 2008), decreased neighborhood attachment (Taylor 1996), and decreased the willingness of neighbors to cooperate to prevent crime (Skogan 1990; Hipp 2016). Police-initiated broken-windows policing was credited by some for the drop in crime in New York City in the 1990s (Bratton and Knobler 1998; Guiliani and Kurson 2002). However, there is irony in this policing approach. The aggressive enforcement of minor public-order offenses to fix broken windows and reduce fear in neighborhoods makes residents more fearful, thereby less likely to work with the police and neighbors to keep neighborhoods safe (Hinkle and Weisburd 2008).

While the strengths and limitations of hyper-enforcement for social control were being debated in the 1990s, scholars at the University of Chicago offered new insights about the link between disorder and crime (Sampson and Raudenbush 1999). Both crime and disorder had common roots in the social structure (concentrated poverty, racial and economic inequality) and social processes, that is, the relationships in neighborhoods. Sampson and Raudenbush (1999: 603) found that *collective efficacy*, defined as "cohesion among residents combined with shared expectations for social control in public space," mitigated the effect of structural disadvantage for both disorder and crime. The persistent enforcement of public-order offenses in disadvantaged neighborhoods, particularly over long periods of time, work against collective efficacy by stigmatizing the streets and people living there. It increases bias by race and class; it increases fear; it contributes to mass incarceration; and it reduces trust in the police institution and criminal justice system (Wilson and Kelling 1982; Alexander 2012; Weisburd et al. 2024). When the routine practice of enforcing public-order laws in local places becomes counterproductive, we call this over-enforcement.

In 2004, *situational policing* was introduced as a conceptual framework that considers levels of crime and disorder on one hand, and level of collective efficacy on the other. In this way, it identifies neighborhood types that are more or less likely to benefit in the short term from hyper-enforcement. This is particularly true in high-crime neighborhoods that are lacking informal organization and controls and steeped in fear. In these places, called *anomic* neighborhoods, short-term law enforcement action by police can provide temporary relief from crime and violence, giving time and space for relationships among residents and between the police and community to grow stronger. The situational policing framework views the police and community as partners working together to build strong, safe places (Nolan, Conti, and McDevitt 2004: Nolan, DeKeseredy, and Brownstein 2022). From a situational policing perspective, the distinction between appropriate enforcement and over-enforcement is assessed by the extent to which it makes communities stronger and safer. It is a means to an end rather than an end in itself. We describe the elements of situational policing in more detail in Q30.

Further Reading

Alexander, Michelle. 2012. *The New Jim Crow: Mass Incarceration in the Age of Colorblindness*. New York: New Press.

Bratton, William J., and Peter Knobler. 1998. *Turnaround: How America's Top Cop Reversed the Crime Epidemic*. New York: Random House.

Guiliani, Rudolph W., and Ken Kurson. 2002. *Leadership*. New York: Hyperion.

Hinkle, Joshua C., and David Weisburd. 2008. "The Irony of Broken Windows Policing: A Micro-place Study of the Relationship between Disorder, Focused Police Crackdowns and Fear of Crime." *Journal of Criminal Justice* 36, no. 6: 503–12.

Hipp, John R. 2016. "Collective Efficacy: How Is It Conceptualized, How Is It Measured, and Does It Really Matter for Understanding Perceived Neighborhood Crime and Disorder?" *Journal of Criminal Justice* 46: 32–44.
Nolan, James J., Norman Conti, and Jack McDevitt. 2004. "Situational Policing: Neigh bourhood Development and Crime Control." *Policing and Society* 14, no. 2: 99–117.
Nolan, James J., Walter S. DeKeseredy, and Henry H. Brownstein. 2022. "Police Ethics in Rural Contexts: A Left Realist Consequentialist View." *International Journal of Rural Criminology* 7, no. 1: 2–21.
Sampson, Robert J., and Stephen W. Raudenbush. 1999. "Systematic Social Observation of Public Spaces: A New Look at Disorder in Urban Neighborhoods." *American Journal of Sociology* 105, no. 3: 603–51.
Skogan, Wesley G. 1990. *Disorder and Decline*. New York: Free Press.
Taylor, Ralph B. 1996. "Neighborhood Responses to Disorder and Local Attachments: The Systemic Model of Attachment, Social Disorganization and Neighborhood Use Value." *Sociological Forum* 11, no. 1: 41–74.
Weisburd, David, Clair V. Uding, Joshua C. Hinkle, and Kiseong Kuen. 2024. "Broken Windows and Community Social Control: Evidence from a Study of Street Segments." *Journal of Research in Crime and Delinquency* 61, no. 5: 727–71.
Wilson, James Q., and George Kelling. 1982. "Broken Windows: The Police and Neighborhood Safety." *Atlantic Monthly* March: 29–38.

Q9: Can excessive and deadly force in American policing be explained by rising violence against officers?

Answer: Probably not. There is no doubt that the police profession is very dangerous. The number of assaults against the police has remained relatively stable since the late 1990s. The number of police officers feloniously killed over the past three decades has also remained relatively stable, albeit with a gradual decline. However, during the Covid-19 pandemic, especially in 2021, the police have suffered significant increases in annual deaths attributed to line-of-duty contact. This reveals some of the increasing risks in policing in our current times, although not directly related to violence against the police.

The Facts: The police profession is very dangerous. To prepare officers for "survival," they often receive training that is informed by policy research from inside and outside the profession. In 1992, the FBI released findings from its study *Killed in the Line of Duty* (Pinizzotto, Davis, and Miller 1992). During structured interviews with fifty cop killers, FBI researchers identified the behavioral characteristics of officers who are at highest risk for violent assaults against them. These include excessive friendliness, a "laid back" and "easy going" temperament, and a belief they can "read others" (so they tend to let their guards down). Officers at high risk were found to consider the use of force only as a last resort and view the profession as public relations rather than law enforcement (ibid.: 32). These findings made their way into many street-survival police trainings throughout the country, including those offered at the FBI National Academy, where more than one thousand police leaders are trained each year.

Fast forward to 2023, and in a sweeping rebuke of this FBI research, the *New Yorker* columnist David Kirkpatrick linked this study's findings to the hypervigilant and violent police culture of today that contributed to the brutal police killing of Tyre Nichols in Nashville in 2023. The study, according to Kirkpatrick (2023), helped produce the rise in violent special police units such as the Rampart unit in Los Angeles and the Gun Trace Task Force in Baltimore, which target high-crime neighborhoods. More broadly, the study bolstered a certain kind of police folklore. As Kirkpatrick wrote,

> The study's core lesson about the imperative to dominate dovetailed with the nineties-era turn in law-enforcement culture toward what was known as a "warrior mind-set" teaching officers to see almost any civilian as a potentially lethal assassin—an approach that many police trainers still advise, even as the cops-vs.-citizen mentality has fallen out of favor among many police chiefs.

It may be true that the threat of harm to police officers is overstated in police training, but there are still many police officers killed and assaulted in the line of duty each year. Between 2015 and 2022, according to the FBI, 437 police officers were feloniously killed in the line of duty. Of these officer deaths, 389 (89 percent) were shot and killed with firearms (FBI 2023). To get a sense of the nature of this violence against the police, we provide a few examples from the FBI's 2023 Law Enforcement Officers Killed and Assaulted (LEOKA) report:

> In the early morning on a winter day a 30-year-old patrol officer was shot and killed while responding to a disturbance in a commercial area. The patrol officer … was dispatched to a motel after an anonymous caller reported a suspicious person. When the officer approached the motel room where the complaint was registered, a subject opened the door and fired three rounds at the officer with a .50 caliber semiautomatic handgun. (FBI 2023: 1)

> On an early winter evening, two police officers were shot and killed while responding to a report of a domestic disturbance at an apartment. Three officers responded and spoke with the complainant in a living room. Body camera footage

> shows that two of the officers, who were both wearing body armor, walked down a hallway to speak to the subject who was in a bedroom at the rear of the apartment. The subject exited the bedroom and began firing shots from a .45-caliber semiautomatic handgun. (ibid.: 3)

> A 46-year-old police corporal and a 27-year-old police officer were shot and killed while responding to a disturbance ... The officer's body camera footage showed that, as the corporal and the officer attempted to arrest the suspect, he resisted and pulled a 9 mm semiautomatic handgun from the waistband of his pants. The suspect shot the corporal and the officer at close range. The corporal was fatally struck in the rear head, side head, and front upper torso/chest as the round entered through the armhole or shoulder area of his body armor vest. The officer, who was also wearing body armor, returned fire but was struck in the rear head and in the arms/hands. The suspect then stole the corporal's patrol vehicle and fled the scene. (ibid.: 2)

In addition to the number of officers feloniously killed in the line of duty, there were many more officers seriously injured. The FBI reports that, between 2014 and 2021, there were 130,500 police officers injured either by a firearm, knife, physical force, or some other weapon (James Nolan's analysis of FBI 2023). This level of violence against the police keeps officers hypervigilant and suspicious of strangers, often putting them at odds with the community. In this perpetual state of readiness for violence, the police and the community alike are at high risk for serious harm. A closer look at the data on officers assaulted and killed over the past two decades can reveal if the problem has gotten worse and help to evaluate the claim that rising rates of excessive and deadly force by the police is a response to rising violence against them.

In 2023, 79,091 police officers were assaulted in the line of duty. This number represents 13 percent of 600,120 police officers employed in police agencies that submitted police-assault data to the FBI. Of those police officers assaulted, 26,689 were injured. This means 4.4 percent of police officers were injured in the line of duty in 2023. Figure 3.1 shows the trend in total assaults on police officers and assaults with injuries from 1996 to 2023, indicating a steady decline in assaults on US police from 1998 to 2014. Since 2015, the rate of assaults on police officers appears to be rising. However, the FBI made changes to the LEOKA program in 2015 and 2016, which complicates this trend analysis. Beginning in 2015, the FBI included, in its LEOKA data, assaults against civilians who were serving at the request of law enforcement agencies. This includes unpaid reserve officers who are assaulted helping on-duty police officers. Then, in 2016, the FBI added LEOKA criteria to include military and civilian police at the Department of Defense

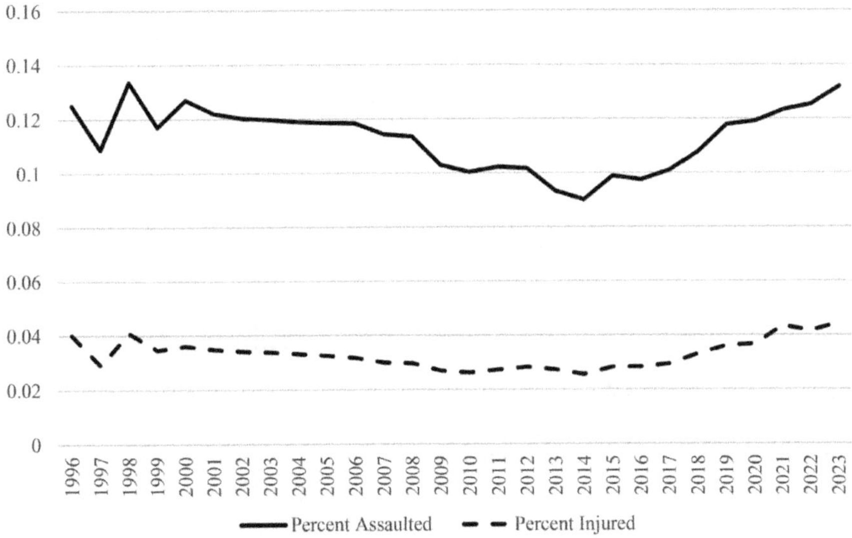

Figure 3.1 Trends in police officers assaulted and assaulted with injured in the line of duty, 1996–2023.

Source: Data from FBI, Law Enforcement Officers Killed and Assaulted (LEOKA), 1996–2023, https://cde.ucr.cjis.gov/LATEST/webapp/#/pages/le/leoka.

(DOD) when they are working as law enforcement officers in the United States. It is uncertain whether these changes affected recent trends in police assaults. Still, the rate of officer assaults at its peak in 2023 is slightly lower than it was in 1998.

According to the FBI, between 1993 and 2022, 3,500 US police officers were killed in the line of duty. The FBI makes a distinction between officers who were feloniously killed and those who were accidentally killed. A felonious killing refers to an incident in which the willful and intentional actions of offenders results in the death of officers acting in their official capacity. An accidental death refers to an incident in which the officer is killed, but there was no willful intent on the part of the offender (FBI 2023).

Figure 3.2 shows the total number of US police officers killed in the line of duty between 1993 and 2022 and indicates whether these officers died because of an intentional act on the part of an offender (feloniously killed) or were accidentally killed while acting in an official capacity as a police officer. During this thirty-year period, the number of police officers feloniously or accidentally killed has remained relatively stable, but with a slight decline since 2007. Between 1998 and 2010, the number of accidental deaths remained higher than the number of felonious police officer killings. In recent years, these two types of fatalities have been occurring at about the same rate.

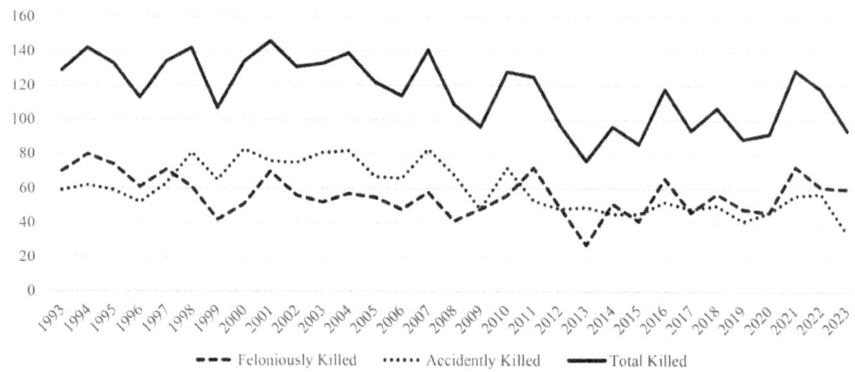

Figure 3.2 Number of police officers feloniously and accidently killed in the line of duty, 1993–2023.

Source: Data from the FBI, Law Enforcement Officers Killed and Assaulted (LEOKA), 1996–2023, https://cde.ucr.cjis.gov/LATEST/webapp/#/pages/le/leoka.

In addition to the FBI data, the Officer Down Memorial Page, Inc. (ODMP) collects similar information. ODMP is a nonprofit organization dedicated to honoring police officers killed and wounded in the line of duty. Like the FBI, ODMP gathers information about felonious and accidental deaths of police officers. It also collects information about the deaths of police officers who die of natural causes (such as heart attacks) while performing law enforcement duties. Figure 3.3 presents the annual totals of police line-of-duty deaths for the fifty-year period 1973–2022. Because the data include deaths by natural causes while performing official duties, the ODMP numbers are a little higher than that of the FBI. However, the same downward trend in officer deaths is observed from 1973 until 2021. The sudden spike in police officer deaths in 2021 is related to on-duty exposure to the Covid-19 virus.

The link between rising rates of deadly force by the police and increasing violence against them is dubious. The fatal or accidental killing of police officers in the line of duty has remained relatively stable since the 1970s, and the assaults on police officers since the late 1990s has declined but may be rising slightly since 2015. This does not mean that the practice of policing is not dangerous. It just means there may be different explanations for it, including the institutional perspective offered in Chapter 1. That is, the police mandate for crime and social control through law enforcement creates logic for action and a disposition in officers that keeps them hypervigilant for danger. The research by the FBI in the 1990s clearly accentuated the law enforcement disposition in a way that makes officers more prepared to use deadly force. However, it is not likely a single study alone could be responsible for

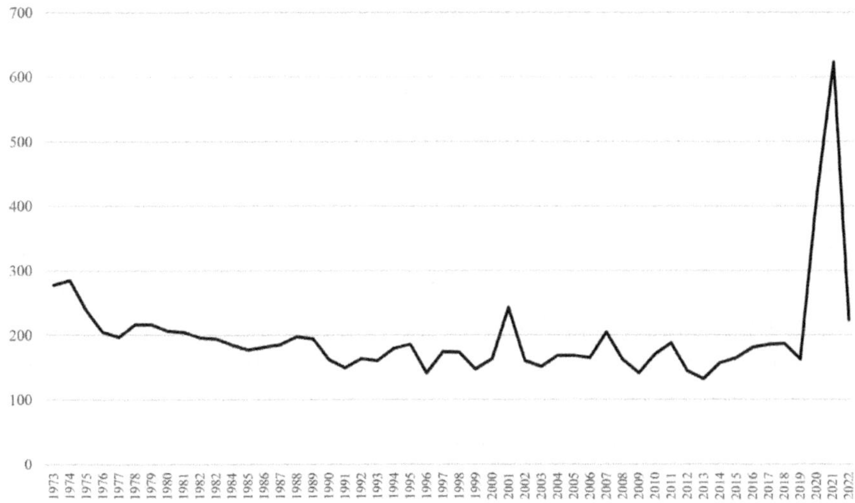

Figure 3.3 Police fatalities in the line of duty, 1973–2022.
Source: Data from Officer Down Memorial Page, https://www.odmp.org.

so much deadly violence in policing. In Q11 we examine some of the legal, policy, and ethical guidelines that may shed more light on this issue.

Further Reading

Federal Bureau of Investigation (FBI). 2023. "Law Enforcement Officers Killed and Assaulted, 2023." Washington, DC. https://cde.ucr.cjis.gov/LATEST/webapp/#/pages/le/leoka.

Kirkpatrick, David D. 2023. "The Police Folklore That Helped Kill Tyre Nichols." *New Yorker*. January 28. https://www.newyorker.com/news/daily-comment/the-police-folklore-that-helped-kill-tyre-nichols

Officer Down Memorial Page (ODMP). n.d. Accessed 2024. https://www.odmp.org/.

Pinizzotto, Anthony, Edward F. Davis, and Charles E. Miller. 1992. *Killed in the Line of Duty: A Study of Selected Felonious Killings of Law Enforcement Officers*. Washington, DC: US Department of Justice, Federal Bureau of Investigation.

Q10: Is implicit bias the reason for discrimination in American policing?

Answer: Implicit bias in policing simply refers to the automatic associations that influence how officers think, feel, and act. Because of this, implicit bias is sometimes considered a *root cause* of racial and ethnic disparities in policing. However, implicit (and explicit) biases are symptoms of larger structural inequities by race, class, and gender.

The police are certainly affected by these things like everyone else. However, it is the organization of the American police as law enforcement—with a mandate to fight crime and secure social control—in a society steeped in racial and economic inequality that is the source of discrimination in American policing. In other words, even if there were no implicit, or explicit, biases in the ranks of the police (which is certainly not the case), it is likely there would still be racial and ethnic disparities in all aspects of policing. This is because the *game* and *scorecard* associated with the American police mandate (see Chapter 1) emphasize arrests, citations, and other forms of coercive social control as the *raison d'être* of the profession. These law enforcement *scores*, and the status associated with them, are most easily accessible in disadvantaged places and among disadvantaged groups reflective of racial, ethnic, and class inequality in American society.

The Facts: Implicit bias refers to associations or assumptions that are often tied to racial, ethnic, and gender stereotypes. Implicit biases influence feelings, thoughts, and behavioral tendencies, even though they operate outside of our awareness or consciousness (Spencer, Charbonneau, and Glaser 2016). This type of bias may influence the judgments some police officers make, but it is difficult to explain the pervasive discrimination at all levels of American policing in this way.

Let's consider some cases of police abuse that made national headlines in recent years—all involving the killing of unarmed black men. In 2014, eighteen-year-old Michael Brown was fatally shot and killed by a white police officer in Ferguson, Missouri. Also in 2014, Dontre Hamilton was shot fourteen times and killed by a white police officer in Milwaukee, Wisconsin. That same year, Eric Garner was killed in New York City by a white police officer who performed an illegal chokehold. Even with repeated complaints by Garner, exclaiming "I can't breathe," police did not let up. In 2015, Tony Robinson of Madison, Wisconsin, was shot and killed by police due to reports of a traffic disturbance. That same year, Freddie Gray was arrested by police in Baltimore, Maryland, on a minor charge. During the transport to the police station, Gray sustained a broken neck (Gordon 2015). Of the six officers charged for Gray's death, three were white and three were black. In 2020, George Floyd was murdered by white police officer

Derek Chauvin in Minneapolis, Minnesota, after Chauvin held his knee on the back of Floyd's neck for nine minutes. In 2023, Tyre Nichols was beaten to death by five Memphis, Tennessee, police officers, all black (Cardia et al. 2023).

In each of these fatal encounters between the police and unarmed citizens, the victims were black. However, the police officers involved were both white and black. Although research suggests that black and white officers may have different views regarding the plight of blacks in American society (DeSilver, Lipka, and Fahmy 2020), both are subject to the same institutional forces that produce racial disparities in arrests and other forms of law enforcement action (Pyo 2023; Nolan, Crispino, and Parsons 2021). For example, 45 percent of the population in Washington, DC, and 50 percent of the district's Metropolitan Police Department are black; yet the arrest rate is ten times higher for blacks than whites in that city. Similarly, in Philadelphia, the arrest rate is 100 percent higher for blacks compared to whites, even though 30 percent of the department is black (authors' computations based on FBI n.d.; BJS 2020; U.S. Census n.d.).

In addition, consider an example from the state of Texas. One quarter of the resident population in Dallas is black and 25 percent of the Dallas Police Department (DPD) is also black. According to the FBI, the arrest rate was two times higher for blacks than whites in 2022 (FBI n.d.). Moreover, 57 percent of the 3,408 use-of-force incidents reported by the DPD in 2020 involved black citizens. White officers were responsible for 55 percent of the use-of-force incidents, Hispanic officers, 24 percent, and black officers, 15 percent. While white and Hispanic officers use force to compel compliance more often than black officers, the rate at which black officers use force against black citizens is 12 percent higher than that of white or Hispanic officers (James Nolan's computations based on City of Dallas 2020).

The American police mandate for crime and social control through law enforcement is an institutional structure producing consistently high rates of discrimination in the practice of law enforcement. The mandate creates a disposition and worldview in officers that helps them earn status in the profession. There is little doubt that police officers want to do the right things. They are recognized and rewarded for law enforcement outputs such as arrests and the seizure of illegal guns and drugs. Therefore, it is these enforcement actions that count on a police officer's scorecard. Implicit biases that emerge from structured racial, ethnic, and economic inequality may be a catalyst for police discrimination, but they are probably not its root cause (Nolan, Crispino, and Parsons 2021; Spencer, Charbonneau, and Glaser 2016).

Further Reading

Bureau of Justice Statistics (BJS). 2020. Law Enforcement Management & Statistics (LEMAS) 2020 Survey. https://bjs.ojp.gov/data-collection/law-enforcement-management-and-administrative-statistics-lemas.

Cardia, Alexander, Jason Kao, Christopher Koettl, Eleanor Lutz, Anjali Singhvi, and Robin Stein. 2023. "A Timeline of Tyre Nichols's Lethal Police Encounter." *New York Times*. January 28. Accessed January 10, 2025. https://www.nytimes.com/interactive/2023/01/27/us/tyre-nichols-police-beating-timeline.html.

City of Dallas, Open Data, Police Response to Resistance. 2020. https://www.dallasopendata.com/Public-Safety/Police-Response-to-Resistance-2020/nufk-2iqn.

DeSilver, Drew, Michael Lipka, and Dalia Fahmy. 2020. "10 Things We Know about Race and Policing in the U.S." Washington, DC: Pew Research. June 3. https://www.pewresearch.org/short-reads/2020/06/03/10-things-we-know-about-race-and-policing-in-the-u-s/.

Federal Bureau of Investigation (FBI). n. d. Uniform Crime Reporting System. Accessed 2024. https://cde.ucr.cjis.gov/LATEST/webapp/#/pages/home.

Gordon, Kalani. 2015. "Latest Updates on Baltimore Unrest and Freddie Gray Case." *Baltimore Sun*. May 1.

Nolan, James J., Frank Crispino, and Timothy Parsons, eds. 2021. *Policing in an Age of Reform: An Agenda for Research and Practice*. London: Palgrave Macmillan.

Pyo, Sunyoun. 2023. "Does an Increased Share of Black Police Officers Decrease Racial Discrimination in Law Enforcement?" *Urban Affairs Review* 59, no. 2: 534–79.

Spencer, Katherine B., Amanda K. Charbonneau, and Jack Glaser. 2016. "Implicit Bias and Policing." *Social and Personality Psychology Compass* 10, no. 1: 50–63.

U.S. Census Bureau. n.d. Quick Facts. Accessed 2024. https://www.census.gov/quickfacts/fact/table/US/HCN010217.

Q11: Are legal, policy, and ethical frameworks helpful in evaluating the use of force in American policing?

Answer: Yes, but they only help us evaluate police use of force in specific cases of police-citizen encounters rather than the necessity and severity of force in routine institutional practices. Legal frameworks tell us if the police followed the law. Policy frameworks help determine if the police followed agency protocols. Ethical frameworks focus on whether the behavior of officers aligned with law or policy, or whether the outcome of the police use of force was just and necessary.

The Facts: There is no general agreement about limits on the use of force used by the police (Gerber and Jackson 2017). When the police use physical force against a citizen, especially when it results in serious injury or death, there is a belief among many that it could have been avoided. However, the debate within police circles rarely takes this on. Instead, the focus of the review is fixed on whether the police officer followed policy and the law. The institution rarely asks, for example, "Could this incident have been avoided?" or "Did it result in preventable harm to families or neighborhoods?" The moral framework does not even consider whether the use of force by police is perceived to be unjust or excessive by a community standard. To explain this a little further, we examine the three main frameworks used to determine the limits on force used by the police: law, police policy, and police ethics.

In the United States, police officers are permitted to use force if it is objectively reasonable. In determining reasonableness, courts consider the facts of a case including the severity of the crime, whether the suspect is a threat to the safety of the officer or others, or whether the suspect is resisting arrest and attempting to flee. The courts tend to recognize that police officers have to make split-second judgments under difficult situations. Therefore, the standard of reasonableness applies to a reasonable officer on the scene rather than "20/20 vision of hindsight" of others (*Graham v. Conner* 1989).

This standard of reasonableness applies to all levels of force including deadly force. US courts generally hold that the police must believe the suspect poses an imminent danger of death or serious physical injury to the officer or another person. However, there are limits to this. For example, the police may not use deadly force solely to prevent a suspect from getting away. Firearms may not be used to disable moving vehicles unless the vehicle is being used as a deadly weapon against the officer or others. Deadly force may not be used against persons who threaten only their own lives, unless it involves danger to others in proximity. Typically, officers are expected to give verbal warnings to the suspect prior to using deadly force. Warning shots are generally not permitted (US Department of Justice n.d.).

In addition, the US courts have ruled that police officers do not have to be absolutely sure of the seriousness of the threat in order to use deadly force (*Elliott v. Leavitt* 1996). Police officers are also not required to wait until they see a weapon before employing deadly force on a fleeing suspect who moves as though to draw a gun (*Thompson v. Hubbard* 2001). And the use of force by police to terminate a vehicle pursuit in order to protect the public is not prohibited by the US Constitution even if it results in serious injury or death (*Scott v. Harris* 2007). These are just a few examples of the legal framework in the United States regarding the police use of force.

Police policies generally follow the law and significant court decisions. They typically require officers to consider ways to de-escalate dangerous situations before using force. They also require officers to use only the amount of force necessary to overcome resistance. However, the police are not required to retreat or back down to avoid using force. As an example, consider the policy statement by the Ann Arbor, Michigan, Police Department. We use this example because the agency is accredited by the Commission on Accreditation for Law Enforcement (CALEA). Therefore, it is likely to be consistent with professional law enforcement standards everywhere.

> Ann Arbor Police shall use only that amount of force reasonably necessary to accomplish lawful objectives and apply de-escalation techniques when possible. Officers are justified in using the amount of force that is reasonable to affect a lawful arrest. *Officers need not retreat or desist from efforts to make a lawful arrest because of resistance or threatened resistance to an arrest.* An officer is also justified in using reasonable force against another when and to the extent the officer believes that such force is necessary to defend the officer or another person. (emphasis added; CALEA 2023)

We added the italics in the foregoing quotation to highlight something we referenced in Chapter 1, that is, the logic and common sense of the law enforcement game. To briefly review, the professional mandate in American policing is crime control and social order via law enforcement. In Chapter 1, we referred to this as the game. It is this law enforcement game that produces a logic for action. It also gives rise to a police officer disposition and worldview. It is the internalized logic of the law enforcement game that helps officers navigate the nuances and contingencies that unfold on the field. On the field of American policing, a *common sense* emerges that predicts what the police will do and not do. What officers will do is take control when faced with opposition, standing ready to apply force. What they will not do is retreat or desist. They often will not even wait temporarily until backup officers arrive, or for a relative or other community member to be contacted to assist. They must take control and demand compliance, never backing down even in the short term.

One set of policy guidelines employed is the use-of-force continuum. This is a model that is widely used in policing and part of standard police training (NIJ 2009). It generally begins with verbal directions by officers, which compel a person to do something. The level of force increases incrementally through a series of nonlethal approaches and up to the use of deadly force. It should be noted, however, that the term "continuum" is discouraged by the International Association of Chiefs of Police (IACP). This is because it is often misapplied to mean officers should systematically try everything in linear order before using the level of force called for in the situation. Rather, the IACP recommends that officers choose a level of force based on legal principles (IACP 2020).

The IACP's National Consensus Policy on the Use of Force (IACP 2020: 10) defines deadly force as "any use of force that creates substantial risk of causing death or serious bodily injury." In addition, the IACP defines less-than-lethal force as "any force other than that which is considered deadly force that involves physical effort to control, restrain, or overcome the resistance of another." This includes physical techniques such as come-along holds and other manual restraints. It also includes the use of electronic control weapons, pepper spray, and impact projectiles, but does not include verbal commands or de-escalation techniques. The IACP's consensus policy bans certain types of less-than-lethal impact weapons, including slapjacks, blackjacks, brass knuckles, and nunchucks and other martial arts weapons. It also suggests that officers give verbal commands and, if possible, wait enough time for the subject to comply before using force.

According to the consensus policy, the protection of property is not a proper justification for the use of deadly force. Suicide or threats of suicide are also not a justification to use deadly force, except when the suicide risks the lives of those in proximity. In addition, firing shots at moving vehicles, or from vehicles, is prohibited unless there is immediate risk to the life of the officer or others. Also, chokeholds and vascular neck restraints are only to be used in situations where deadly force is called for (IACP 2020: 15).

Most police agencies in the United States create policies and practices that conform to professional and accrediting organizations like the IACP and the CALEA. These policies and practices become the rules of the game. In the game of crime control and social order via law enforcement, the use of force is common sense. The ability to skillfully and effectively use force to demand compliance is an asset on a field where many people really do not want to comply with police commands. If this law enforcement game remains the same, the need for coercive force will continue.

In addition to legal and policy frameworks described, ethical frameworks are often used by the police and others to determine what is moral conduct. As mentioned previously, there are more than 18,000 police agencies in the United States. Most have adopted the IACP code of ethics as the standard. This code begins as follows:

> As a law enforcement officer, my fundamental duty is to serve the community; to safeguard lives and properly protect the innocent against deception, the weak against oppression or intimidation and the peaceful against violence and disorder; and to respect the constitutional rights of all to liberty, equality, and justice. (IACP 1957)

The IACP code of ethics continues with personal pledges that are intended to guide officers in making ethical decisions on and off duty. These include the promise not to bring discredit to the police agency, to always remain courageous and calm, to be mindful of the welfare of others, to be honest in thought and deed, to be obedient to the laws and rules of the department, and to be unbiased and relentless in the prosecution of criminals. The code of ethics ends with this final line: "I will constantly strive to achieve these objectives and ideals, dedicating myself before God to my chosen profession … law enforcement."

The first thing to notice in this widely adopted code of ethics is that the police profession is referred to as "law enforcement." As we discussed in Chapter 1, this is significant in that the law enforcement identity shapes the disposition and worldview of officers. This fact often puts police officers at odds with the very people they want to serve and protect. The code sets up "the criminal" as society's eternal enemy and who must be the target of relentless action on the policing field. This is consistent with the notion that the root causes of crime are criminals; therefore, the right thing to do is to pursue them.

In addition, the code further obscures the fact that the law enforcement approach to the profession is socially constructed and changeable. The line, "dedicating myself before God to my chosen profession," is an acknowledgment that the profession is sacred and worthy of divine approval. The danger in misrecognizing the law enforcement approach to policing as natural and divine rather than socially constructed and changeable is that the underlying assumptions are rarely examined.

Most importantly, those who pledge to safeguard, protect, respect, remain courageous and calm, and be honest, unbiased, and relentless in the prosecution of criminals are not required to think about the consequences of behavior—only whether the behavior conforms to ethical principle or moral code. As mentioned in the introduction to this book, this is known as a *deontological* approach to ethics. On the other hand, a consequentialist code of ethics would judge the rightness of action in its outcome (Sahakian and Sahakian 1966). To do the latter, the police would have to identify a desired end at which the profession aims (Pojman 1999). By doing so, ethical action by the police would be judged by the degree to which the behavior led toward or away from this end. In recent years, there have been several studies that explore this alternative view of police ethics (Nolan, Parsons, and Crispino 2021; Nolan, DeKeseredy, and Brownstein 2022).

To set the stage for a discussion of police abuse from legal, policy, and ethical frameworks, we present four case examples. In each case, the police used lethal or nonlethal force against a person. The legitimacy of the use of force in each case is contested. This means that some people claim it is a justified use of force, while others say it is an unjustifiable abuse of force. As you read each passage, see if you think the use of force was justified or not, and why.

North Carolina. When Charlotte, North Carolina, police officer M. S. Connor observed Dethorne Graham enter a convenience store then exit almost immediately, he thought this behavior was suspicious. Then he noticed Graham get into the passenger side of a car waiting for him outside the store. He saw the car quickly pull away. Suspecting a crime may have occurred, Officer Connor followed the vehicle, stopping it about a half mile away. When Officer Connor approached the vehicle, Graham told the officer that he was having a "sugar reaction" due to diabetes. Officer Connor told Graham and the driver of the vehicle to wait in the car while he asked assisting police units to check on things at the convenience store. When Officer Connor went back to his police car, he saw Graham exit his car and run around it several times. After a few minutes, Graham sat down and passed out. When he woke up, Graham discovered he had been handcuffed behind the back. He also observed more police officers had arrived at the scene. It was at this time that Graham attempted to reach for his wallet to show officers his diabetic identification card. For their safety, officers stopped him from reaching for the wallet. They then forcibly put him in the back of the police car, while Graham struggled vigorously. Ultimately, the police discovered that Graham was, in fact, having an insulin reaction and that no crime had occurred at the convenience store. Officer Connor decided not to file charges and returned Graham to his home. During the incident Graham suffered multiple injuries, including a broken foot. He claimed the officers used excessive force causing his serious physical injuries (*Graham v. Connor* 1989).

Georgia. A Georgia sheriff's deputy clocked a speeder going 73 mph in a 55 mph zone. The deputy turned on his blue lights, but the speeder, Harris, refused to stop. A second deputy, Scott, who was on patrol in the area of the offense, heard the radio transmissions about the fleeing traffic offender and joined in the chase. The chase was captured on the deputy's in-car video system. It reached speeds of approximately 90 mph down two- and four-lane roads and lasted for nearly ten minutes. When Harris drove into a shopping center, officers tried to box him in, but Harris evaded the trap, collided with Scott's vehicle, and then continued down a two-lane road. Following the collision in the parking lot, Scott took over as the lead pursuit vehicle. About ten miles later, Scott decided to try to terminate the pursuit. He radioed in for permission to apply alternative means to make the vehicle driven by Harris stop. Then Scott hit the rear of Harris's car with his front push bumper. Harris lost control of his vehicle, ran down an embankment, overturned, and crashed. Harris was rendered a quadriplegic from the collision. He claimed the officer used excessive force (*Scott v. Harris* 2007).

Maryland. Police officer Jason Leavitt stopped motorist Archie Elliott and noticed a strong odor of alcohol on his breath. Officer Leavitt called for a backup and conducted several sobriety tests. The officer told Elliott he was under arrest and handcuffed him. Officer Leavitt briefly searched Elliott for weapons and contraband but found none. When backup officers arrived, they helped secure Elliott in the front seat of Leavitt's police car to be transported for booking. While officers were talking outside the police car, they noticed Elliott moving around. Then they suddenly noticed Elliott had a gun with his finger on the trigger. Officer Leavitt yelled "gun" and ordered Elliott to drop it. Officer Leavitt and another officer opened fire, killing Elliott. Elliott's parents brought a suit against the police for abuse of force (*Elliott v. Leavitt* 1996).

Missouri. Officer Bryan Hubbard was responding to a call regarding an armed robbery with shots fired. On the way to the scene, he observed Ravone Thompson getting into a car. Thompson fit the description of one of the robbery suspects. Upon being stopped, Thompson initially complied with Officer Hubbard's commands. Then suddenly, Thompson fled on foot. Officer Hubbard chased Thompson between two buildings and over a fence. According to Officer Hubbard, Thompson appeared to be reaching for a weapon and so Hubbard fired a single shot into his back. Thompson died from the wound. No weapon was found. His family claimed this was abuse of force (*Thompson v. Hubbard* 2001).

Table 3.1 shows how these cases are evaluated according to legal and ethical standards and explains the difference. In all four cases, the courts ruled that the behavior of the police was justified by law. In the North Carolina case, the US Supreme Court cited the "objective" factors justifying the police behavior. These include the severity of the suspected crime, the immediate threat to officer or public safety, and the active resistance of the person injured. Police policies generally permit police officers to use force to prevent harm to the officer or others. A deontological ethic suggests that any behavior that aligns with policy

Table 3.1 Determining Whether Use of Force Is Justified: Four Case Examples

Use-of-Force Case	Legal Framework: Actual Court Decision	Police-Policy Framework	Ethical Framework
North Carolina Police used physical force to control a person experiencing an insulin reaction.	Justified. Court considered "objective" factors: —Severity of crime —Suspect posed immediate threat to officer or public safety —Suspect actively resisted *Graham v. Connor* (1989)	Justified. Police policies permit the use of force to prevent harm to the officer or others.	*Deontological*: Justified. It follows law or policy. *Consequential*: Unjustified. Police response seriously injured someone having a medical crisis.
Georgia Case Police officer intentionally bumped the back of a speeding car to end a chase.	Justified. Police attempts to terminate a dangerous high-speed chase to protect the public is not prohibited. *Scott v. Harris* (2007)	Unjustified. Even though the law does not prohibit bumping a vehicle to end a pursuit, some police policies do.	*Deontological*: Justified. It follows law or policy. *Consequential*: Unjustified. Police action created a harmful outcome.
Maryland Case Police fatally shot a man in their custody. The man was handcuffed but had a gun.	Justified. No citizen should draw a gun on the police, and no police officer needs to be absolutely sure of the threat. *Elliott v. Leavitt* (1996)	Justified, But with a caveat. The police were justified in shooting an armed suspect who posed a serious risk. However, placing a man with a gun in the vehicle in handcuffs may be a separate violation of policy.	*Deontological*: Justified. It follows law or policy. *Consequential*: Justified. Although the police should learn from the encounter about searching suspects for weapons, the threat was real and so officers had little choice.

(*Continued*)

Table 3.1 (*Continued*)

Use-of-Force Case	Legal Framework: Actual Court Decision	Police-Policy Framework	Ethical Framework
Missouri Case Police shot and killed a fleeing suspect in the back, thinking he was armed.	Justified. A police officer is not required to wait until he sees a weapon before employing deadly force on a fleeing suspect who moves as though to draw a gun. *Thompson v. Hubbard* (2001)	Justified. Police policies generally allow use of deadly force when, considering the circumstances, the officer has probable cause to believe that the suspect poses an immediate threat of death or serious physical injury to the officer or others.	*Deontological*: Justified. It follows law or policy. *Consequential*: Unjustified. There are less violent alternatives that could be considered. Plus, the use of force was based on an error in perception.

or law would be justified. However, a consequentialist ethic would find the behavior of officers in North Carolina unjustified and unethical because the force used by the police created serious injury to a person having a medical crisis.

The use of force by police in Georgia to end a vehicle chase was justified by the US Supreme Court, which held that an officer's attempt to end a dangerous chase by bumping the speeding car was not prohibited by law. Some model police policies prohibit the use of bumping a vehicle to end a chase in this way. A deontological ethic might see it both ways. On one hand, the behavior followed the law. On the other hand, it may have violated police policy. A review of this case through a consequentialist lens might find the car bumping unjustified because the serious injury that resulted could have been prevented, albeit while possibly endangering others.

In the Maryland case, the US Supreme Court decided that the behavior of officers in using deadly force was justified. They held that officers do not have to be absolutely sure that a suspect poses a deadly threat before using deadly force. This is generally the position from a police policy perspective as well. However, most police policies dictate that suspects must be searched thoroughly before being placed in a police vehicle in handcuffs. From an ethical perspective, both the deontological and consequentialist approaches would probably find the use of deadly force justifiable.

Finally, in the Missouri case, the US Supreme Court found the use of deadly force by shooting a fleeing suspect in the back—and where the officer wrongly believed that the suspect was armed—was justified. Most police policies require probable cause to believe the suspect presents a serious risk of deadly violence, but this does not have to rise to the level of absolute certainty. Therefore, the Missouri shooting would likely be justified. Deontologists would agree that the behavior is justified because it follows the law and police policy. The consequentialist, to the contrary, would probably say that the behavior is unjustified, since an unarmed man was shot in the back and killed by officers, owing to a preventable mistake.

In summary, the police, as law enforcement officers, must follow the law and police policy. Therefore, the use of force is often judged by appellate courts to be right or wrong from this perspective. To be right from a deontological ethical view means to be *in the right*, that is, following police policy and the law. In contrast, the consequentialists say following policies and laws that lead to harmful consequences is wrong. Whether one judges the use of force by the police as right or wrong often can be traced back to these competing frameworks.

Further Reading

CALEA Accredited Use of Force Policy for Ann Arbor, Michigan Police. 2023. https://public.powerdms.com/a2gov/documents/2051.

Elliott v. Leavitt, 99 F. 3d. 640 (1996).

Gerber, Monica M., and Jonathan Jackson. 2017. "Justifying Violence: Legitimacy, Ideology, and Public Support for Police Use of Force." *Psychology, Crime, and Law*, 23 no. 1: 79–95.

Graham v. Connor, 490 U.S. 386 (1989).

International Association of Chiefs of Police (IACP). 1957. *Law Enforcement Code of Ethics*. https://www.theiacp.org/resources/law-enforcementcode-of-ethics.

International Association of Chiefs of Police (IACP). 2020. *National Consensus Policy and Discussion Paper on the Use of Force*, 2020. https://www.theiacp.org/sites/default/files/2020-07/National_Consensus_Policy_On_Use_Of_Force%2007102020%20v3.pdf.

National Institute of Justice (NIJ). 2009. "The Use-of-Force Continuum," August 3. https://nij.ojp.gov/topics/articles/use-force-continuum.

Nolan, James J., Timothy Parsons, and Frank Crispino. 2021. "'Doing Right': Police Ethics in an Age of Reform." In James J. Nolan, Frank Crispino, and Timothy

Parsons, eds., *Policing in an Age of Reform: An Agenda for Research and Practice*, 233–50. London: Palgrave Macmillan.

Nolan, James J., Walter S. DeKeseredy, and Henry H. Brownstein. 2022. "Police Ethics in a Rural Context: A Left Realist Consequentialist View." *International Journal of Rural Criminology* 7, no. 1: 1–23.

Pojman, Louis P. 1999. *Ethics: Discovering Right and Wrong*, 3rd ed. New York: Wadsworth Publishing Company.

Sahakian, William S., and Mabel Sahakian. 1966. *Ideas of Great Philosophers*. New York: Barnes & Noble.

Scott v. Harris, 550 U.S. 372 (2007).

Thompson v. Hubbard, 257 F. 3d 896 (2001).

US Department of Justice. n. d. Policy on Use of Force. Accessed 2024. https://www.justice.gov/jm/1-16000-department-justice-policy-use-force.

Q12: Are "bad apples" a problem in policing, and why is it so hard to eliminate them?

Answer: Although bad apples exist and are a problem, they are just one part of the larger systemic issues in policing discussed in this book. The American law enforcement game makes policing in general problematic and foments widespread abuses through over-enforcement, excessive force, and discrimination, as discussed in Chapters 1 and 2. In addition, however, the US legal system affords police officers special protections that make it hard to keep officer misconduct in check, even where such conduct may violate the Constitution, police department policy, or both. There are two kinds of police officer special protections. One is the legal doctrine of qualified immunity; the other is the Law Enforcement Officers' Bill of Rights (LEOBOR), which lawmakers have passed in many states.

The Facts: The police in American society are given the legal authority to use coercive force, both lethal and nonlethal, to deprive citizens of their liberty (Bittner 1970). This authority has helped shape the professional practice of policing as crime control and social order through law enforcement mandate. Due to the nature of this work, the police receive two special protections: qualified immunity and an officers' bill of rights.

Qualified immunity is a legal doctrine that protects police officials from civil liability in certain cases when police deprive citizens of their statutory or constitutional rights. The US Supreme Court has ruled that qualified immunity balances the need to hold public officials accountable while at the same time shielding them from harassment when they perform their duties reasonably. Qualified immunity protects officers not just against civil damages, but also against the need to defend themselves in litigation altogether. As the term implies, it is not complete immunity. Instead, it simply shields those officers who act competently and without knowingly violating the law.

In recent years, there have been attempts in Congress to end or modify qualified immunity. The George Floyd Justice in Policing Act of 2021, which Congress did not pass, is an example of this (US Congress 2021). Section 102 of the act pertains to qualified immunity and states

> It shall not be a defense or immunity in any action brought under this section against a local law enforcement officer … that—
>
> (1) the defendant (officer) was acting in good faith, or believed … that his or her conduct was lawful at the time when the conduct was committed; or
> (2) the rights, privileges, or immunities secured by the Constitution and laws were not clearly established at the time (they were deprived by the officer), or that … the defendant (officer) could not reasonably have been expected to know whether his or her conduct was lawful.

This kind of change would have had significant implications for the police. As such, it is strongly opposed by professional law enforcement groups who argue it would prevent anyone from wanting to become a police officer.

The second type of protection is the LEOBOR. LEOBOR refers to the due process provisions in state statutes and collective bargaining agreements that protect police officers during internal investigations (Keenan and Walker 2005). LEOBOR statutes give officers the right to advance notice of an internal investigation, the nature of the violation, and findings of the investigation. Other rights and protections afforded to police by LEOBOR include the right to counsel; protection from threats or inducements; the right to a hearing and to review transcripts; the right to add written comments in one's personnel file; and protection against retaliation for exercise of rights established in LEOBOR. Many argue that LEOBOR minimizes accountability and transparency within police departments by granting rights to police officers not offered to other public officials (Elliott 2021). In Delaware, for example, the LEOBOR statute specifies that records from an internal investigation or disciplinary procedure "are confidential and shall not be released to the public" (Del. Code Title 11, Section 92).

In summary, qualified immunity and LEOBOR offer protections to all police officers. These protections assume that officers are doing their job in good faith, which means that bad-apple cops are sometimes shielded from public scrutiny. Still, the problems of violence and discrimination in American policing are *primarily* rooted in the professional mandate for crime control and social order via law enforcement, and not in bad apples per se. From this point of view, the debates about qualified immunity and LEOBOR are necessary but insufficient for reforming the American police system in ways that reduce police abuse.

Further Reading

Bittner, Egon. 1970. *The Function of Police in Modern Society*. Washington, DC: National Institute of Mental Health.

Del. Code Title 11, Section 92 (12). https://delcode.delaware.gov/title11/c092/.

Elliott, Richard D. 2021. "Impact of the Law Enforcement Officers' Bill of Rights on Police Transparency & Accountability." Southern Political Science Association. http://dx.doi.org/10.2139/ssrn.3690641.

Keenan, Kevin M., and Samuel Walker. 2005. "An Impediment to Police Accountability: An Analysis of Statutory Law Enforcement Officers' Bills of Rights." *Public Interest Law Journal* 14: 185–244.

US Congress, House. 2021. *George Floyd Justice in Policing Act of 2021*. HR 1280, 117th Congress. Introduced February 24. https://www.congress.gov/bill/117th-congress/house-bill/1280.

4

Historical Patterns in American Police Reform

The early settlers in America probably gave little thought to police administration. After all, they were busy subduing a continent (Smith 1949). However, as cities grew larger and more diverse, a need arose for a more formalized policing system. The American police had become so intertwined with politics that it was difficult to separate the two. Notwithstanding, the early colonists were able to draw from the English heritage to help shape the contours of an emerging American policing system.

The enduring features of this system include limitations on police authority, as articulated in the Bill of Rights; local political control of the police; and a fragmented system of relatively independent agencies that, today, number over 18,000 (Walker 1998). The decentralized structure and control of American policing makes the system extraordinarily resistant to reform, as compared to its European counterparts (Hirschfield 2020).

The American policing system has been described as developing linearly through predictable stages from informal to formal or modern (Lundman 1980). In the early colonies, the first policing system was *informal*, meaning it was characterized by citizens sharing responsibility with the police for maintaining order (ibid.). Fast forward to the twentieth century, when a formal, *modern* policing had emerged, which included salaried personnel in a single organization with 24/7 citywide responsibilities and accountability to a government authority (ibid.). This is still how we think of the police today.

The informal and modern policing systems were the anchor points in this linear progression, but there was also an intermediate stage called a *transitional* policing system. The transitional system included elements of the informal while anticipating the modern. The slave patrols in the Southern states have been described as transitional policing (ibid.). They had begun as informal control with all white citizens involved in the enforcement of slavery laws.

Later, they took a more modern form, having men assigned to full-time law enforcement duties. This style of policing—full-time law enforcement—had yet to appear elsewhere, and it is likely to have been a precursor to the modern law enforcement approach.

The push for modernization centered on the growing need for formal social control. As populations grew and became more diverse, the informal controls provided by families, neighborhoods, and communities became insufficient for keeping communities safe. In a review of the literature, sociologist Richard Lundman (1980: 24) found that four factors influenced the development of formal social control: (1) an increase in crime (real or perceived), (2) public riots, (3) public intoxication, and (4) a need to control the "dangerous classes." In addition, scholars have also maintained that the origin of modern policing is a consequence of the division of society into dominant and subordinate classes with antagonistic interests. Therefore, social control function needed to move out of communities and be ensured by the police. From this view, the police institution was created and is maintained by the dominant class as an instrument for the preservation of its class interests (Robinson and Scaglion 1987: 109).

The history of the American police is often reported as occurring in three discernable eras, such as the political era (1830s–1900), the professional era (1900–1960s), and the era of conflicting pressures (1960s–present). This framing, and others like it, is biased in favor of Northern urban areas, such as Boston, Chicago, New York, and Philadelphia. It gives little attention to the role of the police in sustaining slavery, segregation, and discrimination throughout our nation's history (Williams and Murphy 1990). Moreover, it excludes experiences of minoritized populations who suffered the most and benefited the least from all police reforms. These omitted historical facts are what continue to shape police behavior toward black populations today, that is, "keep[ing] them under control" (ibid.: 2). The racial disparities in all aspects of policing today (see Chapter 2) thus reflect a significant historical continuity.

In this chapter, we examine the historical developments in American policing. We begin with the *informal* policing system used in colonial America. Then, we look at *transitional* policing in the South, specifically the slave patrols. Finally, we examine the first two attempts at modernizing the police, one political and the other professional. In Chapters 5 through 8, we describe how conflicting pressures in the police profession repeatedly prompt loud cries for police reform. However, none of these has yet to deliver a vision for change that moves us beyond the law enforcement approach that emerged in the twentieth century and continues today. In Chapter 9, we conclude the book by evaluating conventional reform and examining potential alternatives.

Further Reading

Hirschfield, Paul. 2020. "Policing the Police: U.S. and European Models." *Journal of Democracy* 31, no. 4: 166–81.

Lundman, Richard J. 1980. *Police and Policing: An Introduction*. New York: Holt.

Robinson, Cyril D., and Richard Scaglion. 1987. "The Origin and Evolution of the Police Function in Society: Notes Toward a Theory." *Law and Society Review* 21, no. 1: 109–53.

Smith, Bruce. 1949. *Police Systems in the United States*, 2nd ed. New York: Harper Row.

Walker, Samuel. 1988. *Popular Justice: A History of American Criminal Justice*, 2nd ed. New York: Oxford University Press.

Williams, Hubert, and Patrick V. Murphy. 1990. "The Evolving Strategy of Police: A Minority View." *Perspectives on Policing*. Washington, DC: National Institute of Justice.

Q13: How did American policing begin, and how has it evolved?

Answer: The origin of American policing goes back to English heritage. In the early colonies, the sheriff, constable, and watch served the functions of the police. In the Southern colonies, policing took shape as slave patrols organized to prevent slave revolts and to seek out and return runaway slaves (Walker and Katz 2011). Industrialization and European immigration to America created a need for more sophisticated models of policing, including those focused on crime prevention. The idea of preventive patrol in the American system can be traced to the London Metropolitan Police Act of 1829 (UK Public Acts 1829). However, unlike the more centralized policing strategy in London, the first professional police departments in American cities were decentralized and attached to local political factions. Officers were recruited by political leaders in wards or precincts. The police earned the respect of the community by knowing what was expected of them and behaving accordingly. However, widespread corruption and political patronage that emerged from this decentralized system would eventually lead to calls to professionalize the police (Uchida 2005). A professional model of policing emerged with an emphasis on crime and social control through law enforcement. This professional model of policing continues to the present day with only minor attempts at change.

The Facts: The first form of policing in the American colonies had its roots in the English heritage (Walker and Katz 2011). It was an informal policing style in that citizens shared responsibility for keeping the community safe (Lundman 1980). The *night watch* was a service obligation of all adult men, whose primary duty was to look for fires and other impending dangers. Some men tried to evade this service, while others paid replacements to serve. Service to the night watch was also a punishment meted out to those who refused military service. The watch was supervised by *constables*. These were official law enforcement officers who were elected by the people and paid for their services. Constables had a variety of responsibilities including the service of warrants, the elimination of health hazards, and escorting people to court (Uchida 2005). In addition to the constable and watch, the position of *sheriff* (along with deputies and marshals) served a law enforcement function, but it did not have regular patrol responsibilities like the watch (Monkkonen 1981). There was some variation in the way the watch, constable, and sheriff evolved in different regions of the country, but these were the essential components of the informal policing system (Uchida 2005).

Policing in the Southern colonies took the form of slave patrols. At first this was mostly done informally by way of citizen participation. For example, in South Carolina in the seventeenth century, white citizens had a legal duty to "apprehend, chastise, and send home any slave found off his/her plantation without authority" (qtd. in Reichel 1988: 57). And in 1705, a statute in Virginia made it legal "for any person or persons whatsoever, to kill or destroy such slaves (i.e., runaways) without accusation or impeachment of any crime for same" (qtd. in ibid.: 57). These informal means for controlling slaves was insufficient, so Southern colonies began passing legislation enabling the enactment of routine slave patrols. A statute in South Carolina from 1740 provides an example.

> As any late horrible and barbarous massacres have been actually committed and more designed, on the white inhabitants of this Province, by negro slaves, who are generally prone to such current practices, which makes it highly necessary that constant patrols should be established. (Cooper 1838: 568, qtd. in Reichel 1988: 55)

Unlike the watch, constables, and sheriffs, who had many non-law-enforcement duties, slave patrols operated solely for law enforcement purposes. They are, therefore, viewed as a *transition* from informal colonial policing systems to the more modern and formal systems of today.

The first modern police departments in the United States were established in the mid-nineteenth century, often referred to as the *political era* in policing. This is because officers were selected primarily because of their ethnic backgrounds and political connections. There were no education or physical fitness requirements and officers often had criminal records (Walker and Katz 2011). Police officers during this period were basically political operatives who owed their "allegiance to the ward boss and police captain who chose him" (Uchida 2005: 27). They were paid well but had terrible job security, as political changes often also meant a change in police staffing.

Police officers typically walked a beat and spent time at the stationhouse. However, outside the stationhouse, the officers were not under close supervision and were easily lured into illegal enterprises. Criminologist Craig Uchida (2005: 29) recounts,

> Because police officers worked alone or in small groups, there were ample opportunities to shake down peddlers and small businesses. Detectives allowed con men, pickpockets, and thieves to go about their business in return for a share of the proceeds. Captains often established regular payment schedules for houses of prostitution depending upon the number of girls in the house and the rates charged by them.

In all, the American police in this political era were praised and criticized. Officers often drank alcohol on duty, and they could be extremely brutal, particularly to black Americans and people from immigrant groups and with party affiliations outside their own. Notwithstanding, the police in the nineteenth century also took care of the homeless, ran soup kitchens for the poor, and provided many social welfare services in the community. However, by the end of the nineteenth century, a progressive movement pushed to professionalize the police—moving it toward the next stage, known as the professional era (1900–60).

It was not until the early part of the twentieth century that a movement from within the ranks of the police, and propelled by external forces, that a second wave of modernization came to fruition. This is sometimes referred to as the reform or professional era (Kelling and Moore 1988). In the 1920s, Richard Sylwester, the chief of the Washington, DC, police and president of the International Association of Chiefs of Police (IACP) began rallying police chiefs behind the idea of professionalism (Uchida 2005). He was joined by August Vollmer, the police chief of Berkeley, California, who is often recognized as the leading figure in the police professionalism movement. At the time, Vollmer was respected among his police colleagues for developing university-level police education programs and for his use of forensic science in solving crimes (Kelling and Moore 1988). Vollmer wanted to improve the stature of the profession. This meant recruiting and selecting a higher quality of officers who would become capable experts. He recruited college students to the profession and instituted intelligence and psychological testing to the selection process.

During the professional era, the police function narrowed to crimefighting. Crime prevention at this time meant asserting control over those deemed deviant, threatening, or undesirable, and doing so through the enforcement of laws. This was a huge shift in the police institution. Police agencies became law enforcement agencies, a move that separated the police from the community. The Uniform Crime Reporting Program (UCR) was born in this era and administered by the FBI. Consistent with the new professional mandate, the UCR established crime-related metrics as a standard for policing throughout the nation. The underlying assumption in the professional model was that crime and violence in American society can be suppressed by high-quality, well-trained, technologically equipped, thoroughly disciplined police officers who target the source of crime—the criminal. Of course, this completely ignores the economic and social conditions that produce high rates of criminality and violence in the first place. It also ignores the fact that the police are part of the social system that creates and maintains these conditions. The view of the police as professional crimefighters has led to more problems and further calls for police reform. We explore these in Chapters 5 through 8.

The American police have been described as having two sides. One is described as an iron fist and the other a velvet glove (Center for Research on Criminal Justice 1977). The iron fist represents the coercive aspect of policing. It is the most prominent side in American policing today and arguably the source of the police abuse triad (see Chapter 2). The velvet glove is the public service and community relations side of policing. This includes helping people in trouble, attending community meetings, foot and bike patrols, directing traffic, and so on. In the original formulation of the iron fist and velvet glove aspects of American policing, the iron fist provides the muscle to protect the interests of the ruling class. The velvet glove provides legitimacy to the police institution so the iron fist can continue unimpeded. This critical view of American police organized to serve race and class interests is controversial and outside the scope of this book. However, the images of the iron fist and velvet glove can help us see why the American police are struggling to find a more effective policing system.

Criminal justice scholars Samuel Walker and Charles Katz (2011: 41) describe the post-1960s in American policing simply as an era of "conflicting pressures." The police must respond to emerging realities, such as US Supreme Court decisions, competing political demands, citizen oversight, body and phone cameras, claims of racism and rising crime, and the loss of legitimacy. Since the late 1960s, there have been several attempts to forge a new era in policing. Researchers George Kelling and Mark Moore (1988: 10) called this time the community problem-solving era. Coming out of the iron fist era of the 1960s, when the police had used extreme violence to quell civil rights protests, the need emerged to prioritize the velvet glove side of the profession. Foot patrols and community policing became popular again. Problem-oriented policing took center stage (Goldstein 1990). This involved decentralizing decision-making so officers could work with residents to solve neighborhood problems. The velvet glove wouldn't stay on for long, however. Into the 1980s and 1990s, during the fiercest fighting in the war on drugs, the iron fist reemerged in the form of military equipment and SWAT teams (Balko 2014; Kraska 2017). The struggle for a new, more effective, less violent and discriminatory way to organize the American police continues today. In Chapters 5–8, we describe some of the major attempts to reform the police since the 1960s.

Further Reading

Balko, Radley. 2014. *Rise of the Warrior Cop: The Militarization of America's Police Forces.* New York: Public Affairs.

Center for Research on Criminal Justice. 1977. *The Iron Fist and the Velvet Glove: An Analysis of the U.S. Police*, 2nd ed. Berkeley, CA.

Cooper, Thomas, ed. 1838. *Statutes at Large of South Carolina,* vol. 3, part 2. Columbia, SC: A. S. Johnston.

Goldstein, Herman. 1990. *Problem-Oriented Policing.* New York: McGraw-Hill.

Kelling, George L., and Mark H. Moore. 1988. "The Evolving Strategy of Policing." *Perspectives on Policing* 4. Washington, DC: National Institute of Justice.

Kraska, Peter. 2017. "Militarization and Policing—Its Relevance to 21st Century Police." *Policing* 1, no. 4: 501–13.

Lundman, Richard J. 1980. *Police and Policing: An Introduction.* New York: Holt, Rinehart and Winston.

Monkkonen, Eric H. 1981. *Police in Urban America, 1860–1920.* London: Cambridge University Press.

Reichel, Philip L. 1988. "Southern Slave Patrols as a Transitional Police Type." *American Journal of Police* 7, no. 2: 51–78.

Uchida, Craig. 2005. "The Development of the American Police." In Roger G. Dunham and Geoffrey P. Alpert, eds., *Critical Issues in Policing: Contemporary Readings*, 5th ed., 20–40. Long Grove, IL: Waveland Press.
UK Public Acts. 1829. *Metropolitan Police Act*, 10 Geo. 4. C. 44.
Walker, Samuel, and Charles Katz. 2011. *The Police in America: An Introduction*, 7th ed. New York: McGraw Hill.

Q14: What processes are involved in the evolution of American police reform?

Answer: One way to think about reform in any institution is to see it as a process of *destabilizing*, *moving*, and *restabilizing* (Lewin 1997). For our purposes, this means that at various times in the evolution of American policing systems (informal > transition > first modern > second modern), as discussed in Q13, equilibrium had to be disrupted. This destabilization enabled reform (movement) to occur. Once the new system was in place, equilibrium had to be reestablished, restabilizing the system. For example, transition from the first modern (political) policing system to the second modern (professional) system meant strengthening forces for change while weakening those opposing it. The destabilizing intensified with growing dissatisfaction with the status quo. Scholars assisted through critical works comparing well-organized European policing systems with the disorganized, dysfunctional American systems. This enabled movement toward the new professional policing system. Visionary leaders from inside the ranks of the police, like Berkeley Police Chief August Vollmer, aligned with influential groups on the outside, such as a presidential committee known as the Wickersham Commission, to destabilize the forces holding the political system in place and to push movement forward. Once the new professional policing system was in place, equilibrium had to be reestablished. It was restabilized through the mechanism of the FBI's Uniform Crime Reporting (UCR) program and organizational policies and practices in local places that aligned with international groups such as the International Association of Chiefs of Police. The stabilization process continues today through linguistic and scientific mechanisms that hold the professional law enforcement approach tightly in place.

The Facts: As American policing systems evolved, so did the specific duties and expectations of police officers. Initially, the concern was community safety and the orderly functioning of cities. Catching criminals was only a minor concern. In the mid- to late nineteenth century, the concern shifted to maintaining political control and controlling the dangerous classes, which included immigrants and black Americans. The growing emphasis on crime control continued into the twentieth century, and it is still a primary focus in policing today (Monkkonen 1981).

An important lesson we can take from the evolutionary developments in American policing is the way reform happens. Much like individuals, the behavior of social institutions is maintained by social forces. At any one time, there are sets of forces driving for change and those opposing it. These *driving* and *restraining* forces stabilize institutional behaviors in a way that is sometimes referred to as quasi-stationary equilibrium (Lewin 1997). When the behavior is viewed as problematic, a process of *destabilizing*, *moving*, and *restabilizing* occurs. The following paragraphs provide examples of this process and are not meant to be comprehensive.

The term *destabilizing* refers to disrupting the balance of competing social forces so that change can occur. This happens by weaking or strengthening the driving and restraining forces holding the institution in a state of quasi-stationary equilibrium. During the late nineteenth century, for example, urban reformers became a driving force for change as they railed against political corruption, wanting to rescue the police from its influence. However, driving forces were matched by the restraining forces from political factions who sought to retain control of their private armies. As dissatisfaction grew, the driving forces were augmented by the work of scholars like Raymond Fosdick whose book *American Police Systems* (1920) made highly critical comparisons of the well-organized and functional European policing systems to the disorganized, dysfunctional American system. Fosdick wrote the following about the state of American policing during this era.

> There is little conception of policing as a profession or a science to be matured and developed. It is a *job*, held, perhaps by the grace of some mysterious political influence, and conducted in an atmosphere sordid and unhealthy. It is a treadmill, worked without imagination or aim, and with little incentive except the desire to keep out of trouble … . In the interim between spasms of (negative) publicity the average police force sinks in its rut, while crime and violence flourish. (380)

As the driving forces increased and intensified, the existing policing system was thrown into disequilibrium, enabling movement toward the new professional policing system (see Figure 4.1).

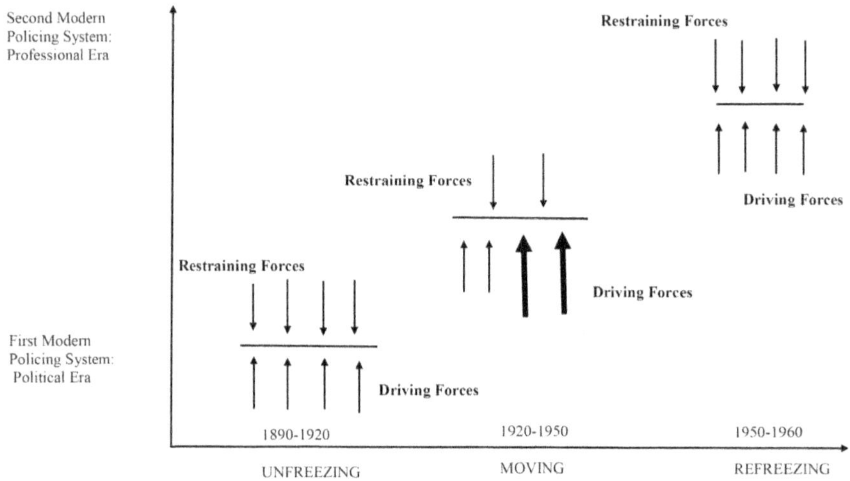

Figure 4.1 The process of reform from first to second modern policing system. Source: Figure created by James Nolan.

The strengthening of driving forces for change in the early decades of the twentieth century far outpowered the restraining forces. This destabilized the system and enabled movement toward a new policing system. This is indicated by the heavy dark arrows in Figure 4.1. One of the more significant driving forces was police insider August Vollmer, the police chief of Berkeley, California. At the time, Vollmer was a capable spokesperson for reform who made a compelling case for a new policing system that aimed at "objective and aggressive law enforcement" (Carte and Carte 1975: 3). Restraining forces at this time included other chiefs of police who thought the police should retain their generalist function to provide strong-arm support for municipal departments rather than focus solely on crimefighting.

Then, in 1925, President Herbert Hoover established the National Commission on Law Observance and Enforcement, more popularly known as the Wickersham Commission. Vollmer's appointment to this commission elevated his influence. He was assigned to help write the policing section of the report, which was to articulate standards and goals in policing. Most importantly, the report established as a first priority the removal of politics from policing and the independence of the police function (Carte and Carte 1975: 67). It also included careful screening and the comprehensive training of officers. Professionalism meant the search for the "perfect man" who could use modern technology for suppressing crime (ibid.: 84). According to Vollmer, the enemy of the people was the criminal and the professional police officer was the best way to wage battle.

As the new professional model of police took hold nationally, the need arose to restabilize the institution. The restabilizing included new metrics for police success, written organizational policies and practices that operationalize the professional model, and other restabilizing forces such as linguistic and scientific mechanisms. The UCR program was born during the movement to professionalize the American police, introduced by the IACP in its book, *Uniform Crime Reporting* (1929). Since 1930, the FBI has managed the UCR data collection and published annual reports of its findings. The foreword to *Uniform Crime Reporting* (1929: vii) expressed the need to establish the metrics for crime control that are best located with the police.

> The urgent need for national crime statistics in the United States is so well recognized as to require no debate. Criminal justice administrators and others engaged in the prevention and suppression of crime have for many years expressed regret upon the absence of reliable information concerning crime and criminals …
>
> Compilations of the number of persons tried, convicted and imprisoned do not, and cannot, provide an index of crime and criminality. Only a police record of known offenses will do this. Likewise, the police alone know the number and nature of persons apprehended for committing offenses. Thus at the start we are compelled to recognize that crime statistics must originate with the police and that without police support there can be no crime statistics.

The UCR provided metrics for success in what was now being called a "law enforcement" profession. These related to crime control (rather than political control). The things that were "essential to the police executive, the legislator, the sociologist, and the public generally" included summary counts of seven crimes deemed most likely to come to the attention of the police (IACP 1929: 16). These were called Part I crimes. These included felonious homicide, rape, robbery, aggravated assault, burglary, larceny theft, and motor vehicle theft. The count of these seven crimes were to become the "index" of crime for the United States. The UCR also sought to collect statistics on crimes that were less serious or less likely to come to the attention of the police. These Part II crimes included simple assault, forgery or counterfeiting, embezzlement and fraud, weapons violations, sex offenses (other than rape), offenses against the family and children, drug and liquor law violations, driving while intoxicated, disorderly conduct and vagrancy, gambling, traffic and motor vehicle violations, and other offenses against the public order (IACP 1929: 25).

In one sense, the impetus of police executives to develop a national statistical program emerged from the public's unrealistic expectation that the police alone would be responsible for the control of crime. In fact, some police agencies were hesitant to compile and publish crime data because they knew the public viewed rising crime rates as a failure of the police. However, national police leaders knew that false or misleading information about crime could be even more harmful to the police and community. This sentiment was expressed as follows:

> In the absence of data on (crime), irresponsible parties have often manufactured so-called "crime waves" ... to the discredit of police departments and the confusion of the public concerning the effective measures for reducing the volume of crime. (ibid.: 17)

The fear of being blamed for high crime rates was allayed by police leaders with examples from other professions such as public health, which collected data on the prevalence of disease and produced statistical tables in the public's interest. Like disease, crime was a "social misfortune, which requires a similar cooperation between public and private agencies if it is to be successfully combated and treated" (ibid.: 2). Crime data generated by the police through the UCR program reflected the spirit of the professional policing system and continue to stabilize professional law enforcement practices today.

The professional policing system that was developed nationally had to be implemented locally to restabilize the institution. The professional model was to do the following things: separate the police from politics, organize departments hierarchically and bureaucratically, target criminals and crime-prone places, detach from the community, and stand ready to use coercive force for social control. One way to examine how reforms in the early part of the twentieth century materialized in police practice is to look at policy manuals from the time. For example, the following paragraphs explore excerpts from the Rules and Regulations of the Bureau of Police in Wilmington, Delaware, issued in 1932 (Bureau of Police 1932) to illustrate how the Wilmington policy followed the themes developed as part of the national professional model.

In Wilmington, the police were prohibited from participating in politics. This was made explicit in the department's rules: "No member of the force will be permitted to take part in any way in the political or partisan convention, nor in any other matter in which political action will be required of him" (65). The WPD organizational structure was described as bureaucratic and hierarchical. Positions in the department followed a US military rank structure. The movement of officers was also in accord with military formations. The Bureau of Police rule put it this way: "Captains or Sergeants, while proceeding with a body of police to perform any duty, or when returning from the performance of a duty, shall see that the men under their command march in military order" (68). The military style associated with the professional law enforcement organization is further established in the following directive:

> Any member of the police force in full uniform, or partial uniform, on meeting or passing a superior officer, when he is in uniform, shall salute him in the manner hereinafter specified: First—It is the duty of the subordinate to offer first the prescribed salutation and of the officer to return it. Second—The salute will be made by raising the right hand to the brim of the hat. Third—Members of the force on duty in citizens' dress are not required to salute. (71)

The new police profession assumed sole responsibility for preventing crime in local places. Its unrealistic expectation that the police alone could prevent crime is detectable in the Wilmington policy manual, which states, "Each patrolman must, by his vigilance, render it extremely difficult, if not impossible, for anyone to commit a crime on his district" (61). This meant that police officers would prevent crime by looking for criminals.

> Patrolmen must strictly watch the conduct of all persons of suspected or known bad character, in such a manner that it will be evident to such persons that they are watched … (he must) note the time of the appearance of any person of known bad character on their district, the circumstances relating thereto, the premises that said person may enter and leave, and report the same to their commanding officer. (62)

Along with looking for criminals, the police were to identify crime-prone places: "Patrolmen must pay particular attention to all suspicious or questionable places on their districts" (63).

Although its primary responsibility was crime control, the police were not expected to build relationships between the police and community or build connections among residents, businesses, or other stakeholders in the community. In fact, the police were not permitted to have interactions with citizens unless it related to *police business*. This expectation is expressed as follows: "Patrolmen must not walk or talk with citizens while on patrol duty, except on police business; then he will stand and hear what the business is; if it requires his immediate attention, attend to it; if not, he will direct the person or persons seeing the information to the Central Station" (63). In addition, the police profession was predominately male, and officers remained under strict orders not to engage in conversations with females unless it was for the purpose of crime control.

> Members of the police force will not be allowed to stand and converse with females in the street, unless upon matters appertaining to their duty, and their Sergeants are strictly enjoined that it is their duty to report all such cases, and the neglect to do so will be visited on the Sergeant himself. (63)

The social control aspect of the professional police mandate included the use of coercive force for maintaining order. "It shall be the duty of all members of the police force while on duty to disperse all crowds who may be found loitering at the corners or upon the streets, or near public places" (69). One can see from the policy manual of this urban police agency in the 1930s that professional police practice was apolitical, organized as a paramilitary bureaucracy, separated from the community, and focused on the control of crime, which meant the control of "dangerous" people and "dangerous" places.

In addition to UCR and local police policy manuals, the professional policing system, along with the law enforcement identity it produces, is stabilized through language. Consider the way we talk about the profession as "law enforcement." The term *law enforcement* is used everywhere to symbolize the police profession. It is found in criminology textbooks (Walker and Katz 2021); in presidential commission and task force reports (President's Commission 1968; President's Task Force 2015); in professional organizations like the International Association of Chiefs of Police, the National Sheriffs' Association, and the National Organization of Black Law Enforcement Professionals; in professional accreditation organizations, such as the Commission on Accreditation for Law Enforcement Standards, in state and local omnibus crime bills; in popular media; and in routine discourse. To underscore the point about how pervasive this is, there is now a national Law Enforcement Appreciation Day!

Even in the field of evidence-based policing, which prioritizes scientific rigor and object standards, scholars seem blind to this linguistic trap shaping both research questions and findings. In addition, the Center for Evidence Based Crime Policy at George Mason University hosts an Evidence-Based Policing Hall of Fame, which recognizes "innovative *law enforcement* practitioners who have been central to the implementation of a high-quality research program in their agency and are relentless champions of institutionalizing evidence-based practices" (emphasis added).

In closing this chapter, we include the critical remarks of criminologists Gene and Elaine Carte in their book *Police Reform in the United States: The Era of August Vollmer* (1975: 122).

> Profound social conflicts can only be resolved when the groups involved have access to the democratic exchange process; there is no other mechanism in the United States for problem solving. Vollmer's professional policing, by placing the maintenance of order (social control) above the rights of all groups to have such access, perpetuates the very situation that it used to justify its existence. Although the police are not an important institution in themselves, their position as the maintainers of this inequity makes it imperative that control of policing be dispersed.

The following chapters examine the major police reform initiatives that have taken place since the 1960s. These reforms continue to embrace the professional policing system established more than a hundred years ago. Rather than moving toward a new system, the current era's reforms simply respond to conflicting pressures. In Chapter 9, we discuss potential alternatives that could reinvent the American police institution.

Further Reading

Bureau of Police. 1932. *Rules and Regulations of the Bureau of Police*. Wilmington, DE: Wilmington Bureau of Police.

Carte, Gene E., and Elaine H. Carte. 1975. *Police Reform in the United States: The Era of August Vollmer*. Berkeley: University of California Press.

Evidence-Based Policing Hall of Fame at George Mason University. n. d. Accessed 2024. https://cebcp.org/hall-of-fame/.

Fosdick, Raymond B. 1920. *American Police Systems*. New York: The Century.

International Association of Chiefs of Police (IACP), Committee on Uniform Crime Records. 1929. *Uniform Crime Reporting*. New York: J.J. Little and Ives.

Lewin, Kurt. 1997. *Resolving Social Conflicts and Field Theory in Social Science*. Washington, DC: American Psychological Association.

Monkkonen, Eric H. 1981. *Police in Urban America, 1860–1920*. London: Cambridge University Press.

President's Commission on Law Enforcement and Administration of Justice. 1968. *The Challenge of Crime in a Free Society*. New York: Dutton.

President's Task Force on 21st Century Policing. 2015. *Final Report of the President's Task Force on 21st Century Policing*. Washington, DC: Community Oriented Policing Services.

Walker, Samuel, and Charles M. Katz. 2021. *The Police in America: An Introduction*, 10th ed. New York: McGraw Hill.

5

The Turbulent 1960s and Policy Debates

Questions lurk over issues of crime, policing, and public safety in America. Why are we handling crime primarily through the policing and prison systems? Wouldn't a better approach get to the heart of the matter by offering gainful employment to all able adults, rich programs for youth, and a robust social safety net that fills the remaining gaps? Evidence that poverty and inequality feed crime has long been recognized by scholarly and government sources. Indeed, President Lyndon Johnson's Crime Commission stated in its 1967 report

> Warring on poverty, inadequate housing and unemployment, is warring on crime. A civil rights law is a law against crime. Money for schools is money against crime. Medical, psychiatric, and family-counseling services are services against crime. More broadly and most importantly every effort to improve life in America's "inner cities" is an effort against crime. A community's most enduring protection against crime is to right the wrongs and cure the illnesses that tempt men to harm their neighbors. (President's Commission 1968: 69)

Many years later, a police reform task force convened by President Barack Obama echoed similar sentiments. "The justice system alone cannot solve many of the underlying conditions that give rise to crime" (President's Task Force 2015: 8). The body advised the president to "promote programs that take a comprehensive and inclusive look at community-based initiatives that address the core issues of poverty, education, health, and safety." Such recommendations are sound. Ample studies have documented how the nations with more generous welfare states, such as the Nordic countries, produce not only less poverty and inequality but also lower rates of homicide (Lappi-Seppälä and Tonry 2011; Reiner 2007: 103–10).

If such insights about "the roots of crime" have been known for many decades, why then does the United States remain so reliant on a punitive approach to crime, with the world's highest incarceration rate (Fair and Walmsley 2021), and yet with small anti-poverty and safety-net programs as compared to other developed countries (Alesina and Glaeser 2004)? This remains a matter of wide scholarly debate (see Reitz 2018), and the present volume does not attempt an answer as such. However, as matters of police abuse and reform are helpfully studied within economic and political contexts, this chapter examines events of the 1960s as a way to provide particular insights about policing and social policy. What gives the 1960s notable historic significance is that the debate over how to address crime and urban unrest was more frontal in American politics than is the case today. And American government at that time was far more committed to providing social programs than it has been since the Reagan era began a trend toward dismantling such programs (Midgley 1992).

The national debate on domestic and urban policy in the 1960s—pitting the call for law and order against the call for expansive social programs—was waged amid certain historic developments. One was the civil rights movement and its milestone victories achieved under Johnson, with a host of "war on poverty" initiatives, the Civil Rights Act of 1964, and Voting Rights Act of 1965. A second development was a national rise in crime that began in the late 1950s and extended through the next decade. In New York City, for example, robberies rose from 6,600 in 1962 to 78,000 in 1972 (Flamm 2005: 5). A third development was the outbreak of urban riots, with over 750 local revolts between 1963 and 1972 (Levy 2018), the largest being in Los Angeles in 1965 and in Detroit and Newark in 1967. In one sense, the national debate was about how best to maintain order and safety in our cities; in another sense, the debate was about race, since both the major crime growth and the riots were based in the highly segregated urban black communities.

The liberal position in this debate, best represented by Johnson, embraced a mixed remedy—social programs and civil rights legislation, on the one hand, and bolstered policing, on the other. The conservative position, led by Arizona senator Barry Goldwater, who lost to Johnson in the 1964 presidential race but launched a new conservative movement in the process, opposed the welfare state and sought to limit the government's role to enforcing law and order, maintaining a stable fiscal climate, and "encouraging a free and a competitive economy" (Goldwater 1964). A third and radical left posture, advanced by civil rights leaders A. Philip Randolph and Martin Luther King Jr., demanded a "Freedom Budget" that would take Johnson's social programs much further through a federal jobs guarantee and the full elimination of poverty (Le Blanc and Yates 2013). The radical posture took a major blow in April 1968 with King's assassination, touching off widespread riots, which, in turn, helped moved the country as a whole toward a politics of law and order.

Questions 15, 16, and 17 delve into the 1960s' debate with particular attention to the liberal and conservative positions. Question 18 presents pertinent lessons from the 1960s, including the decade's mixed legacy on issues of police reform.

Further Reading

Alesina, Alberto, and Edward Glaeser. 2004. *Fighting Poverty in the US and Europe: A World of Difference*. New York: Oxford University Press.

Fair, Helen, and Roy Walmsley. 2021. *World Prison Population List*, 13th ed. London: Institute for Criminal Policy Research, University of London. Accessed January 8, 2025. https://www.prisonstudies.org/resources/world-prison-population-list-13th-edition.

Flamm, Michael W. 2005. *Law and Order: Street Crime, Civil Unrest, and the Crisis of Liberalism in the 1960s*. New York: Columbia University Press.

Goldwater, Barry M. 1964. "Address Accepting the Presidential Nomination at the Republican National Convention in San Francisco." July 16. American Presidency Project. Accessed January 8, 2025. https://www.presidency.ucsb.edu/documents/address-accepting-the-presidential-nomination-the-republican-national-convention-san.

Lappi-Seppälä, Tapio, and Michael Tonry. 2011. "Crime, Criminal Justice, and Criminology in the Nordic Countries." *Crime and Justice* 40: 1–32.

Le Blanc, Paul, and Michael D. Yates. 2013. *A Freedom Budget for All Americans: Recapturing the Promise of the Civil Rights Movement in the Struggle for Economic Justice Today*. New York: Monthly Review.

Levy, Peter B. 2018. *The Great Uprising: Race Riots in Urban America during the 1960s*. Cambridge, UK: Cambridge University Press.

Midgley, James. 1992. "Introduction: American Social Policy and the Reagan Legacy." Special issue. *Journal of Sociology and Social Welfare* 19, no. 1: 3–11.

President's Commission on Law Enforcement and Administration of Justice. 1968. *The Challenge of Crime in a Free Society*. New York: Dutton.

President's Task Force on 21st Century Policing. 2015. *Final Report of the President's Task Force on 21st Century Policing*. Washington, DC: Community Oriented Policing Services.

Reiner, Robert. 2007. *Law and Order: An Honest Citizen's Guide to Crime and Control*. Malden, MA: Polity Press.

Reitz, Kevin R., ed. 2018. *American Exceptionalism in Crime and Punishment*. New York: Oxford University Press.

Q15: What caused the urban disorders—riots and rising crime—of the 1960s?

Answer: The era's riots and crime rise are best understood in relation to the twentieth-century black migration, as some 6 million people fled the rural South and its collapsed sharecropper system to seek job opportunities in cities of the North and West (Wilkerson 2011). The new arrivals found ample jobs in the 1940s but fewer opportunities from the 1950s forward amid emerging patterns of automation and deindustrialization. The migrants also encountered racial barriers that were nearly as onerous as the Jim Crow conditions they had left behind in the South. Segregated conditions in the North and West, joined with poor employment prospects, fomented black crime, while police harassment added insult to injury and triggered many of the riots. The postwar baby boom has also been cited as a contributing factor in the 1960s crime wave (Clegg and Usmani 2019: 19–21).

The Facts: Urban disorder and race were plainly interconnected in the 1960s. "Black men displaced white ethnics as the new face of urban violence" starting in the late 1950s, historian Michael Flamm (2005: 5) observes in his study of law and order during the era. The annual robbery arrest rate for black juveniles was around twenty times as high as for white juveniles during the 1960s, Flamm adds (188, note 14). Behind the crime, and clearly so behind the riots—which historian Gerald Horne (1995: 41) likens to a "toothache" alerting the body politic that "something is dangerously awry"—lay histories of discrimination and exclusion in employment, housing, and schools. At the same time, the civil rights movement and the Nation of Islam, with its powerful speaker Malcolm X, conveyed to many black youth that it was time to fight back. Horne describes the buildup of events leading to the August 1965 uprising with its epicenter in the Watts district of South Los Angeles.

> In April 1964 tensions involving young blacks and police erupted at Jefferson High School. During the summer of 1964 a report was filed with Democratic governor Pat Brown detailing the deteriorating conditions and attitudes in South LA. No vigorous action was taken. Worse, the initiative on the fall ballot, Proposition 14, was viewed widely among African-Americans as a crude attempt to maintain housing segregation and keep blacks penned in South LA; this measure would overturn moderate fair-housing legislation. This could mean a return to the bad old days of de facto racially restrictive covenants in deeds. (46)

Proposition 14 was passed by California voters but was later held to be unconstitutional by the state's supreme court.

In March 1965, Horne continues, the police brutal suppression of protests over segregation and voting rights in Selma, Alabama, built tension in Los Angeles.

> A number of demonstrations were held in sympathy and solidarity [with Selma], while others focused on similar local grievances … . Van de Kamp's, a chain of restaurants, had been targeted by local activists because of its reluctance to hire "Negro waitresses" on the grounds that they would not comport with its "Dutch motif." Other targets of protest were Sears Roebuck, Safeway, Thriftimart, and other companies accused of discriminatory hiring practices. (46–7)

Amid raucous Selma solidarity protests at the federal building in West Los Angeles, the targeting of local companies for alleged discrimination, a June 1965 protest at the office of Los Angeles mayor Sam Yorty over his blocking the dissemination of anti-poverty funds from Washington, and an "apparent deterioration of police-community relations" that the city's Human Relations Commission was attempting to settle—Horne remarks that "any one who merely followed the public record of what was going on would not have been surprised by the fires of August" (49).

In the triggering episode of August 11, a state highway patrolman attempted to arrest a young man, Marquette Frye, for drunken driving. Frye resisted arrest, aided by his mother, and a scuffle ensued that included an officer striking Frye on the forehead with his baton. A crowd gathered to watch, growing to a thousand, while more police were sent to the scene. After the police departed, with Frye and his mother and brother taken into custody, false rumors about what had occurred during the arrests promptly spread through the area, according to a riot commission appointed by Governor Pat Brown. The crowd broke into small groups that vandalized the area and pulled white motorists from their cars and beat them. The following evening and for several days, the city was swept by fires and looting (Governor's Commission 1965: 12–16).

In July 1967, amid a summer of race riots in over 150 cities, President Johnson appointed a commission to investigate causes and make policy recommendations. The report of the Kerner Commission, chaired by Illinois governor Otto Kerner, included profiles of ten of the cities struck by revolt—including Detroit, Newark, Cincinnati, and Atlanta. These revealed black community grievances and histories of protest that roughly mirrored what Horne describes in Los Angeles. Surveys and interviews conducted by the commission in twenty of the cities revealed patterns that may be viewed as the primary drivers of the 1960s' riots generally. Among twelve identified areas of grievance, two ranked the highest in intensity and were found to be problematic in all twenty cities. One was police practices, where the commission heard

> complaints about physical or verbal abuse of Negro citizens by police officers, the lack of adequate channels for complaints against police, discriminatory police employment and promotion practices, a general lack of respect for Negroes by police officers, and the failure of police departments to provide adequate protection to Negroes. (National Advisory Commission 1968: 81)

The second high-ranked area, unemployment and underemployment, was expressed "in terms of joblessness or inadequate jobs and discriminatory practices by labor unions, local and state governments, state employment services and private employment agencies" (81). Other heavily cited complaints included inadequate housing, inadequate education, poor recreation facilities and programs, and unresponsive local political structures and grievance mechanisms (82).

Further Reading

Clegg, John, and Adaner Usmani. 2019. "The Economic Origins of Mass Incarceration." *Catalyst* 3, no. 3: 9–53.

Flamm, Michael W. 2005. *Law and Order: Street Crime, Civil Unrest, and the Crisis of Liberalism in the 1960s*. New York: Columbia University Press, 2005.

Governor's Commission on the Los Angeles Riots. 1965. *Violence in the City—An End or a Beginning?* Los Angeles, CA: Governor's Office, State of California. December 2. Accessed January 8, 2025. https://archive.org/details/ViolenceInCity/page/n3/mode/2up.

Horne, Gerald. 1995. *Fire This Time: The Watts Uprising and the 1960s*. Charlottesville, VA: University Press of Virginia.

National Advisory Commission on Civil Disorders. 1968. *Report of the National Advisory Commission on Civil Disorders*. Washington, DC: US Government Printing Office.

Wilkerson, Isabel. 2011. *The Warmth of Other Suns: The Epic Story of America's Great Migration*. New York: Vintage.

Q16: What remedies did liberal leaders advance?

Answer: The decade's pivotal maker of liberal domestic policy, after President John Kennedy's assassination in November 1963, was Lyndon Johnson, who presided in the White House through January 1969. Johnson's response to the urban crisis enacted three lines of policy. Two of these—racial equality and anti-poverty—addressed what may be considered the social roots of crime. The third, toward more and better policing, addressed law and order more conventionally, though its call for better police-community relations reflected a new thrust.

The Facts: Johnson's major race legislation, the Civil Rights Act of 1964, had been introduced by Kennedy in June 1963. Johnson helped push it through Congress the next year. Upon signing the bill, he remarked: "We believe that all men are created equal. Yet many are denied equal treatment. … because of the color of their skin." Those who are equal before God, he said, "shall now also be equal in the polling booths, in the classrooms, in the factories," and in restaurants and other public accommodations (Johnson 1964b). The act included voting rights; desegregation of schools and public accommodations; nondiscrimination in employment; and nondiscrimination in access to federal funds or assistance, such as in welfare or housing benefits. Some of the act's provisions were later strengthened through the Voting Rights Act of 1965, Fair Housing Act of 1968, and Equal Employment Opportunity Act of 1972.

Johnson coupled civil rights legislation with a "war on poverty," introduced during his January 1964 State of the Union address (Johnson 1964a). Let this session of Congress, he urged, be known as the one that declared "all-out war on human poverty and unemployment in these United States." The plan would help every American fulfill hopes for "a full-time job on full-time pay," "a decent home for his family in a decent community," "a good school for his children with good teachers," and "security when faced with sickness or unemployment or old age." The war on poverty consisted of a host of initiatives, the most important four being:

- Economic Opportunity Act of 1964, establishing the Office of Economic Opportunity, which oversaw the war on poverty. Its prominent programs included Job Corps, VISTA, and Head Start.
- Food Stamp Act of 1964, addressing nutrition and food access for low-income households.
- Social Security Act of 1965, creating Medicare and Medicaid, and expanding Social Security benefits for retirees, widows, the disabled, and college-aged students.
- Elementary and Secondary Education Act of 1965, establishing the Title I program that subsidizes school districts with a large share of impoverished students.

The president's anti-poverty initiatives, though historic and impactful, did not nearly constitute an adequate safety net that guarantees basics such as living-wage jobs, health care, and housing for all. That a more far-reaching remedy was required did gain official acknowledgment. Following scores of urban riots in summer 1967, Johnson condemned the widespread violence but also appointed the Kerner Commission to seek remedies, and he suggested its mandate:

> The only genuine, long-range solution for what has happened lies in an attack—mounted at every level—upon the conditions that breed despair and violence. All of us know what those conditions are: ignorance, discrimination, slums, poverty, disease, not enough jobs. We should attack these conditions—not because we are frightened by conflict, but because we are fired by conscience. We should attack them because there is simply no other way to achieve a decent and orderly society in America. (Johnson 1967)

The commission, whose 1968 report was reproduced by Bantam Books and became a national bestseller, did indeed rise to Johnson's call for urgent action. On employment, the commission advised:

> Take immediate action to create 2 million new jobs over the next 3 years—1 million in the public sector and 1 million in the private sector—to absorb the hard-core unemployed and materially reduce the level of underemployment for all workers, black and white. We propose 250,000 public sector and 300,000 private sector jobs in the first year. (National Advisory Commission 1968: 11)

This would include on-the-job training supported by federal funding. On housing, the commission proposed that the government bring, within the next five years, 6 million new and existing units of decent housing. These would be "within the reach of low- and moderate-income families," and "beginning with 600,000 units in the next year" (13).

However, the president's earlier call for "an attack—mounted at every level" on the conditions underlying the unrest was intended within the limits of Washington politics. Johnson had expected his commission to bring more restraint. He took no action in response, and later commented in his memoir (Johnson 1971: 173) that the panel had not acknowledged the budget constraints he faced:

> The [commission's] recommendations would cost in the vicinity of $30 billion, in addition to the $30 billion plus already in the budget for the poor.
>
> That was the problem—money. At the moment I received the report I was having one of the toughest fights of my life, trying to persuade Congress to pass the 10 per

> cent tax surcharge without imposing deep cuts in our most critical Great Society programs. I will never understand how the commission expected me to get this same Congress to turn 180 degrees overnight and appropriate an additional $30 billion for the same programs that it was demanding I cut by $6 billion.

Johnson's decision was not well received in civil rights quarters. Roger Wilkins, son of NAACP president Roy Wilkins and director of the US Justice Department's Community Relations Service, observed, "There is widespread disappointment in the Negro community that the president has not embraced this report more enthusiastically" (qtd. in Flamm 2005: 110).

The other important part of Johnson's response to the urban crisis lay in policing. Here his major initiatives were the Law Enforcement Assistance Act of 1965 and the Omnibus Crime Control and Safe Streets Act of 1968. The first appointed a President's Crime Commission and established an Office of Law Enforcement Assistance (OLEA). The second transformed the OLEA into a larger Law Enforcement Assistance Administration (LEAA). Together, these initiatives engaged federal government as never before in supporting state and local police agencies—with technical expertise; training programs, often coordinated with universities; and grant programs that would expand through the 1970s. Thus, as historian Elizabeth Hinton observes in *America on Fire* (2021: 22), "The federal allocation for local police forces went from nothing in 1964 to $10 million in 1965, $20.6 million in 1966, $63 million in 1968, $100 million in 1969, and $300 million in 1970." The $300 million figure is equivalent to over $2 billion today.

Policing, as advocated under Johnson and subsequently under Nixon, had two faces that were at odds with one another. There was a "hard" face that sought to clamp down in a muscular, even warlike manner on the forces of crime and disorder; and there was a "soft" face that underscored good police-community relations. Both would bear on the future of US policing; but it was clearly the hard face that was dominant in the 1960s. So, Johnson's Crime Commission (President's Commission 1968: 45) included soft strategies: police departments were urged to establish "effective citizen advisory committees" in minority group neighborhoods; make "special efforts to recruit minority group officers and to deploy and promote them fairly"; and set up "rigorous internal investigation units to examine complaints of misconduct." Yet, funding for police-community relations projects never reached 5 percent of the LEAA's annual action grant budget (Hornbostel 2022: 612). Grants were more often used to enlarge police forces or to introduce new kinds of equipment and technology, much of it geared to riot control:

> Riot-control training, military-grade weapons such as AR15s and M4 carbines, steel helmets, three-foot batons, masks, armored vehicles, two-way radios, tear gas—these and other techniques, weapons, and tools flowed into cities, even small ones across the United States. … The Los Angeles Police Department, still recovering from the Watts rebellion in 1965, received the second largest grant, as well as a helicopter, in 1967. (Hinton 2021: 11)

Hinton (2021: 23) points out, "Preventing rebellion 'with muscle and with toughness' became the dominant strategy for fighting disorder." The model equally became policing's dominant response to rising crime. Policing became more aggressive and intrusive, and particularly so in black communities.

Further Reading

Flamm, Michael W. 2005. *Law and Order: Street Crime, Civil Unrest, and the Crisis of Liberalism in the 1960s*. New York: Columbia University Press.

Hinton, Elizabeth. 2021. *America on Fire: The Untold History of Police Violence and Black Rebellion since the 1960s*. New York: Liveright Publishing.

Hornbostel, Brendan. 2022. "'Public Order Is the First Business of Government': The Law Enforcement Assistance Administration and the Making of a Liberal Counterinsurgent Police-Industrial Complex." *Small Wars and Insurgencies* 3, no. 4–5: 607–32.

Johnson, Lyndon B. 1964a. "Annual Message to Congress on State of the Union." January 8. American Presidency Project. Accessed January 8, 2025. https://www.presidency.ucsb.edu/documents/annual-message-the-congress-the-state-the-union-25.

Johnson, Lyndon B. 1964b. "Radio and Television Remarks upon Signing the Civil Rights Bill." July 2. American Presidency Project. Accessed January 8, 2025. https://www.presidency.ucsb.edu/documents/radio-and-television-remarks-upon-signing-the-civil-rights-bill.

Johnson, Lyndon B. 1967. "The President's Address to the Nation on Civil Disorders." July 27. American Presidency Project. Accessed January 8, 2025. https://www.presidency.ucsb.edu/documents/the-presidents-address-the-nation-civil-disorders.

Johnson, Lyndon B. 1971. *The Vantage Point: Perspectives of the Presidency 1963–1969*. New York: Holt.

National Advisory Commission on Civil Disorders. 1968. *Report of the National Advisory Commission on Civil Disorders*. Washington, DC: US Government Printing Office.

President's Commission on Law Enforcement and Administration of Justice. 1968. *The Challenge of Crime in a Free Society*. New York: Dutton.

Q17: What remedies did conservative leaders advance?

Answer: Urban crime and disorder, according to conservatives in the 1960s, should be addressed through vigorous law-and-order policing and, as Senator Barry Goldwater expressed during his 1964 presidential campaign, through our faith in "the self-reliance, enterprise and initiative of the individual and family" (Goldwater 1964). Very importantly, conservatives also opposed the liberal roots-of-crime remedies—that is, civil rights legislation and anti-poverty programs. President Nixon did not quite fit that pattern: although he expanded policing and its militarization, he did keep Johnson's social programs intact, and he supported racial equality by widening affirmative action in employment (Kotlowski 1998) and by signing the Equal Opportunity Employment Act of 1972. It was Goldwater who most clearly defined the new conservatism that would become an increasingly powerful force in US politics.

The Facts: The conservative domestic platform in the 1960s highlighted law and order, and self-reliance rather than social programs, while it looked sternly on civil rights. In a closing statement of his 1964 presidential bid (Goldwater 1964), published in the *New York Times* on November 1, Goldwater underscored the first two themes but did not mention civil rights. The senator pointed to an "alarming breakdown" of law and order:

> Crime is growing five times as fast as population. Our nation's capital itself ranks first among large cities in its rate of major crimes against persons. … We are not plagued with this crisis in lawlessness because we are poor. We are the richest nation on earth … . The cause is deeper and more dangerous. Our traditional values of individual responsibility and moral obligation have been slipping away at a quickened pace.

In this vein, Goldwater took aim at the US Supreme Court. The court was much criticized by conservatives during the 1960s, as its liberal majority under Chief Justice Earl Warren was expanding the constitutional rights of criminal suspects and defendants (Chemerinsky 2021: part III). For example, in *Mapp v. Ohio* (1961), the court ruled that evidence obtained illegally could not be used in court. This "exclusionary rule" had previously applied only to the federal government; *Mapp* extended it to state government. In *Escobedo v. Illinois* (1964), the court held that suspects have the right to counsel during police interrogations. Goldwater remarked: "Our highest court has been steadily taking away from local law enforcement agencies the powers needed to control law and order. The freedom and rights of law-abiding citizens have been jeopardized by obsessive concern for the criminal defendant."

Goldwater's campaign statement (1964) also challenged Johnson's war on poverty: "Now we are told government can make us free from poverty—free from worry and responsibility. Does anybody really believe that government can make us rich and happy and confident and secure?" He argued, "Thirty-five years ago, the Federal Government commanded only 4 per cent" of our income through taxation. "Today it commands 25 per cent." He added: "Government must be cut down to size or we will surely lose our free society. We will go the age-old way of tyranny and oppression."

The conservative movement with which Goldwater aligned had roots stretching back to the 1930s, when many business leaders spoke out against President Roosevelt's New Deal. Goldwater, whose family owned a Phoenix-based department store chain, had called Roosevelt to task in a 1938 editorial: "In five years my taxes have increased over 250 percent and I fear greatly that 'I ain't seen nothin' yet.'" Furthermore, he wrote, Roosevelt's labor laws had "turned over to the racketeering practices of ill-organized unions the future of the workingman. Witness the chaos they are creating in the eastern cities" (Goldwater 2012a: 34). Now Goldwater directed similar critique at Johnson. In a September 1964 campaign speech in Charleston, West Virginia, amid the persistent poverty and unemployment of Appalachia, the senator suggested that the president's anti-poverty program was meant to maintain Johnson in power. "Human misery is not to be trifled with just to get votes in an election," he remarked. The anti-poverty program was a "hodgepodge of handouts … . You don't want to throw your money away on this worthless nostrum any more than I do" (qtd. in Mohr 1964).

Regarding civil rights, Goldwater preferred to avoid the topic during his presidential campaign. He was careful to distance himself from segregationists such as Alabama governor George Wallace (Edwards 1995: 241–2). Nevertheless, Goldwater had opposed the 1964 Civil Rights Act. On June 18 of that year, the day before the historic measure was passed by the Senate, Goldwater told the assembly: "I am unalterably opposed to discrimination or segregation on the basis of race, color, or creed, or on any other basis" (Goldwater 2012b: 200). Yet, there were portions of the bill that he could not support, specifically those prohibiting discrimination by private enterprises—in public accommodations such as restaurants and hotels (Title II), and in employment (Title VII). He explained:

> I find no constitutional basis for the exercise of federal regulatory authority in either of these areas; and I believe the attempted usurpation of such power to be a grave threat to the very essence of our basic system of government; namely, that of a constitutional republic in which fifty sovereign States have reserved to themselves and to the people those powers not specifically granted to the central or federal government. (ibid.: 202)

The enforcement of such prohibitions, Goldwater warned, would "require the creation of a federal police force of mammoth proportions." It would also lead to the rise of an informer psychology with "neighbors spying on neighbors, workers spying on workers, business spying on businessmen—where those who would harass their fellow citizens for selfish and narrow purposes will have ample inducement to do so" (ibid.: 203).

Further Reading

Chemerinsky, Erwin. 2021. *Presumed Guilty: How the Supreme Court Empowered the Police and Subverted Civil Rights.* New York: Liveright Publishing.

Edwards, Lee. 1995. *Goldwater: The Man Who Made a Revolution.* Washington, DC: Regnery Publishing.

Goldwater, Barry. 1964. "Goldwater Spells Out the Issues." *New York Times*, November 1.

Goldwater, Barry M. 2012a. "A Fireside Chat with Mr. Roosevelt," *Phoenix Gazette*, June 23, 1938. In Leonard Schlup and James Manley, eds., *The Political Principles of Senator Barry M. Goldwater as Revealed in His Speeches and Writings: A Source Book*, 34–6. Lewiston, NY: Edwin Mellen Press.

Goldwater, Barry M. 2012b. "Civil Rights Bill of 1964: Remarks Before the U.S. Senate." In Leonard Schlup and James Manley, eds., *The Political Principles of Senator Barry M. Goldwater as Revealed in His Speeches and Writings: A Source Book*, 200–5. Lewiston, NY: Edwin Mellen Press.

Kotlowski, Dean J. 1998. "Richard Nixon and the Origins of Affirmative Action." *The Historian* 60, no. 3: 523–41.

Mohr, Charles. 1964. "Goldwater Derides Antipoverty Drive in Appalachia Talk." *New York Times*, September 19.

Q18: What historic lessons may be derived from the 1960s about policing and social policy?

Answer: The urban problems of the 1960s—crime and unrest, poverty and unemployment, racial and other inequities—remain as pertinent today as ever. That elected officials such as Johnson not only talked about the roots of crime, but enacted remedial social policy reminiscent of Roosevelt's New Deal, distinguishes the decade from our current era. Even if the civil rights and anti-poverty measures were not adequate, they did make a difference in millions of lives and still do so today. A closer look at the decade can inform our current discussions and search for social policy remedies. The 1960s can likewise inform how we talk about policing—for example, whether its role in addressing urban crises should be large or small, and whether different models of policing can make a difference in social outcomes.

The Facts: The Johnson initiatives must be recognized for both what they accomplished and failed to accomplish. Let's glance at the first before turning to the second. Blacks, women, and other groups would gain new economic and educational access from the 1960s forward. One employer that was impacted by the Civil Rights Act of 1964 (CRA) was Duke Power Company in North Carolina. When the bill was passed by the Congress, as political scientist Robert Smith (1995: 58–9) recounts, the company

> abandoned its overtly racist policy relegating blacks to jobs in the low-skill, low-wage laborer category. However, the company simultaneously introduced a [high-school] diploma and successful completion of two general intelligence tests as requirements to transfer to any nonlabor category or for initial hiring in such categories.

The new policy was challenged by Willie Griggs and twelve other black employees. In *Griggs v. Duke Power Company* (1971), the US Supreme Court found that the new requirements had discriminatory effect, since black workers were less likely than white workers to have graduated high school. Only 12 percent of the state's black males were high-school graduates, versus 54 percent of white males. Furthermore, the requirements were not found to be necessary to, or predictive of satisfactory performance in, the jobs in question. The company policy was thus found to be in violation of CRA. The Voting Rights Act (VRA) would also bear impact: in another North Carolina case, *Gaston County v. United States* (1969), the US Supreme Court found that a literacy test used for voter eligibility was in violation of VRA.

The decade's anti-discrimination thrust bore notable impact in police hiring, as did the wide calls for a more diverse police force. Blacks are historically underrepresented in policing and even more so in policing's senior ranks. In many cities prior to the 1960s, as Marvin Dulaney describes in *Black Police in America* (1996), black officers were less than full-fledged members of their departments and, for example, were not allowed to arrest white suspects. Chicago was one of many cities that saw significant change in its police force composition during the 1960s. Innovative police superintendent O. W. Wilson added 500 black officers (from about 700 to 1,200) during his tenure from 1960 to 1967. In addition, he appointed fifty black sergeants and three black police captains (Dulaney 1996: 71). Often the departmental changes were pressed forward by the black officers themselves, who organized black officer associations and spoke out against internal discrimination within their departments as well as police brutality in the community (Dulaney 1996: chap. 6). Today, although much more remains to be done, several cities now have police forces whose racial composition is comparable, or nearly so, to that of the respective city populations. So, if the goal is to achieve full equity between the ratio of non-white officers and the non-white percentage of the city population, Baltimore had reached 79 percent of this goal by 2019; New York City, 93 percent; Oakland, California, 99 percent; while Atlanta and Washington, DC, had both exceeded 100 percent (US Department of Justice 2023).

Johnson's war on poverty bore impact as well. US poverty, as federally defined and drawing here on US census data, fell from 19 percent in 1964 to a historic low of 11 percent in 1973. The sharpest change over time would lay in poverty reduction among the elderly, which fell from 35 percent in 1959 to 9 percent in 2016. The food stamps program, now called the Supplemental Nutrition Assistance Program (SNAP), has since become "one of the most effective antipoverty programs overall and is particularly effective at lifting nonelderly households with children out of deep poverty" (Bartfeld et al. 2016: 2). Here, it should be noted, researchers have long challenged the federal government's official definition of poverty, which is widely believed to understate the extent of US poverty (Edelman 2013: 26–9). Some researchers instead use a "twice-poverty rate," where income below twice the official poverty line is considered a more accurate measure of households that struggle to make ends meet. Economist Lawrence Mishel and others (2012: 422) thus found a US twice-poverty rate of 34 percent in 2010, versus an official poverty rate of 15 percent.

With respect to racial equality, the long-term outcomes of the 1960s' initiatives have been mixed. In their 2017 review of studies on discrimination in hiring, sociologist Lincoln Quillian and others (2017: 10870) see "no change in the level of hiring discrimination against African Americans over the past 25 years," and find that white job applicants receive on average 36 percent more callbacks than do African Americans. Law professor Samuel Bagenstos (2006: 8) adds that antidiscrimination law in employment has been largely ineffective as biases have become more covert and unconscious. Even assuming that actions based on unconscious bias violate the law as a formal matter, he comments, "such violations are extremely difficult to prove." The gap between black poverty and white poverty *has* narrowed since the early 1970s, when the black poverty rate was four times that of the white rate. But in 2021, according to the US census, black poverty (19.5 percent) was still double that of white poverty (10.0 percent).

America's level of national commitment to remedying poverty is best viewed in comparative terms. Mishel et al. (2012: 450) compare the "relative poverty" of the United States and twenty-two peer countries including Canada, Australia, Japan, and a host of European countries. The United States is at the bottom of the list, with the highest relative poverty. In addition, the authors find that America's social programs—or redistributive "tax-and-transfer" programs—achieve less poverty reduction than do the tax-and-transfer programs of all other countries in the sample.

Finally, the general direction of US policing advanced in the 1960s did not alleviate rising crime or urban unrest, nor make communities safer overall. As noted earlier in this chapter, many of the decade's riots were triggered by conflicts between communities and police, though underlying causes were more complex. The consequent attention given to police-community relations was contradicted by the larger new emphasis on aggressive and often militarized policing. As historian Elizabeth Hinton describes in her book, *From the War on Poverty to the War on Crime* (2016: chap. 4), the federally backed push for more, and more aggressive, policing soon produced rising incarceration: "Under the auspices of the Nixon administration the federal government began to construct prisons at unprecedented rates" (163). As that trend continued at state and federal levels, buttressed by harsher penalties and longer sentencing, America's incarceration rates would quadruple over the next four decades (Travis, Western, and Redburn 2014: 35).

Although solutions to the country's race problems were unclear in the 1960s—antidiscrimination laws were necessary but insufficient—civil rights leaders believed that economic justice, such as through job and income guarantees, could provide an essential floor that would ease racism and ease competition between workers. In his address to the 1963 March on Washington for Jobs and Freedom, civil rights and labor leader A. Philip Randolph explained:

> Yes, we want all public accommodations open to all citizens, but these accommodations will mean little to those who cannot afford to use them. Yes, we want a Fair Employment Practices Act, but what good will it do if profit-geared

automation destroys the jobs of millions of workers, black and white? (qtd. in Kersten and Lucander 2014: 261)

One central lesson from the 1960s is that discussions of policing and police reform are best framed in expansive terms and in connection to broad questions about social policy and social justice. An important question is raised by the 1960s as well. If it is well known that remedies to urban crises must include deep-going social programs—and the Kerner Commission clearly recognized this—what is to be done if our elected leaders claim that such course of action is unrealistic, as did Johnson?

Further Reading

Bagenstos, Samuel R. 2006. "The Structural Turn and the Limits of Antidiscrimination Law." *California Law Review* 94, no. 1: 1–47.

Bartfeld, Judith, Craig Gundersen, Timothy M. Smeeding, and James P. Ziliak, eds. 2016. *SNAP Matters: How Food Stamps Affect Health and Well-Being.* Stanford, CA: Stanford University Press.

Dulaney, W. Marvin. 1996. *Black Police in America.* Bloomington: Indiana University Press.

Edelman, Peter. 2013. *So Rich, So Poor: Why It's So Hard to End Poverty in America.* New York: New Press.

Hinton, Elizabeth. 2016. *From the War on Poverty to the War on Crime: The Making of Mass Incarceration in America.* Cambridge, MA: Harvard University Press.

Kersten, Andrew E., and David Lucander, eds. 2014. *For Jobs and Freedom: Selected Speeches and Writings of A. Philip Randolph.* Amherst: University of Massachusetts Press.

Mishel, Lawrence, Josh Bivens, Elise Gould, and Heidi Shierholz. 2012. *The State of Working America,* 12th ed. Ithaca, NY: ILR Press.

Quillian, Lincoln, Devah Pager, Ole Hexel, and Amfinn H. Midtbøen. 2017. "Meta-analysis of Field Experiments Shows No Change in Racial Discrimination in Hiring Over Time." *Proceedings of the National Academy of Sciences* 114, no. 41: 10870–5.

Smith, Robert C. 1995. *Racism in the Post-Civil Rights Era: Now You See It. Now You Don't.* Albany: State University of New York Press.

Travis, Jeremy, Bruce Western, and Steve Redburn, eds. 2014. *The Growth of Incarceration in the United States: Exploring Causes and Consequences.* Washington, DC: National Academies Press.

US Department of Justice. 2023. Office of Justice Programs. Bureau of Justice Statistics. Law Enforcement Management and Administrative Statistics (LEMAS), 2020. Inter-university Consortium for Political and Social Research (distributor), March 7. Accessed January 8, 2025. https://doi.org/10.3886/ICPSR38651.v1.

6

Rodney King Beating, L.A. Riots, and Department of Justice Investigations

It was just past midnight on March 3, 1991, when Rodney King, driving his Hyundai westbound on the Foothill Freeway in the northeast of Los Angeles, passed a California Highway Patrol (CHP) car, which promptly turned on its flashing red lights, ran its siren, and began pursuit. This was a frightening moment for King. He and his two passengers, Bryant Allen and Freddie Helms, had been having a relaxing evening. The three black men, friends since their teens and now in their twenties, had been chatting, drinking Olde English 800 malt liquor, and watching some basketball. Life was on upswing for King. He had recently been paroled after spending a year in prison for robbing a small market, and he had begun a job as a laborer at Dodger Stadium. Now he was caught speeding, and he was intoxicated; a police stop could return him to prison. He slowed down but didn't stop. He exited the freeway and continued on surface streets. The CHP patrol, upon entering Los Angeles Police Department (LAPD) jurisdiction, had radioed that department. King was now being followed by a CHP car, an LAPD car, and a Los Angeles Unified School District police car. After a ten-minute chase, King finally pulled over and came to a stop near an apartment complex in Lake View Village. The Hyundai was promptly surrounded by squad cars.

Using a loudspeaker, CHP officer Melanie Singer along with her partner and husband, Timothy, ordered King out of his car and directed him to lie flat on the ground. On the other side of the car, another officer had ordered Allen and Helms to do the same. But while Allen and Helms had complied and were now lying on the ground, their hands cuffed behind their backs, King had resisted and was acting oddly. He moved about in a kind of dance; then, instead of lying flat, he went down on all fours, slapped the ground, and shook his rear suggestively at Officer Singer (Domanick 1994: 370). Meanwhile, more officers arrived, along with a helicopter, hovering above and shining a bright light on the encounter. Twenty-seven officers in all had come to either offer assistance or merely to watch.

Four LAPD officers then proceeded not just to restrain King but to punish him. In less than two minutes, as a mayor-appointed inquiry commission would later recount, King received two high-voltage Taser stun darts, fifty-six blows from the officers' two-foot-long aluminum batons, and six kicks (Christopher 1991: 7). The assault was conducted by Officers Laurence Powell, Timothy Wind, and Theodore Briseno, as directed by their sergeant, Stacey Koon. "Hit his joints, hit his wrists, hit his elbows, hit his knees, hit his ankles," Koon instructed (qtd. in ibid.: 7). King was then hogtied, his hands and feet bound together behind him, and he was dragged on his stomach to the side of the road to await arrival of an ambulance. King wound up with a broken cheekbone, cracks to the bones that hold his right eye in its socket, fractured bones at the base of his skull, a serious concussion, facial-nerve damage, a broken ankle, and the loss of several of the fillings from his teeth (Domanick 1994: 375).

The King assault was severe, even by LAPD's aggressive standards. What made this event even more unusual was that George Holliday, who lived in the adjacent apartment building and was awakened by the sirens and lights, grabbed his newly purchased Handycam and videotaped the beating from his balcony. Holliday would provide his recording to KTLA, a local television station, which put it on the air and then shared it with CNN. The King beating was broadcast globally and repeatedly in the coming weeks. L.A.'s black community was furious.

Politicians mobilized to take remedial action. President George W. Bush told reporters, "It's sickening to see the beating that was rendered" (qtd. in Reed 1991). His justice department, at the urging of the congressional Black Caucus, announced a review of all complaints of police brutality to the federal government over the previous six years—about 15,000 cases in all (Domanick 1994: 386–7). Also in Washington, the House Judiciary Subcommittee on the Constitution, Civil Rights, and Civil Liberties promptly held hearings on police brutality as a national problem, including on root causes of the King incident. House Democratic leaders then proposed reform through the Police Accountability Act; the act was incorporated into a larger Omnibus Crime Control Act of 1991, but this failed to pass (Rushin 2014: 3207–38). A similar and significant reform measure did pass Congress in 1994 (discussed later). Locally, L.A. mayor Tom Bradley announced his appointment of a commission, chaired by prominent attorney Warren Christopher, to inquire into the LAPD and the underlying causes of the videotaped beating. The findings and recommendations of the Christopher Commission were released in July 1991 (Christopher 1991; Wilkinson, Ford, and Wood 1991).

Yet, the city's problems were magnified a thousandfold on April 29, 1992. That was when verdicts were announced for the four officers involved in the King beating. They had each been charged with assault with a deadly weapon, and excessive force by an officer under color of authority; two were additionally charged with filing a false police report. The venue for their trial had been moved to suburban Simi Valley, a heavily white and conservative suburb forty miles northwest of downtown L.A. where many police officers lived. The jury proved sympathetic to the officers and their defense, acquitting them of all charges, except that it deadlocked over the excessive force charge against Powell. The acquittals were a shock to the city and the nation, given especially the powerful videotaped evidence. The government's credibility was lost: L.A. saw six days of riots in what would become one of the largest urban rebellions in American history. By the time order was reestablished with help from the National Guard, the 1992 unrest had brought 198 deaths; 11,900 arrests; fires in 10,000 buildings; and an estimated $1 billion in damages (Upton and Jeffries 2010: 32).

Further efforts to secure a more accountable LAPD followed the riots. Koon, Powell, Wind, and Briseno were retried under federal jurisdiction, charged with violating King's civil rights. In April 1993, two of them—Koon and Powell—were convicted but were given only eighteen months in federal prison, the minimum sentence possible (Domanick 1994: 438). Then, in June 1992, L.A. voters gave strong approval to Charter Amendment F, which implemented part of the Christopher Commission's reform recommendations. Its provisions included giving City Hall more power to remove the chief of police; limiting the chief's tenure to two five-year terms; and providing more civilian review of officer misconduct. Many other of the commission's proposals would be taken up by a special committee of the city council (Rainey and Sahagun 1992). At the same time, Chief Daryl Gates, who had run the LAPD since 1978, resigned that June; he was replaced by an outsider, Willie Williams, formerly Philadelphia's police commissioner, who would be L.A.'s first black police chief.

Finally, and perhaps more impactful than the various local steps taken after the King beating and the unrest, came a police reform provision that was added to a major crime bill signed by President Bill Clinton. Section 14141 of the Violent Crime Control and Law Enforcement Act of 1994 gave the US attorney general the power to initiate reform litigation against local police departments that engage in a "pattern or practice" of unconstitutional conduct (Rushin 2014: 3207–15). The process typically begins with a Department of Justice (DOJ) investigation into the police agency where the misconduct is alleged; over sixty such investigations have been conducted since passing of the 1994 law. Based on its findings, the DOJ makes reform recommendations. This is normally followed by a settlement between the DOJ and the local city government, under which the latter agrees to implement the reforms. The agreement takes the form of a "consent decree" supervised by a local judge (Thurgood Marshall Institute n.d.). Among the many agencies that have undergone reform through DOJ consent decrees is the LAPD itself. That process began not with the King beating but with a later debacle—a corruption scandal in the late 1990s involving dozens of officers in a gang enforcement unit housed in the LAPD's Rampart Division (Rushin 2017: 180).

More than any prior act of police violence, the Rodney King beating marked a turning point in the recognition of police abuse as a grave American problem. The riots a year later, prompted by the exoneration of the four officers charged in the assault, made the need for remedial action around police abuse, and many related urban problems, all the more apparent. The rise of federal DOJ intervention in police unconstitutional conduct, as authorized by the Clinton crime bill, represents the broadest reform initiative achieved in response to King. Question 19 sets the King beating and subsequent riots in wider context. Question 20 then asks about the effectiveness of the DOJ investigations and court-ordered consent decrees in securing police reform nationally, while Question 21 explores the DOJ intervention in Baltimore as a case study.

Further Reading

Christopher, Warren. 1991. *Report of the Independent Commission on the Los Angeles Police Department.* Los Angeles, CA.

Domanick, Joe. 1994. *To Protect and to Serve: The LAPD's Century of War in the City of Dreams.* New York: Pocket Books.

Rainey, James, and Louis Sahagun. 1992. "Local Elections: Measure F Vote Called Just Start of Police Reform." *Los Angeles Times.* June 4.

Reed, Christopher. 1991. "A Vicious Assault on a Black Motorist by a Group of White Los Angeles Policemen Has Turned into a National Issue." *Guardian.* March 22.

Rushin, Stephen. 2014. "Federal Enforcement of Police Reform." *Fordham Law Review* 82, no. 6: 3189–247.

Rushin, Stephen. 2017. *Federal Intervention in American Police Departments.* New York: Cambridge University Press.

Thurgood Marshall Institute, National Police Funding Database. n. d. "Consent Decrees." Accessed January 8, 2025.https://policefundingdatabase.org/explore-the-database/consent-decrees.

Upton, James N., and Judson L. Jeffries. 2010. "Comparing a Major American City and Its Rebellions against Itself: Los Angeles of 1965 and 1992." *Journal of History and Social Sciences* 1, no. 2: 11–32.

Wilkinson, Tracy, Andrea Ford, and Tracy Wood. 1991. "Panel Urges Gates to Retire: Report on Police Cites Racism, Excess Force." *Los Angeles Times.* July 10.

Q19: From the L.A. Riots of 1965 to the L.A. Riots of 1992, had things changed in American society and policing?

Answer: Fundamentally, no. Some conditions had changed for blacks and others, growing out of the civil rights and anti-poverty initiatives of the 1960s. But the deprivations and inequities that underlay the riots in both instances, and the abusive and harassing forms of policing that fomented the sharpest anger, remained squarely in place.

The Facts: As described in Chapter 5, unemployment and racial discrimination set the context for the riots in Los Angeles and nationally in the 1960s, while abuse or disrespect from police often served as trigger for black rebellion. A similar confluence affected South Central L.A. in 1992. The area did emerge from the 1960s with a still-vital manufacturing industry, including a large General Motors assembly plant in nearby South Gate, where many blacks found decent-paying jobs. Blacks were also gaining better access to the city's public sector jobs. Yet, as journalist Lou Cannon (1997: 8–12) describes in his study of the 1992 riots and their impact, multiple factors took an economic toll on South Central and across California for more than a decade prior to the 1992 riots. Auto and other manufacturing industries shut down plants and moved jobs abroad in pursuit of cheaper labor. The aerospace industry, which had thrived in the 1950s and 1960s in Southern California, was weakened as the Cold War wound down, and this bore a ripple effect across the local economy. Adding to the downturn, many city and county jobs were lost as a consequence of Proposition 13, passed by California voters in 1978, which provided property tax relief but at the expense of public services. The measure meant a loss of social services just as more services were needed owing to lost industry. Such trends were further exacerbated by the pullback of federal jobs programs (e.g.,

Job Corps, and the Comprehensive Employment and Training Act) and social programs under the Reagan administration.

One further demographic and economic shift that would bear impact on the area was the heavy Latino immigration from Mexico and Central America from the 1970s forward. Many of the new arrivals settled in South Central, as well as in the Mid-City area situated just north of South Central and west of downtown. There was growing competition for jobs, while the area's poverty became more diverse in character. Significantly, the 1992 riots were also more diverse: whereas the 1960s' rioters were primarily black, such was not the case in 1992, where arrestees were 38 percent black but 51 percent Latino (Webster 1992: appendix 8–12). In fact, as social critic Mike Davis points out, the predominantly Latino Mid-City area experienced a greater density of riot-related incidents than did the predominantly black South Central. The Mid-City unrest, Davis comments (1998: 371–2), "was driven by empty bellies and broken dreams, not by outrage over the acquittal of the cops who beat Rodney King. It was the culmination of a decade of declining economic opportunity and rising poverty followed by two years of recession that tripled unemployment in Los Angeles's immigrant neighborhoods."

Beyond economics, the King beating and the city's long history of police brutality and racism clearly did light the fuse in 1992. One characteristic of the LAPD that had been a constant for decades and that helped bring about these events was the department's unchecked power. As award-winning investigative journalist Joe Domanick documents in his lively history, *To Protect and to Serve: The LAPD's Century of War in the City of Dreams* (1994), the LAPD's power has often rivaled that of the city's elected officials and business leaders. In the 1920s and 1930s, the interrelationships between city politics, business, organized crime, and the police helped put the police on equal footing with the other players. The police capacity to spy and maintain files on its critics and departmental foes would further embolden the chief of police. In 1936, Chief James Davis decided that something had to be done about the tens of thousands of unemployed who were migrating to California amid the 1930s' depression. Declaring a "bum blockade," he sent LAPD officers to guard major entry points into L.A. and into California. Domanick describes the procedure at the Arizona border, where Davis's officers asked arriving travelers, "Any money? Any work?" As Domanick writes, "When the answer was no, the travelers were given a blunt choice: thirty to eighty days at hard labor for vagrancy and nonpayment of train fare, or turning around and going back from where they came" (Domanick 1994: 61). Domanick notes that California's Republican governor Frank Merriam was remarkably circumspect about this "wildly unconstitutional" blockade. The governor later commented that it was "up to them, if they can get away with it" (qtd. in ibid.: 61).

Under the enormously influential William Parker, LAPD chief from 1950 to 1966, the department largely halted its prior engagement in graft and corruption and instead established a reputation for professionalism that made LAPD an admired model nationally. Parker had an assistant write an operations manual; he set up a department of planning and research; streamlined tracking of employees, crime analysis, and officer deployment; and reduced traffic accidents through enforcement (ibid.: 104–6). Parker did insist, though, on the department's independent power. "The police commission doesn't run the police department," he would say. "*I* run the police department" (qtd. in ibid.: 13; emphasis in original). Parker's protégé Daryl Gates, LAPD chief from 1978 until his resignation in the wake of the 1992 riots, echoed his mentor's sense of entitlement and power. In 1990, for example, he told a US Senate committee that casual drug users "ought to be taken out and shot." Afterwards, he refused to retract the statement, telling officers and supporters at a luncheon, "Yeah, I mean it!" (qtd. in Serrano and Fritch 1990).

Parker also emphasized a proactive, militaristic, commandist policing philosophy that, from his tenure forward, would be received by the entire department "as if sent down by Moses from the Mount," writes Domanick, who summarizes the perspective as follows (1994: 12):

> Give no slack and take no shit from anyone. Confront and command. Control the streets at all times. Always be aggressive. Stop crimes before they happen. Seek them out. Shake them down. Make that arrest. And never, never, admit the department had done anything wrong.

The approach promised a police culture that not only tolerated excessive force in the mold of Rodney King but that appeared to celebrate it. Law professor Laurie Levenson (1993: 514, note 13) points out that, in the fourteen months prior to the King event alone, the *L.A. Times* ran over sixty stories reporting incidents of the police use of excessive force in the greater L.A. area.

Among the striking findings from the Christopher Commission report was the extent to which both racism and the use of brutal force permeated LAPD culture, underscoring that the King beating was no aberration. The commission found evidence of such in its review of Mobile Digital Terminal (MDT) communications, drawn from six sample months. The MDT system was a messaging technology used by LAPD patrol officers at that time for their field operations. Here are some excerpts reflecting officer attitudes toward the use of force (qtd. in Christopher 1991: 49, 50):

> We got a little physical w/ a [name omitted] on Colombus … it was fun … we had to teach him a little respect … for the police … hahahahaha … we had fun … no stick time though.
>
> U missed out bro, we backed 2X53 [a patrol unit] on a poss shots fired from veh. some of the susps had some big boot marks on their heads, once they were in custody.
>
> I obviously didn't beat this guy enough. He got right back up and is still being obnoxious.

Here are some excerpts reflecting officer racial attitudes (qtd. in ibid.: 72):

> If you encounter these negroes shoot first and ask questions later.
>
> Well … I'm back over here in the projects, pissing off the natives
>
> I would love to drive down Slauson with a flame thrower … we would have a barbeque.

Slauson Avenue is a major street that runs through predominantly black neighborhoods in South L.A. The Christopher report points out, "The racist comments freely exchanged over the MDT system stand in sharp contrast to the LAPD's official policy against 'racially or ethnically oriented remarks'" (ibid.: 73).

In addition to what the King beating itself conveyed about LAPD culture, various statements and testimony in the event's wake further suggest the troubling attitudes and practices that marked the department. For example, black officer Janine Bouey told the *L.A. Times* that, when she worked at the Foothill Station in 1988–9—this being the station where the four officers who assaulted King were assigned—white officers freely used derogatory language against black officers. One day, she discovered a Ku Klux Klan business card on her car, which was parked in the station's secure lot. The card proclaimed, "Racial Purity Is America's Security." Another black officer at the station found such a card in his locker, according to Bouey. When she complained to the station's captain, he told her racism did not exist at the station (Serrano and Soble 1991).

The views of some officers toward the use of force was underscored during the Simi Valley trial over the King beating. A nurse who had attended to King at Pacifica Hospital, a few miles from the site of the assault, testified that Officer Powell taunted King as he lay in the emergency room. During the assault, Powell had clubbed King in the head repeatedly, wielding his baton with a baseball player's swing, according to the prosecution. The nurse recalled that, after King indicated that he worked at Dodger Stadium, Powell made needling statements: "We had a pretty good hardball game tonight"; "We hit quite a few home runs"; and "You lost the ballgame, didn't you?" (qtd. in Deutsch 1992).

In its pursuit of a better LAPD and following a Christopher Commission recommendation, the L.A. city council made its first priority securing greater control over the department. Specifically, the council placed Charter Amendment F on the June 1992 ballot, which included provisions strengthening control over the police chief by the mayor-appointed police commission. The strategy was apropos: the city could not reform that which it could not control.

A series of events in 1976 described by Domanick (1994) illustrated well the control and accountability issues. Wayne Satz, an investigative reporter for local television station KABC, had written to then chief Ed Davis and to the police commission asking for detailed information about shootings involving LAPD officers. Satz and his news director, Dennis Swanson,

> had been observing a pattern of unarmed civilians being shot and killed by the LAPD, followed only by a few terse lines in the city news service. That was it. No public discussion, no questions asked. He wanted to know, Satz wrote Davis, how many people they had shot in the past, what the circumstances were, how many of the suspects had been unarmed, and what the disposition of the cases had been. (Domanick 1994: 267)

Satz, however, received no response. "It was astonishing to us that we could make an inquiry and that it would simply be ignored," Satz later told Domanick. "They didn't think they had any public accountability whatsoever. Their arrogance was incredible" (qtd. in ibid.: 268).

KABC produced "The Accountability of the LAPD," a critical report aired daily on its evening news hour, and which interviewed witnesses to shootings and provided versions of events that "often differed dramatically from the official LAPD version." The station interviewed an LAPD whistleblower cop, disguised in a scuba diver's hood and a mask, who said that most of the officers he worked with in South Central's 77th Division were racist and, moreover, "extremely eager to be in a shooting" (qtd. in ibid.: 268).

Chief Davis was outraged, Domanick reports, and launched a countercampaign. The chief went on the LAPD's in-house, closed-circuit television system and denounced KABC and Satz, calling the reporter an enemy of law enforcement, and then distributed dubs of his denouncements to his troops and to local news stations. Bumper stickers announcing "Satz Sucks" began appearing on LAPD squad cars; Satz received threatening phone calls; and targets at the LAPD academy firing range popped up with Satz's picture on them (ibid.: 269).

As the city approached its 1992 vote on Charter Amendment F to address the matter of control, the measure was actively opposed by Chief Gates and by the police officers' union. Voters nonetheless approved it by a two-to-one margin (Sahagun and Schwada 1992). Enormous work would yet remain toward reforming the department and holding it democratically to account.

Further Reading

Cannon, Lou. 1997. *Official Negligence: How Rodney King and the Riots Changed Los Angeles and the LAPD*. New York: Times Books.

Christopher, Warren. 1991. *Report of the Independent Commission on the Los Angeles Police Department*. Los Angeles, CA.

Davis, Mike. 1998. *Ecology of Fear: Los Angeles and the Imagination of Disaster*. New York: Metropolitan Books.

Deutsch, Linda. 1992. "King Target of Taunts, Nurse Says." *Los Angeles Times*. March 14.

Domanick, Joe. 1994. *To Protect and to Serve: The LAPD's Century of War in the City of Dreams*. New York: Pocket Books.

Levenson, Laurie L. 1993. "The Future of State and Federal Civil Rights Prosecutions: The Lessons of the Rodney King Trial." *UCLA Law Review* 41, no. 3: 509–608.

Sahagun, Louis, and John Schwada. 1992. "Measure to Reform LAPD Wins Decisively." *Los Angeles Times*. June 3.

Serrano, Richard A., and Jane Fritsch. 1990. "'Yeah, I Mean It!' Gates Says of Idea to Shoot Drug Users." *Los Angeles Times*. September 8.

Serrano, Richard A., and Ronald L. Soble. 1991. "Grand Jury Widens Probe of King Beating." *Los Angeles Times*. March 29.

Webster, William H. 1992. *The City in Crisis: A Report by the Special Advisor to the Board of Police Commissioners on the Civil Disorder in Los Angeles*. Los Angeles, CA. October 21.

Q20: Have the Department of Justice investigations into local police agencies and court-ordered consent decrees aided reform?

Answer: Yes and no. Civil rights advocates often do need assistance from state or federal oversight agencies, and from the courts, to secure local police reform. Department of Justice (DOJ) investigations into local police agencies, together with consent decrees—that is, reform requirements set out by the DOJ and agreed to by local government, with a federal judge supervising compliance—have in many cases led to real improvements. Yet, the gains are achieved slowly—the DOJ-led reform process can take a decade or longer—and at high financial cost to the municipality. Some sites show impressive progress but then backtrack when the federal monitoring ends; others seem to make little headway at all. One challenge is that policing's underlying purpose and priorities need inquiry and broad public discussion as part of a deep reform process; however, the DOJ defines its scope narrowly in terms of enforcing the Constitution and disinclines to ask questions that fall outside that purview. A second challenge is the fragmented nature of American policing, with over 18,000 agencies and under predominantly local government control. The DOJ has the capacity to intervene in only a small number of agencies. So, under the existing system, with or without DOJ involvement, responsibility for holding police accountable ultimately lies with local, not federal, government. The effectiveness of DOJ interventions, then, must bear in mind these relationships and responsibilities.

The Facts: Section 14141 of the 1994 Clinton crime bill has been an aid to American police reform but still a mixed one. One consistent benefit of the DOJ pattern-or-practice investigations is that they produce detailed public reports, shedding light on local institutions that historically lack transparency, and documenting a range of internal problems and malfunctions that need addressing. Thus, the DOJ investigation of the Minneapolis Police Department in the wake of the 2020 police murder of George Floyd revealed that the problem was not limited to just a few bad officers but indicative of a department where racial discrimination and poor accountability were systemic (US Department of Justice 2023). Although the DOJ intervention may or may not make a difference, the very documentation of issues and how a local police department functions has undeniable value to communities and civil rights groups.

Sometimes the process does produce a timely difference. As discussed in the next chapter, the DOJ intervention in Ferguson, Missouri, that followed the 2014 police killing of Michael Brown and subsequent uprising, led to concrete remedies for some of the underlying issues—such as the need to racially diversify the police department and to end the city's unconstitutional reliance on fines and court fees for municipal revenues. The DOJ consent decree in L.A., which stretched from 2001 to 2013, led to multiple improvements including reduced "categorical" (i.e., serious) use of force, better handling of civilian complaints, and establishing a computer system that tracks officer performance and identifies patterns that need supervisory attention (Stone, Foglesong, and Cole 2009).

What the DOJ process does not do nearly as well is produce remedies that are locally sustainable after the DOJ's departure.

> The available evidence suggests that some cities may revert back to problematic practices after federal regulators leave town. For example, some have accused departments like the Pittsburgh Bureau of Police of sliding back into patterns of unconstitutional misconduct after federal overseers left the city. Without any formal mechanism in place, the sustainability of reforms after federal intervention remains uncertain. (Rushin 2017: 19)

Civil rights lawyer Sunita Patel (2016: 796) believes that a more democratic DOJ reform process, with stronger community engagement—in developing and implementing reforms; in monitoring or evaluation of the reform process—can aid reform's sustainability and transparency. Although the consent decrees often do include a community engagement provision, Patel finds that the community engagement component is rarely robust and notes that the DOJ has denied community groups' official standing as intervenors in the reform process (799):

> A distinct pattern has emerged in many of the examined jurisdictions: the community engagement body responsible for voicing the views of community members has felt inadequately represented by the DOJ. In several cities, courts denied community groups' attempts to intervene as official parties. Such rejection always rests upon the DOJ's view that the community engagement entities or advocacy groups do not have a separate, protectable interest beyond that of the government's.

Here, Patel takes issue with the legal assumptions of both the DOJ and the courts and believes that community groups representing highly policed communities have a legitimate stake in the reforms.

The much-praised DOJ intervention in L.A. exemplifies the trend wherein initial reform successes have not necessarily sustained well. In 2021, the *L.A. Times* editorialized:

> The LAPD is now the most reformed, and perhaps the most reform-minded, large police department in the nation. Yet it remains one of the most problematic. It took a series of Los Angeles Times stories, for example, flagging racial bias in police vehicle stops for the LAPD to modify the practice. Separately, officers have been charged with falsifying records to enter the names of non-gang members into a gang database. ("The More LAPD Changes" 2021)

Nor has the LAPD's proclivity for excessive force been wholly remedied. L.A. was one of several cities met by fierce protests in June 2020 over the police killing of George Floyd. In a subsequent class-action lawsuit, Black Lives Matter and others charged that the LAPD responded in a brutal and unconstitutional manner. Amid the over three thousand arrests, plaintiffs allege that police chief Michel Moore ordered the types of force that can severely wound demonstrators, including the firing of foam and sponge bullets into crowds, and that arrestees were held for hours in crowded buses, risking exposure to coronavirus. A *Times* investigation confirmed that LAPD officers wounded many demonstrators and in ways that "likely violated protocol" (Rector 2020; Rector, Karlamangla, and Winton 2020).

As discussed in Chapter 1, American policing follows a game that values "outputs" such as arrests, citations, and the seizure of illegal drugs and guns, rather than looking to community safety as the vital measure of success. Too often, police reform efforts fail to question policing's core assumptions, and such limitation applies equally to the DOJ and its interventions. Here, police practices that violate the Constitution—such as excessive force and discrimination—are put under scrutiny, as they should be. But many practices may pass constitutional muster, yet produce community harms by over-criminalizing populations or by undermining police-community trust. The DOJ-led reforms, if reworked, could potentially become more effective by not only enhancing community engagement, as Patel (2016) suggests, but also fostering new standards for policing that put community safety and well-being front and center. Criminal justice as a field of scholarship widely accepts conventional policing assumptions and may benefit from a rethinking along the same lines. Consider, for example, the widely cited Harvard study by Christopher Stone, Todd Foglesong, and Christine M. Cole on LAPD's reform under a DOJ consent decree. Stone and colleagues commend the LAPD for reducing high levels of force and making other improvements, and doing so while at the same time "doubling ... both pedestrian stops and vehicle stops" and with rising arrests (2009: i). Moreover, the authors emphasize, this activity involved a proportional increase in the "quality of stops" (meaning those resulting in arrest) and "quality of arrests" (meaning those resulting in felony charges filed by the district attorney), as compared to past performance. Surely, police work *should* involve good stops and good arrests, as appropriate. However, effective reform likely needs to move beyond today's mandate that highlights arrests and the enforcement of laws or that equates these with making communities safer.

It should be noted that, in the same period as the study by Stone and colleagues, the LAPD was implementing a "Safer Cities Initiative" which, from 2006 to 2014, assigned scores of officers to police the poor and the homeless in the Skid Row area of downtown L.A. The initiative's first two years oversaw 19,000 arrests; 24,000 issued citations; the incarceration of 2,000 residents; and the dismantling of 2,800 sites of self-made housing (Dozier 2019: 185). The most frequent police actions were for minor infractions such as jaywalking, littering, and sitting or sleeping on sidewalks. More rarely, as sociologist Forrest Stuart describes in his ethnographic study *Down, Out, and Under Arrest* (2016), residents were charged with drug sales or prostitution. Arrests were often issued for warrants linked to the nonpayment of previous fines. One of the program's key aims, according to Stuart, was to remove the homeless from downtown to make way for gentrification and business development (see also Vitale 2010). With the aid of civil rights groups and activists, some of the arrests were successfully challenged in court as unconstitutional. Many of the police actions in Skid Row may well be considered legal but would not be justifiable on moral or social policy grounds. New reform models that forefront community needs—and especially the needs of economically struggling and marginalized communities—may enable police to serve consistently as community allies and as supporters of community safety and uplift.

Further Reading

Dozier, Deshonay. 2019. "Contested Development: Homeless Property, Police Reform, and Resistance in Skid Row, LA." *International Journal of Urban and Regional Research* 43, no. 1: 179–94.

Patel, Sunita. 2016. "Toward Democratic Police Reform: A Vision for 'Community Engagement' Provisions in DOJ Consent Decrees." *Wake Forest Law Review* 51, no. 4: 793–879.

Rector, Kevin. 2020. "Class-Action Suit against LAPD Adds Fresh Claims of Injury, Anguish among Protesters." *Los Angeles Times.* June 22.
Rector, Kevin, Soumya Karlamangla, and Richard Winton. 2020. "LAPD's Use of Batons, Other Weapons Appears to Violate Rules, Significantly Injuring Protesters, *Times* Review Finds." *Los Angeles Times.* June 11.
Rushin, Stephen. 2017. *Federal Intervention in American Police Departments.* New York: Cambridge University Press.
Stone, Christopher, Todd Foglesong, and Christine M. Cole. 2009. *Policing Los Angeles under a Consent Decree: The Dynamics of Change at the LAPD.* Cambridge, MA: Harvard Kennedy School. Accessed January 8, 2025. https://www.hks.harvard.edu/publications/policing-los-angeles-under-consent-decree-dynamics-change-lapd.
Stuart, Forrest. 2016. *Down, Out, and Under Arrest: Policing and Everyday Life in Skid Row.* Chicago: University of Chicago Press.
"The More LAPD Changes . . . ." *Los Angeles Times.* May 28, 2021. Editorial.
U.S. Department of Justice. 2023. *Investigation of the City of Minneapolis and the Minneapolis Police Department.* Washington: DC, June 16. Accessed January 8, 2025. https://www.justice.gov/opa/press-release/file/1587661/download.
Vitale, Alex S. 2010. "The Safer Cities Initiative and the Removal of the Homeless: Reducing Crime or Promoting Gentrification on Los Angeles' Skid Row?" *Criminology and Public Policy* 9, no. 4: 867–74.

Q21: Has the Department of Justice intervention in Baltimore been successful?

Answer: The Department of Justice's intervention in Baltimore—one of the federal agency's largest in recent years and which is emblematic of DOJ interventions since the 1990s—has had mixed results. It was intended to reduce police abuse, including over-enforcement, excessive force, and discrimination. It also required the Baltimore Police Department (BPD) to work closely with residents to prevent crime in neighborhoods and work collaboratively to solve neighborhood problems. According to the consent decree monitoring team, the use of force in Baltimore has been reduced. Arrests for social order enforcement are also down. However, racial disparities in arrests following the consent decree have actually increased. Violent crime rates continue at high levels in Baltimore and crime clearance rates for homicide and other violent crime have declined significantly. In addition, the community's perception of the police in Baltimore communities, according to a monitoring team report, is poor.

The Facts: Freddie Gray was a young black man stopped by the Baltimore police on April 12, 2015, for possession of a knife—a social control arrest. While in the back of a police transport van, Gray sustained fatal injuries to his cervical spinal cord. The six officers involved (three black and three white) were arrested for murder. Four of the six officers went to trial in state court. Three were acquitted and one ended in a mistrial when the jury failed to reach a verdict. The State Attorney's Office dismissed charges against the other two officers. An independent federal investigation failed to find sufficient evidence to prosecute the officers for civil rights charges, which ended all criminal cases in Gray's death (Barron 2023).

In May 2015, DOJ initiated a pattern-or-practice investigation of the BPD and issued its report the following year. The investigation found that BPD engages in patterns or practices that violate the First and Fourth Amendments of the Constitution. A DOJ press release stated the following:

> BPD makes stops, searches and arrests without the required justification; uses enforcement strategies that unlawfully subject African Americans to disproportionate rates of stops, searches and arrests; uses excessive force; and retaliates against individuals for their constitutionally protected expression. The pattern or practice results from systemic deficiencies that have persisted within BPD for many years and has exacerbated community distrust of the police, particularly in the African American community. (US Department of Justice 2016)

The investigation resulted in a court-enforceable agreement between the city of Baltimore and DOJ to ensure BPD complied with constitutional protections. The consent decree focused on building community trust, creating a culture of community and problem-oriented policing, prohibiting unlawful stops and arrests, preventing discriminatory policing and excessive force, ensuring public and officer safety, and enhancing officer accountability (*United States of America* 2017). With regard to public safety, the consent decree required BPD to "improve public safety and crime prevention through community engagement, including how to establish formal partnerships with community organizations, how to work with communities to set public safety and crime prevention priorities" (ibid.: 6).

A consent decree monitoring team still today oversees progress and conducts regular compliance reviews, which includes surveys of community residents. A June 2023 monitoring-team report said that most respondents in the community survey disagreed that the BPD effectively reduces crime or that BPD has a good working relationship with the community. A typical respondent put it this way:

> I become very frustrated when dealing with law enforcement based on the fact, they took an oath to protect the citizens of Baltimore City. Often as I observe the behavior of the police as they sit, I literally watch them watch criminals break the law and they do nothing. For me it frustrates me because that's not what they're hired to do. They're hired to protect us. I believe higher ups are telling these officers not to do their job. After the Freddie Gray riots nobody is doing their job. These criminals are committing all these crimes they want to commit. It makes me feel like the police have been getting in so much trouble and you can't trust the police to be police. I've observed someone get shot and the police didn't even pursue the suspect ... I have very low faith in the people who are hired to protect it, they have an agenda. (BPD Consent Decree Monitoring Team 2023: 21)

It is true that the police in Baltimore are making fewer arrests, which is most likely the result of the consent decree. It is also true, though, that BPD is clearing fewer homicides and violent crimes. Table 6.1 compares arrest data by BPD for a five-year period before the consent with a five-year period after the consent decree. It also looks at the percentage of unsolved homicides and violent crimes in these two periods. The total number of arrests decreased in the second period by 56 percent and social control arrests decreased by 63.6 percent. Arrests for disorderly conduct dropped by 90 percent. However, unsolved homicides rose from 58 percent to 68 percent, while unsolved violent crimes increased from 60 to 77 percent.

Table 6.2 shows that arrests were down in both white and black racial groups for total arrests and for drug arrests including drug possession. However, the racial disparity in arrests increased in the second period, especially in drug arrests. A racial disparity index of 2.65 means the rate of arrest for black individuals in Baltimore is 2.65 times higher than the rate of arrests for whites. This increased to 2.93 in the second period. The racial disparity in drug arrests increased from 2.94 in the first period to 3.61 in the second. The racial disparity in arrests for drug possession also increased in this second period following the consent decree.

In addition to the aforementioned problems, the violent crime rate in Baltimore has remained high since the DOJ investigation (August 2016) and consent decree (April 2017), and still seems to be increasing. Figure 6.1 shows the monthly volume of violent crime in Baltimore from January 1, 2011, through

Table 6.1 BPD Arrests in Two Time Periods, 2011–15 and 2018–22

Arrests	2011–15	2018–22	Change
Total Arrests	177,429	78,960	–55.5%
Social Control Arrests	123,451	44,953	–63.6%
Murder arrests	372	365	–1.9%
Rape Arrests	314	248	–21.0%
Robbery Arrests	4,033	3,305	–18.1%
Burglary Arrests	5,248	2,735	–47.9%
Larceny Arrests	8,925	1,772	–80.1%
Drug Arrests	54,405	10,055	–81.5%
Disorderly Conduct Arrests	4,189	410	–90.2%
Curfew Arrests	532	49	–90.8%
Liquor Laws Arrests	225	8	–96.4%
Rate of Unsolved Crimes	**2011–15**	**2018–22**	
Unsolved Homicides	58%	68%	
Unsolved Violent Crimes	60%	77%	

Source: Data from Federal Bureau of Investigation, Uniform Crime Reporting Program, https://cde.ucr.cjis.gov/LATEST/webapp/#/pages/home.

Table 6.2 Comparing Race of Arrestees in Two Time Periods, 2011–15 and 2018–22

Racial Disparities	2011–15	2018–22	Change
All Arrests			
Black	148,821	67,436	–54.7%
White	26,106	10,671	–59.1%
Drug Arrests			
Black	46,831	8,806	–81.2%
White	7,387	1,133	–84.7%
Drug Possession (cocaine or opium)			
Black	17,625	3,754	–78.7%
White	5,637	998	–82.3%
Racial Disparity in Arrests			
All Arrests	2.65	2.93	
Drug Arrests	2.94	3.61	
Drug Possession Arrests	1.45	1.75	

Source: Data from Federal Bureau of Investigation, Uniform Crime Reporting Program, https://cde.ucr.cjis.gov/LATEST/webapp/#/pages/home and US Bureau of Census Bureau https://www.census.gov/programs-surveys/sis/resources/data-tools/quickfacts.html.

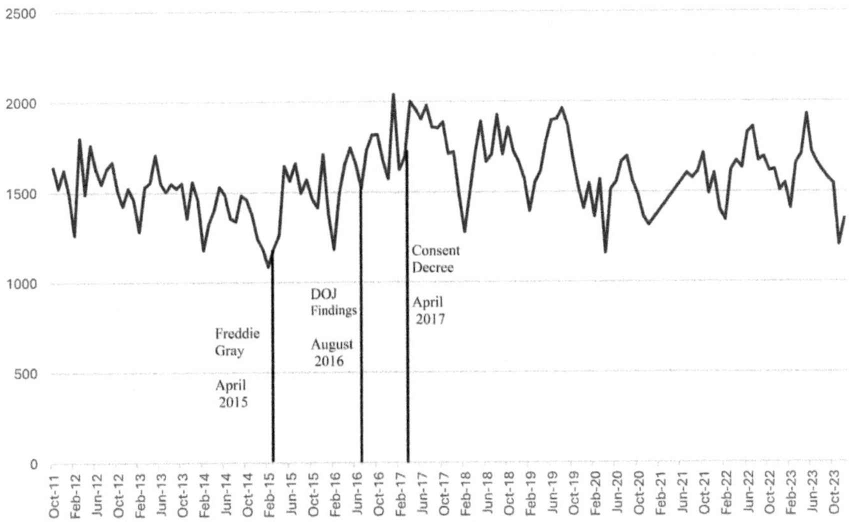

Figure 6.1 Trends in violent crime in Baltimore, 2011–23.
Source: Data from FBI Crime Data Explorer, https://cde.ucr.cjis.gov.

December 31, 2023. From this analysis, it appears that DOJ reforms and oversight have not succeeded in reducing violent crime in that city.

The DOJ pattern-or-practice investigation and resulting court-mandated oversight has changed the *playbook* in Baltimore but not the game (see game analogy introduced in Chapter 1). This change has resulted in fewer arrests by BPD, especially for the purpose of social order. It has also resulted in reduction in the use of force by Baltimore city police officers. However, it has done little to reduce or solve violent crime or reduce the racial disparities endemic in the law enforcement approach to policing. In addition, DOJ required BPD to add transparency and accountability measures to its practices. This is likely to explain—at least in part—why arrests are down in Baltimore. However, no new department purpose has been set in place, nor has a new scorecard been constructed to reflect a new game. It would seem, then, that the DOJ pattern-or-practice approach to police reform in Baltimore has not been fully successful.

Further Reading

Baltimore Police Department (BPD) Consent Decree Monitoring Team. 2023. *The Community's Experiences and Perceptions of the Baltimore City Police Department Survey Draft Report*. Accessed January 8, 2025. https://www.morgan.edu/Documents/ADMINISTRATION/CENTERS/IUR/Research/DOJPoliceReport.pdf.

Barron, Justine. 2023. *They Killed Freddie Gray: The Anatomy of a Police Brutality Cover-Up*. New York: Arcade Publishing.

United States of America v. Police Department of Baltimore City, et al. 2017. Consent Decree. Accessed January 8, 2025. https://www.justice.gov/opa/file/925056/dl.

US Department of Justice. 2010. Press release, August 10. Accessed January 8, 2025. https://www.justice.gov/opa/pr/justice-department-announces-findings-investigation-baltimore-police-department.

7

Ferguson Protests, Black Lives Matter, and the Obama Policing Task Force

On August 9, 2014, the fatal shooting of Michael Brown, an unarmed eighteen-year-old black man, by white police officer Darren Wilson in the St. Louis suburb of Ferguson, Missouri, would touch off events carrying historic and global significance. Brown was walking with his friend Dorian Johnson, twenty-two, down the middle of a two-lane street. Wilson, who was driving by, stopped to tell the two to move to the sidewalk. As he drove on, Wilson later reported, he checked his rearview mirror and realized that the two young men may have been involved in a theft at a nearby convenience store he had heard about on his radio. He reversed his car and pulled it in front of the two, blocking their progress. What happened next is a matter of dispute, but Brown wound up getting struck by several bullets. One witness account that quickly spread in the community was that the young man was shot while surrendering with his hands up. Although several witnesses would state the same, investigators did not find the hands-up account credible or consistent with the evidence (US Department of Justice [hereinafter, US DOJ] 2015a: 8). Wilson would claim that he fired two shots while Brown attempted to grab the officer's gun, and that he fired other shots when Brown was later charging toward him (ibid.: 12–16).

Weeks of protest and some rioting followed. The community was skeptical toward official accounts of the killing, and especially so when, on November 24, St. Louis County Prosecutor Robert McCulloch announced that a grand jury had completed its investigation and would not be indicting Wilson. The Ferguson police force, which was nearly all white amid the town's predominantly black community, further inflamed protests through its militarized response. This included, on August 13, police firing tear gas canisters into a crowd of peaceful protesters after the crowd had refused an order to disperse (Hillstrom 2018: 28).

The Ferguson protests were supported by solidarity demonstrations across the country and globally. In addition, Black Lives Matter (BLM), which had been active since protesting the 2012 killing of black teenager Trayvon Martin, issued a call for a "Freedom Ride" to Ferguson, and 500 volunteers stepped forward to join the movement in Ferguson (Hillstrom 2018: 29). While Ferguson served as a national focal point—drawing sustained protests, intensive media coverage, and investigations by the USDOJ and other agencies—police killings of unarmed blacks in other locales also triggered protests, adding breadth to the rising movement against police violence. Among the victims were Eric Garner, forty-three, who was killed in New York City in July 2014 by a prohibited police chokehold during his arrest for selling loose cigarettes; and Tamir Rice, twelve, who was fatally shot by police in Cleveland that November, where he had been playing in a park with a toy gun.

Ferguson would alter the national policing and social movement landscape in multiple ways. First, it would help BLM cohere as the first-ever and sustained national movement against police violence. BLM incorporated a broad racial justice agenda, pointing up the ways that policing and mass incarceration harmed blacks disproportionately. Through a three-day conference of 1,500 activists at Cleveland State University in July 2015, and followed by major donations from the Ford Foundation and other philanthropies, the new movement established a national organization, Movement for Black Lives (M4BL), as a coalition of some fifty groups and allied with locally based BLM chapters. In 2016, M4BL rolled out a comprehensive program it called "Vision for Black Lives" (Movement n.d.), and many observers now regard BLM generally as today's civil rights movement.

Second, a pattern emerged wherein the most explosive police-triggered protests and riots would draw an official response that includes the DOJ investigating the pertinent police department. Thus, the DOJ intervened not only in Ferguson (US DOJ 2015a, 2015b), but also in Baltimore (US DOJ 2016), which saw several days of protests and riots in response to the in-custody death of Freddie Gray. The DOJ likewise launched an investigation of the Minneapolis Police Department in 2021 (US DOJ 2023), triggered by the police murder of George Floyd and the related national protests of summer 2020. Because the DOJ has finite resources, it cannot investigate every police department alleged to have patterns of misconduct or abuse. The agency must therefore pick and choose its targets; those police departments that are met by massive community protests or disorder now appear likely to draw a vigorous DOJ response.

Note that, in the Ferguson case, the DOJ conducted two separate investigations. One addressed the shooting death of Michael Brown; the other inquired broadly into the Ferguson Police Department (FPD) and the city court system. The two reports were released on the same day, March 4, 2015. One echoed the finding of the St. Louis County grand jury; that is, the DOJ determined that "the evidence does not support charging a violation of federal law" by Officer Wilson (US DOJ 2015a: 4). The other report (US DOJ 2015b), however, found many patterns of unconstitutional misconduct by the FPD, which no doubt had fueled the Ferguson protests as much as had the Brown killing itself. These included excessive use of force, discrimination against blacks and Native Americans, and violations of protesters' and journalists' First Amendment rights.

But the largest core problem identified by the DOJ involved the city's reliance on revenue from court fees and fines. Said the report, "Ferguson police officers from all ranks told us that revenue generation is stressed heavily within the police department, and that the message comes from City leadership" (2015b: 2). Officer "productivity" was measured by the number of citations issued, the DOJ found. "Many officers appear to see some residents, especially those who live in Ferguson's predominantly African-American neighborhoods, less as constituents to be protected than as potential offenders and sources of revenue" (2). This priority also compromised the city court's capacity to deliver justice and honor citizens' constitutional rights, the DOJ asserted. "The municipal court does not act as a neutral arbiter of the law or a check on unlawful police conduct. Instead, the court primarily uses its judicial authority as the means to compel the payment of fines and fees that advance the City's financial interests" (3). This system bore particular harm on the city's heavily low-income black community. "Minor offenses," said the DOJ, "can generate crippling debts, result in jail time because of an inability to pay, and result in the loss of a driver's license, employment, or housing" (4).

The DOJ investigation led to a consent decree under which the City of Ferguson agreed to comply with the DOJ's recommendations (*United States* 2016). Seven years later, a fall 2023 status report from Natashia Tidwell, the consent decree's independent monitor, observed that none of the eleven areas targeted for reform—for example, use of force; bias in policing and the courts; stop, search, citation, and arrest—had been completed and approved (*United States* 2023: 3–4). There was, however, evidence that the Ferguson courts had shifted away from heavy reliance on fines and fees as a source of city revenue. Under a "Comprehensive Amnesty Program," Tidwell points out, 5,851 unresolved court cases had been dismissed by the city as of fall 2018 (*United States* 2023: 11). Many people who could not afford to pay city fines were now enrolled in community service as an alternative. In addition, the police force has diversified. The department's first black police chief was appointed in May 2016 (Karimi and Berlinger 2016). Whereas, in 2015, only four of the FPD's fifty-four officers were black, by 2019, the department had eighteen black officers out of thirty-nine (US DOJ 2015b: 7; Cooperman 2019).

A further significant outcome from the Ferguson protests was President Barack Obama's appointment of the 21st Century Policing Task Force. This was part of a multipronged response rolled out by Obama on December 1, 2014—a week after the non-indictment of Officer Wilson had sparked further protests and rioting in Ferguson. Besides the blue-ribbon task force, Obama proposed a $263 million program advancing police reform and training, including funding for up to 50,000 body-worn cameras. The policing crisis, he declared, is "not a problem simply of Ferguson, Missouri. This is a problem that is national" (qtd. in Feldmann 2014). The task force—led by Charles Ramsey, then commissioner of Philadelphia police, and Laurie Robinson, criminologist at George Mason University—would issue its landmark report the following May (President's Task Force 2015). That report advanced a policing model based on "procedural justice," which refers to policing that applies fair processes to build legitimacy and trust with communities. Likewise, it called for transparency, accountability, reducing racial and other biases, training and monitoring to minimize use of force, and applying best practices when responding to people with drug addictions or mental health crises. The task force report became a "playbook" for police chiefs across the country (Robinson 2020: 229); possibly no prior national police reform initiative would bear its level of influence, especially on police leadership.

A final impact of Ferguson was indicated by an Associated Press analysis one year after the Brown killing (Lieb 2015): "Twenty-four states have passed at least 40 new measures addressing such things as officer-worn cameras, training about racial bias, independent investigations when police use force and new limits on the flow of surplus military equipment to local law enforcement agencies." Ferguson, then, would spawn a movement and would produce a renewed commitment to police reform within the institution and at many levels of government.

Further Reading

Cooperman, Jeannette. 2019. "Ferguson's Former Police Chief Reflects on Recruiting a More Diverse Force and Winning the Community's Trust." *St. Louis Magazine*. July 24.

Feldmann, Linda. 2014. "Ferguson Day at the White House. What Did Obama Accomplish?" *Christian Science Monitor*. December 1.

Hillstrom, Laurie Collier. 2018. *Black Lives Matter: From a Moment to a Movement.* Santa Barbara, CA: Greenwood Publishing.

Karimi, Faith, and Joshua Berlinger. 2016. "Ferguson Swears in New Police Chief." CNN. May 10.

Lieb, David A. 2015. "Ferguson Spurs 40 New State Measures; Activists Want More." *Seattle Times*, August 3.

Movement for Black Lives. Vision for Black Lives, n.d. https://m4bl.org/policy-platforms.

President's Task Force on 21st Century Policing. 2015. *Final Report of the President's Task Force on 21st Century Policing.* Washington, DC: Community Oriented Policing Services.

Robinson, Laurie O. 2020. "Five Years after Ferguson: Reflecting on Police Reform and What's Ahead." *Annals of the American Academy of Political and Social Science* 687, no. 1: 228–39.

United States v. City of Ferguson. 2016. Consent Decree. United States District Court, Eastern District of Missouri, Eastern Division. March 17. Accessed January 8, 2025. https://www.justice.gov/d9/ferguson_consent_decree.pdf.

United States v. City of Ferguson. 2023. Independent Monitor's Fall 2023 Status Report. United States District Court, Eastern District of Missouri, Eastern Division. October 16. Accessed January 8, 2025. https://www.moed.uscourts.gov/mdl/416-cv-180-cdp.

US Department of Justice. 2015a. *Department of Justice Report Regarding the Criminal Investigation into the Shooting Death of Michael Brown by Ferguson, Missouri Police Officer Darren Wilson.* Washington, DC, March 4. Accessed January 8, 2025. https://www.justice.gov/usao/moe/news/2015/march/DOJ%20Report%20on%20Shooting%20of%20Michael%20Brown.pdf.

US Department of Justice. 2015b. *Investigation of the Ferguson Police Department.* Washington, DC, March 4. Accessed January 8, 2025. https://www.justice.gov/sites/default/files/crt/legacy/2015/03/04/ferguson_findings_3-4-15.pdf.

US Department of Justice. 2016. *Investigation of the Baltimore City Police Department.* Washington, DC, August 10. Accessed January 8, 2025. https://www.justice.gov/opa/file/883366/download.

US Department of Justice. 2023. *Investigation of the City of Minneapolis and the Minneapolis Police Department.* Washington, DC, June 16. Accessed January 8, 2025. https://www.justice.gov/opa/press-release/file/1587661/download.

Q22: What were the strengths and limitations of the Black Lives Matter movement in the wake of the Ferguson uprising?

Answer: BLM's key contribution has been that of putting the country and its elected leaders on notice that something must be done about police violence and the larger harms of mass incarceration as well as systemic racism. Its campaigns have also won specific improvements or promising steps in various locales. What the movement did not do—at least not in the aftermath of Ferguson—is provide a clear direction for addressing police abuse as a systemic or national problem. Nor did it offer a strategy for advancing the Vision for Black Lives, as a broad program for economic and social justice, or suggest a path for extending beyond a black focus in order to build a multiracial movement. It was not until the police killing of George Floyd in 2020, when the call for police defunding and abolition came to fore, that an overarching direction did begin taking shape.

The Facts: Before taking measure of BLM's strengths and limitations, it may help to better define BLM as a movement, since an effective movement is much larger than merely the organization that leads it. When BLM cohered as a movement post-Ferguson, it had a national umbrella entity, Movement for Black Lives (M4BL); it built a host of local BLM chapters; and it had an extensive decentralized network of organizations and projects (Ransby 2018). It is not always clear whether a local group does or does not belong to BLM in formal terms. Moreover, when millions protested the Floyd killing in 2020, the *New York Times* identified this outpouring as the "Black Lives Matter movement," even though most of the protesters were probably not affiliated with the movement per se (Buchanan, Bui, and Patel 2020). That alone actually signals a strength of BLM, which is that it truly is a "movement" that has impacted public consciousness beyond that of any organization.

By the same token, those who study social movements (e.g., Della Porta and Diani 2015) might count among a movement's achievements not only what its organization does, but what people do independently because their beliefs or circumstances have been changed by the movement. So, for example, a schoolteacher with no direct movement affiliation becomes inspired by BLM to develop a racial justice unit in her social studies class. Or a police chief, under pressure to effect reform following a series of local BLM protests, implements a use-of-force review process that does in fact reduce the department's abusive practices. Or a lawyer who is sympathetic to BLM decides to run for district attorney on a movement-friendly platform—for example, by promising to end the cash bail system and to hold police accountable to constitutional practices (see Bazelon 2020). All of these may reasonably be counted as BLM achievements.

Along with such impactful but hard-to-measure achievements are the more direct victories from actual BLM campaigns. For example, BLM's Los Angeles chapter spearheaded a campaign for Measure R, which L.A. County voters approved in March 2020. Its provisions included establishing a plan to reduce the county's jail population, offering alternatives to incarceration, increasing access to mental health services and drug treatment, and strengthening the civilian oversight commission that oversees the L.A. County Sheriff's Department (Black Lives Matter Global 2020: 33). In Chicago, Black Youth Project 100, one of the most respected M4BL partner organizations, joined a lawsuit and coalition campaign calling for an end to the Chicago Police Department's Gang Database. As attorney Vanessa del Valle (2020) of the nonprofit MacArthur Justice Center explains, the database had no consistent guidelines and unlimited discretion to add names. The data were shared with other agencies, and many Chicago youth were subjected to "irreparable harm and harassment." Although the coalition's campaign to end the gang database remains ongoing, their lawsuit reached a settlement in September 2020 with several gains for the community, says del Valle. The agreement included greater program transparency, stricter criteria for entering names in the database, and a range of other protections for affected youth; plus, the claims of individual plaintiffs were settled.

Some of BLM's limitations were ones that are common to many grassroots movements, and which involve a lack of clear strategy or direction. As media giant Oprah Winfrey, who had produced the film *Selma* about the civil rights movement, commented during the Ferguson struggle, "I think it's wonderful to march and to protest and it's wonderful to see all across the country, people doing it." But it's not enough to march, she pointed out. "What I'm looking for is some kind of leadership to come out of this to say, 'This is what we want. This is what has to change, and these are the steps that we need to take to make these changes, and this is what we're willing to do to get it'" (qtd. in "Oprah" 2015). BLM post-Ferguson would indeed grapple to find a clear direction. Even where local campaigns would in time notch a host of local victories against police abuse, securing systemic change in the policing or criminal justice arena is a far greater challenge. Moreover, BLM had sights on a larger agenda toward racial and economic justice. Drawing up a Vision for Black Lives is a fine starting point: How will such vision be realized?

In their study of anti-police violence activism in Minneapolis, sociologist Michelle Phelps and colleagues (Phelps, Ward, and Frazier 2021) show how local groups experimented with different strategies over a number of years, and with some debate between them. The main concerned organization prior to the rise of BLM was Communities United Against Police Brutality (CUAPB), which was led by retirement-age white organizers (Phelps, Ward, and Frazier

2021: 428). The largest obstacle to police reform, according to CUAPB, was lack of accountability, which they sought to address by requiring officers to hold personal liability insurance. The group gathered 14,000 signatures to put forward a city ballot initiative requiring officer liability insurance. But that initiative was blocked by the Minnesota Supreme Court, who ruled that it conflicted with state law protecting public employees. In 2014–15, with young and black activists stepping forward in the spirit of BLM, the primary local demand became that of prosecuting officers involved in alleged violence, mirroring the demand in Ferguson. Protest actions also became more militant. In November 2015, responding to the fatal police shooting of Jamar Clark, the local movement held an eighteen-day occupation in front of the Minneapolis Police Department's (MPD's) 4th precinct. But the calls for prosecution brought mixed results: the police killings of Clark in 2015, Philando Castile in 2016, and Justine Damond in 2017 led to an officer's conviction only in the Damond case; and the impact did not necessarily improve officer conduct or reduce abuse. The protests did lead MPD Chief Janeé Harteau to implement a series of reforms in coordination with the National Initiative for Building Community Trust and Justice (see Jannetta et al. 2019). Harteau oversaw community engagement efforts and new trainings on de-escalation and implicit bias. Activists, however, called these reforms "phony" solutions that would not address police violence (Phelps, Ward, and Frazier 2021: 429). The movement attempted further strategies—a strengthened civilian oversight board and fighting the police union through the contract negotiation process.

As Phelps and colleagues recount, there then emerged a trio of groups—MPD150, Reclaim the Block, and Black Visions Collective—guided by police abolitionism. In 2018–19, Reclaim the Block intervened in the city budget process and secured redirection of some funds away from police and to a new Office of Violence Prevention. There was now a division among Minneapolis activists, with some calling for "total abolition" of police and others preferring community control of police (ibid.: 432). Finally, with the May 2020 Floyd killing, the movement against police violence did broadly cohere behind a shared vision, both in Minneapolis and nationally. This was, and remains today, guided by an abolitionist perspective, with police defunding as its transitional strategy. On the other hand, beyond BLM and allied activist circles, police defunding and abolition have not been compelling to the American public. This was signaled not only in polls (Crabtree 2020; Saad 2020) but at the ballot box (Blake 2021; Craig 2021). In the case of Minneapolis, an abolitionist-backed ballot measure to replace the MPD with a new public health-oriented Department of Public

Safety was rejected by 56 percent of voters in November 2021 (Bailey 2021). Thus, although the movement did arrive at a more clear direction, its efficacy remains uncertain. The movement's abolitionist politics are taken up further in Chapter 8.

Further Reading

Bailey, Holly. 2021. "Minneapolis Rejects Measure to Replace Police Department in First Major Electoral Test of Reform Movement after George Floyd's Murder." *Washington Post*, November 2.

Bazelon, Emily. 2020. *Charged: The New Movement to Transform American Prosecution and End Mass Incarceration*. New York: Random House.

Black Lives Matter Global Network. 2020. *Black Lives Matter: 2020 Impact Report*. Accessed January 8, 2025. https://blacklivesmatter.com/wp-content/uploads/2021/02/blm-2020-impact-report.pdf.

Blake, Aaron. 2021. "The Electoral Demise of 'Defund the Police.'" *Washington Post*, November 5.

Buchanan, Larry, Quoctrung Bui, and Jugal K. Patel. 2020. "Black Lives Matter May Be the Largest Movement in U.S. History." *New York Times*, July 3.

Crabtree, Steve. 2020. "Most Americans Say Policing Needs 'Major Changes.'" Gallup. July 22. Accessed January 8, 2025. https://news.gallup.com/poll/315962/americans-say-policing-needs-major-changes.aspx.

Craig, Tim. 2021. "In a Setback for Black Lives Matter, Mayoral Campaigns Shift to 'Law and Order.'" *Washington Post*, October 30.

del Valle, Vanessa. 2020. "Chicagoans for an End to the Gang Database v. City of Chicago." Chicago: MacArthur Justice Center. Accessed January 8, 2025. https://www.macarthurjustice.org/case/chicagoans-for-an-end-to-the-gang-database.

Della Porta, Donatella, and Mario Diani, eds. 2015. *The Oxford Handbook of Social Movements*. New York: Oxford University Press.

Jannetta, Jesse, Sino Esthappan, Jocelyn Fontaine, Mathew Lynch, and Nancy G. La Vigne. 2019. *Learning to Build Police-Community Trust*. Washington, DC: Urban Institute. Accessed January 8, 2025. https://www.urban.org/research/publication/learning-build-police-community-trust.

"Oprah Winfrey's Comments about Recent Protests and Ferguson Spark Controversy." 2015. *People*, January 1.

Phelps, Michelle S., Anneliese Ward, and Dwjuan Frazier. 2021. "From Police Reform to Police Abolition? How Minneapolis Activists Fought to Make Black Lives Matter." *Mobilization* 26, no. 4: 421–41.

Ransby, Barbara. 2018. *Making All Black Lives Matter: Reimagining Freedom in the Twenty-First Century*. Oakland: University of California Press.

Saad, Lydia. 2020. "Black Americans Want Police to Retain Local Presence." Gallup. August 5. Accessed January 8, 2025. https://news.gallup.com/poll/316571/black-americans-police-retain-local-presence.aspx.

Q23: What were the strengths and limitations of the Obama reforms?

Answer: Perhaps the leading achievement of President Obama's Task Force on 21st Century Policing was to focus police leadership in many locales on promoting reform in such areas as racial practice, use of force, and police-community relations. Still, the reality years later is that such problems as racial profiling, excessive force, and weak public accountability continue to deeply mark US policing.

The Facts: Together with the BLM protests, the Obama task force report did bear impact on policing. Task force cochair Laurie Robinson (2020), in an assessment five years after the Ferguson protests, observes that police leaders and their associations were particularly receptive to the panel's report. The International Association of Police Chiefs (IACP), Police Executive Research Forum (PERF), Major Cities Chiefs Association (MCCA), and National Association of Black Law Enforcement Executives (NOBLE) all sent the report to their members and encouraged them to study its recommendations. Robinson adds, "IACP also set up an Institute for Community-Police Relations shortly after the report was issued to provide technical assistance, targeted to small and rural agencies, on how to implement the task force recommendations" (229). Robinson cites a survey conducted jointly by MCCA and the National Police Foundation from 2015 to 2017, involving 47 of the largest US law enforcement agencies. The survey found that 39 percent of the agencies had changed their use-of-force policies and revised their training to incorporate de-escalation. Officer-involved shootings during this period dropped by 21 percent in these agencies, according to the survey (229, citing Stephens 2019).

Despite documenting such progress, Robinson does acknowledge reform's continuing challenges, identifying three major barriers to change (230). First, "the highly decentralized nature of policing in the United States," with some 18,000 state and local departments, means that "change in this field will not be quick or easy." Second is police culture, particularly the warrior mentality that has "'dominated American policing for decades'" (230, quoting Walker

2018: 1796). Third, Robinson's Trump-era article pointed to the more limited role of the DOJ under President Trump's administration, which had directed the DOJ not to pursue new pattern-or-practice lawsuits against police departments, and where the DOJ was not pursuing other reform initiatives as it had under Obama and prior presidents.

In fact, as necessary and appropriate as was Obama's action in appointing his policing task force in response to the rising BLM movement, it may be that no initiative in Washington alone can suffice in tackling America's policing crisis. It may also be that even the most dedicated and well-intended police chief may be incapable of effecting deep change on his or her own, especially in a big urban police department. This was underscored when, not long after Robinson's analysis was published, Minneapolis exploded in protest over the George Floyd killing. Here the MPD had been implementing many Obama-style reforms begun by Chief Harteau in 2015 (see Q22). During the murder trial of Derek Chauvin, the officer who fatally held his knee to Floyd's neck for nine minutes, prosecutors argued that Chauvin had acted in violation of department policy and training regarding the use of neck restraints (Tarm 2021). The three officers who had assisted Chauvin also allegedly violated a department policy that required them to intervene when a fellow officer uses unreasonable force (Associated Press 2020).

When the Obama report is matched to pertinent conditions of American policing today, it appears that virtually every area of recommended reform remains violated on a large scale. The report also failed to significantly address issues with policing's overall mandate. The following paragraphs examine some of the task force recommendations and their outcomes in more detail.

De-escalation. The task force's recommendation regarding de-escalation includes the following statement: "Law enforcement agency policies for training on use of force should emphasize de-escalation" (President's Task Force 2015: 20). The US record on fatal police shootings of civilians since 2015—holding steady at roughly one thousand per year (Washington Post n.d.)—does not suggest a general trend toward de-escalation. Moreover, the US figure towers above outcomes in comparator countries. According to researchers Alex Jones and Wendy Sawyer (2020), who cite the most recent year of available data, police killed two people in Japan, three in England and Wales, and eleven in Germany (Jones and Sawyer 2020).

Use of force data reporting. The task force recommendations for collecting and reporting data on incidents involving police use of force include the following: "Policies on use of force should also require agencies to collect, maintain, and report data to the Federal Government on all officer-involved shootings, whether fatal or nonfatal, as well as any in-custody death" (President's Task Force 2015: 21). No such national policy has been implemented to date. In 2019 and 2020, only 27 percent of US police departments supplied agency data on use of force as requested by the FBI and pursuant to a presidential order (Jackman 2021). In New York state, only 4 of 694 agencies supplied data, covering 2 percent of the state's police officers. Such data provision by state and local agencies is voluntary under the law. Because of this, the nation's data on US killings by police remains reliant on private initiatives such as by the *Washington Post* (n.d.) and Mapping Police Violence (mappingpoliceviolence.org).

Racial profiling. Regarding racial profiling, the task force recommended that "Law enforcement agencies should adopt and enforce policies prohibiting profiling and discrimination based on race, ethnicity, national origin," and other categories (President's Task Force 2015: 28). The Obama report and pertinent recommendations may well have encouraged more initiatives to address racial profiling, which is a well-documented national problem (Pierson et al. 2020). Evidence does suggest, however, that remedies will take far more than legal prohibition. In 2015, California passed a prohibition on racial and identity profiling, including establishing a state board to monitor data and promote best practices ("AB 953" n.d.). Yet, racial profiling by law enforcement has since remained routine in the state. One study of nearly 4 million stops in 2019 involving California's fifteen largest law enforcement agencies (Lofstrom et al. 2021: 3) found that black Californians were more than twice as likely than white Californians to be searched. The searches of black civilians, however, were somewhat less likely to yield contraband or evidence, as compared to searches of white civilians. Blacks were also almost twice as likely as whites to be booked into jail.

Ticket and arrest quotas. The task force report states that "Law enforcement agencies and municipalities should refrain from practices requiring officers to issue a predetermined number of tickets, citations, arrests, or summonses, or to initiate investigative contacts with citizens for reasons not directly related to improving public safety, such as generating revenue" (President's Task Force 2015: 26). Here the task force quotes pertinent testimony from the American Civil Liberties Union: "Cities across the country generate much of their revenue through court fines and fees, with those who can't pay subject to arrest and jail time" (qtd. in ibid.: 27). As discussed in Chapter 1, a central problem in American policing is that its mandate has been defined as enforcing laws rather than advancing public safety and working with communities to solve problems. The Obama report did not directly discuss or challenge policing's law-enforcement mandate. The recommendation does *hint* at the question of police mandate reform but only indirectly—that is, by discussing quotas and city revenues. The quotas *are* a wide problem (Ossei-Owusu 2021), as is the pattern of cities relying on court fines and fees as a source of revenue, which remains the practice in many locales (Subramanian et al. 2022). But the use of tickets, arrests, stops, and frisks as measures of productivity, whether or not actual quotas are enforced, is nearly universal in US policing. As law professors Devon Carbado and Song Richardson point out: "Throughout the nation, policing has become a numbers game, with departments focusing their energies on the 'objectification and quantification of police work.' … Officers are routinely evaluated and rewarded for the number of arrests they make, how many tickets they write, and how many stops and frisks they log" (2018: 2011; quoting Skolnick and Fyfe 1993: 189–90). That the Obama task force declined to initiate a national discussion on the purpose of policing may be the initiative's largest limitation.

Further Reading

"AB 953: The Racial and Identity Profiling Act of 2015." n. d. State of California Department of Justice. Accessed January 8, 2025. https://oag.ca.gov/ab953.

Associated Press. 2020. "Fear, Police Culture Prevented Officers from Stopping Veteran Cop Kneeling on George Floyd, Observers Say." *Oregonian*, June 7. Accessed January 8, 2025. https://www.oregonlive.com.

Carbado, Devon W., and L. Song Richardson. 2018. "The Black Police: Policing Our Own." *Harvard Law Review* 131: 1979–2025.

Jackman, Tom. 2021. "For a Second Year, Most U.S. Police Departments Decline to Share Information on Their Use of Force." *Washington Post*, June 9.

Jones, Alex, and Wendy Sawyer. 2020. "Not Just 'a Few Bad Apples': U.S. Police Kill Civilians at Much Higher Rates Than Other Countries." Prison Policy Initiative, June 5. Accessed January 8, 2025. https://www.prisonpolicy.org/blog/2020/06/05/policekillings.

Lofstrom, Magnus, Joseph Hayes, Brandon Martin, and Deepak Premkumar. 2021. *Racial Disparities in Law Enforcement Stops.* San Francisco: Public Policy Institute of California, October. Accessed January 8, 2025. https://www.ppic.org/publication/racial-disparities-in-law-enforcement-stops.

Mapping Police Violence. n. d. https://mappingpoliceviolence.org.

Ossei-Owusu, Shaun. 2021. "Police Quotas." *New York University Law Review* 96: 529–605.

Pierson, Emma, Camelia Simoiu, Jan Overgoor, Sam Corbett-Davies, Daniel Jenson, Amy Shoemaker, Vignesh Ramachandra et al. 2020. "A Large-Scale Analysis of

Racial Disparities in Police Stops across the United States." *Nature Human Behaviour* 4: 736–45.

President's Task Force on 21st Century Policing. 2015. *Final Report of the President's Task Force on 21st Century Policing.* Washington, DC: Community Oriented Policing Services.

Robinson, Laurie O. 2020. "Five Years after Ferguson: Reflecting on Police Reform and What's Ahead." *Annals of the American Academy of Political and Social Science* 687, no. 1: 228–39.

Skolnick, Jerome H., and James J. Fyfe. 1993. *Above the Law: Police and the Excessive Use of Force.* New York: Free Press.

Stephens, Darrel W. 2019. *Officer Involved Shootings: Incident Executive Summary.* Washington, DC: National Police Foundation & Major Cities Chiefs Association. Accessed January 8, 2025. https://www.policefoundation.org/publication/officer-involved-shootings-incident-executive-summary.

Subramanian, Ram, Jackie Fielding, Lauren-Brooke Eisen, Hernandez Stroud, and Taylor King. 2022. *Revenue over Public Safety: How Perverse Financial Incentives Warp the Criminal Justice System.* New York: Brennan Center for Justice, NYU School of Law, July 6. Accessed January 8, 2025. https://search.issuelab.org/resource/revenue-over-public-safety-how-perverse-financial-incentives-warp-the-criminal-justice-system.html.

Tarm, Michael. 2021. "Explainer: Was Officer's Knee on Floyd's Neck Authorized?" Associated Press, April 5. Accessed January 8, 2025. https://apnews.com.

Walker, Samuel. 2018. "'Not Dead Yet': The National Police Crisis: A New Conversation about Policing, and the Prospects for Accountability-Related Police Reform." *University of Illinois Law Review* 5: 1777–841.

Washington Post. Fatal Force. Fatal police shootings database. n.d. Accessed July 22, 2023. https://www.washingtonpost.com/graphics/investigations/police-shootings-database/?itid=lk_inline_manual_23.

Q24: Can evidence-based policing, which guided the Obama task force, produce a systemic remedy to police abuse?

Answer: Not likely. Evidence-based policing (EBP) (Mitchell and Huey 2019; Sherman 1998) is a narrow, restrictive form of social science that is ill equipped to tackle police abuse or complex social problems generally. An alternative and more robust research framework is needed. Crime control and social order through law enforcement is a paradigm. Within this paradigm, evidence-based methods confirm "what works," or as criminologist Lawrence Sherman (1998: 2) puts it, "Of all the ideas in policing, one stands out as the most powerful force for change: police practices should be based on scientific evidence about what works best." However, evidence-based methods rarely challenge the paradigm itself. However, the narrow kind of science that has become standard in EBP prevents the close examination of the paradigm and its underlying assumptions.

The Facts: EBP, along with related frameworks such as evidence-based crime prevention and evidence-based criminal justice, was pioneered by criminologist Lawrence Sherman in the 1990s. Drawing on medical science models—that is, evidence-based medicine—EBP's core notion, as Sherman and others (2002: 1) explain, is that "effective public policy and practice needs to be based on scientific evidence." The authors remark:

> This is not the standard usually adopted in crime prevention and criminal justice. Anecdotal evidence, program favorites of the month, and political ideology seemingly drive much of the crime policy agenda .... Lawmakers and policymakers are shirking their responsibility to the taxpaying public by not giving funding priority to those programs with evidence of effectiveness in preventing crime.

EBP is today's dominant research framework in the policing field. EBP has become "an anchoring concept for government funding for research and technical assistance in policing," observe Cynthia Lum and Christopher Koper (2017: 3) of George Mason University's Center for Evidence-Based Crime Policy. "The term can be heard in criminal justice undergraduate and graduate programs as well, with new courses on evidence-based crime policy and program evaluation being regularly taught."

EBP was also the guiding framework of the Obama task force. The term appears throughout the body's report—which advises that police apply "evidence-based practices" such as in responding to mass demonstrations, reducing racial bias, or implementing civilian oversight mechanisms (President's Task Force 2015: 20, 24, 26). Laurie Robinson, who cochaired the task force, is a senior fellow at the George Mason crime policy center, while the other cochair, former police chief Charles Ramsey, is a member of that center's Evidence-Based Policing Hall of Fame.

That "research, evaluation, analysis, and scientific processes should have 'a seat at the table' in law enforcement," as Lum and Koper put it (2017: 3–4), makes perfect sense. But what *kind* of science should guide us? Given its medical-model inspiration, EBP favors a controlled, experimental, and highly quantitative kind of science. The Obama task force, for example, describes seminal research that demonstrated a positive impact of body-worn cameras (BWCs) in policing (President's Task Force 2015: 31–2; citing Ariel, Farrar, and Sutherland 2015).

The researchers, as the task force explains, used the "gold standard of research models, a randomized control trial." This is where "the people being studied are randomly assigned either to a control group that does not receive the treatment being studied or to a treatment group that does." The twelve-month study strongly suggested that "the use of BWCs by the police can significantly reduce both officer use of force and complaints against officers" (ibid.: 32).

Another study, also using a randomized control trial, contradicts the task force's claim: it found that the BWCs had little effect on officer use of force or civilian complaints (Yokum, Ravishankar, and Coppock 2019). The point here is not to debate the merits of police body-worn cameras, but to consider the nature of EBP as a mode of science. EBP's enthusiasm for laboratory-style methods turns our view to small and specific things, and away from big-picture and contextual analyses that are hallmarks of a robust, critical social science and criminology (DeKeseredy and Dragiewicz 2018). As management studies scholar Kevin Morrell and criminologist Michael Rowe point out in *Critical Reflections on Evidence-Based Policing* (2020: 117), EBP's focus on "specific outcomes in relation to particular practices" ignores more fundamental issues such as "what are the police for?" and "who call the shots?"

Surely, the small things do matter, whether BWCs or scores of other technical and procedural questions that impact police daily practice. But we equally need a big picture and larger societal goals in order to properly situate the small questions. The Obama task force did not completely neglect the big picture. "The justice system alone cannot solve many of the underlying conditions that give rise to crime," said the report. The president should "promote programs that take a comprehensive and inclusive look at community-based initiatives that address the core issues of poverty, education, health, and safety" (President's Task Force 2015: 8). The roots of crime were unfortunately not more than a passing mention in the Obama report. On the other hand, the work of the Kerner Commission under President Johnson suggests that a national panel *can* inquire jointly into policing and larger matters of racial and economic justice and do both robustly (National Advisory Commission 1968; see also Chapter 5 in the present volume). Perhaps, too, we can imagine approaches to policing that connect immediate reform work with long-term strategies for broad social change.

When racial and economic justice, and core matters of poverty, are added to the study of policing, it becomes more evident why EBP's preference for controlled and medical-style science is inadequate. Winning a war on poverty requires organizing and social movements, as Martin Luther King Jr. (2010) contended. Such complex movements are not very conducive to randomized control trials or controlled experiments. The need for an alternative research framework that integrates policing and criminal justice issues with a larger social justice agenda and with the social movements is suggested by critical criminologist Elliott Currie (2016: 20–1):

> The most promising future for criminology involves the maturing and spreading of a truly structural and globally engaged work that not only puts the larger developments in world society at the forefront of analysis, but also works to create new and more effective ways of linking that intellectual work with movements for social change—which includes a concerted effort to move out beyond our usual academic and governmental constituencies to build stronger working relationships with people who are trying to make change from the ground up.

EBP scholars certainly do not propose that the answers to the historic challenges of poor people's movements can be found through randomized control trials. Rather, such questions are simply not part of EBP research. Offered here, and taken up further in Chapter 8, is that struggles against racism and poverty are not separate from policing issues, but rather belong in the same conversation.

What is more, even when our focus of study is primarily on policing, there are narrower and broader ways of investigating that institution. As Howard Ryan, coauthor of this volume, explores elsewhere (2023), there is a need for new frameworks that help us to study policing and police culture in its fullness. Laurie Robinson, in reflecting on the post-Ferguson era and the impact of the Obama task force, notes some of the large barriers to change within the policing institution—its decentralized structure among 18,000 agencies; its prevailing warrior culture (2020: 230). Yet, Robinson and the other task force members understood these inherent challenges before their panel was convened. So, one might ask, is it enough for a national task force to simply recommend reforms—which, as reviewed in this chapter, remain largely unachieved today? Or, conversely, should an effective task force be more ambitious and ask how its proposed reforms might actually be won? Perhaps, too, such would be a worthwhile conversation for communities and for all students of policing.

Further Reading

Ariel, Barak, William A. Farrar, and Alex Sutherland. 2015. "The Effect of Police Body-Worn Cameras on Use of Force and Citizens' Complaints against the

Police: A Randomized Controlled Trial." *Journal of Quantitative Criminology* 31, no. 3: 509–35.

Currie, Elliott. 2016. "The Violence Divide: Taking 'Ordinary' Crime Seriously in a Volatile World." In Roger Matthews, ed., *What Is to Be Done about Crime and Punishment? Towards a "Public Criminology,"* 9–30. New York: Palgrave.

DeKeseredy, Walter S., and Molly Dragiewicz, eds. 2018. *Routledge Handbook of Critical Criminology*, 2nd ed. New York: Routledge.

King, Martin Luther, Jr. 2010. *Where Do We Go from Here: Chaos or Community?* Boston: Beacon Press.

Lum, Cynthia, and Christopher S. Koper. 2017. *Evidence-Based Policing: Translating Research into Practice.* New York: Oxford University Press.

Mitchell, Renée J., and Laura Huey, eds. 2019. *Evidence Based Policing: An Introduction.* Chicago: Policy Press.

Morrell, Kevin, and Michael Rowe. 2020. "Democracy, Accountability and Evidence-Based Policing: Who Calls the Shots?" In Nigel Fielding, Karen Bullock, and Simon Holdaway, eds., *Critical Reflections on Evidence-Based Policing*, 115–32. New York: Routledge.

National Advisory Commission on Civil Disorders. 1968. *Report of the National Advisory Commission on Civil Disorders.* Washington, DC: US Government Printing Office.

President's Task Force on 21st Century Policing. 2015. *Final Report of the President's Task Force on 21st Century Policing.* Washington: Community Oriented Policing Services.

Robinson, Laurie O. 2020. "Five Years after Ferguson: Reflecting on Police Reform and What's Ahead." *Annals of the American Academy of Political and Social Science* 687, no. 1: 228–39.

Ryan, Howard. 2023. "Critical Policing Studies: Toward a 'Fully Social' Framework." *Critical Criminology* 31, no. 3: 827–42.

Sherman, Lawrence W. 1998. "Evidence-Based Policing." Ideas in American Policing. Washington, DC: Police Foundation, July. https://www.policinginstitute.org/wp-content/uploads/2015/06/Sherman-1998-Evidence-Based-Policing.pdf.

Sherman, Lawrence W., David P. Farrington, Brandon C. Welsh, and Doris Layton MacKenzie. 2002. "Preventing Crime." In Lawrence W. Sherman, David P. Farrington, Brandon C. Welsh, and Doris Layton MacKenzie, eds., *Evidence-Based Crime Prevention*, 1–12. New York: Routledge.

Yokum, David, Anita Ravishankar, and Alexander Coppock. 2019. "A Randomized Control Trial Evaluating the Effects of Police Body-Worn Cameras." *Proceedings of the National Academy of Sciences* 116, no. 21: 10329–32.

8

George Floyd Murder and the Rise of Police Abolitionism

After the May 25, 2020 killing of George Floyd, involving four Minneapolis police officers, with one of them fatally holding his knee to Floyd's neck for nine minutes, the movement against police violence took on a new character nationally. First, the call of Floyd protesters was not primarily about prosecuting the officers, as was demanded in Ferguson (see Chapter 7). The four officers wound up being convicted of various charges, including second-degree murder in the case of Derek Chauvin. Protesters across the country instead called for defunding the police, such as by 50 percent, and that the moneys be redirected to social programs (Levin 2020). Moreover, many of those demanding defunding saw this as part of a police abolitionist strategy and under guidance of an emerging political ideology known simply as *abolition* (Davis 2024; Gilmore 2022). In a related development, many activists became clearer in their belief that police reform—as pursued by officials and policymakers at all levels, and by the Minneapolis Police Department for several years prior to Floyd—was not the answer to police violence, since the police themselves are part of a "violent order" (Correia and Wall 2021). Finally, the movement became more multiracial, engaging white majorities in many of the Floyd protests (Harmon and Tavernise 2020). Although the movement remains widely black-led, with Black Lives Matter serving as an ongoing anchor, many activists now identify with an *abolition movement*. This chapter draws on coauthor Howard Ryan's (2022) article on police abolitionism.

Further Reading

Correia, David, and Tyler Wall, eds. 2021. *Violent Order: Essays on the Nature of the Police*. Chicago: Haymarket.

Davis, Angela Y. 2024. *Abolition: Politics, Practices, Promises*, vol. 1. Chicago: Haymarket.

Gilmore, Ruth Wilson. 2022. *Abolition Geography: Essays towards Liberation*. New York: Verso.

Harmon, Amy, and Sabrina Tavernise. 2020. "One Big Difference about George Floyd Protests: Many White Faces." *New York Times*, June 12.

Levin, Sam. 2020. "Movement to Defund Police Gains 'Unprecedented' Support across the US." *Guardian*, June 4.

Ryan, Howard. 2022. "Police Abolitionism: A Marxist Critique." *Social Justice* 49, no. 1/2: 25–54.

Q25: What did the Floyd murder and the Minneapolis experience tell us about police reform?

Answer: The events tell us that reform efforts failed in Minneapolis, and in that vein, that reforming the police can be tremendously difficult. The larger lessons, however, are matters of ongoing public debate. Does the city's experience tell us that new reform strategies are needed? Or, conversely and as the abolitionists contend, does it demonstrate that the police are incapable of reform and that new ways to imagine public safety are required? Our country has yet to develop adequate answers. Further study is needed, as well as national conversations on police reform, reform versus abolition, and more.

The Facts: The Floyd murder, following as it did several years of Minneapolis Police Department (MPD) reforms (see Janetta et al. 2019; Vitale 2020), signaled a failure of reform in multiple ways. First, Chauvin's neck restraint violated MPD policy and training, according to evidence presented by prosecutors at the ex-officer's murder trial (Tarm 2021). Second, the other three officers expressed concern during Chauvin's action but did not follow department policy requiring them to intervene when a fellow officer uses excessive force (Associated Press 2020). Third, two post-Floyd investigations of the MPD would find systemic problems. One investigation, by Minnesota's Department of Human Rights, found evidence of "a pattern or practice of discriminatory, race-based policing," and "a culture that is averse to oversight and accountability" (Minnesota 2022: 8, 42). The other investigation, by the US Department of Justice (DOJ), found similar results and recommended twenty-eight remedial measures that would help the city and MPD to "improve public safety, build the trust of the Minneapolis community, and comply with the Constitution and federal law" (US Department of Justice 2023: 85).

One of the DOJ's findings—that the MPD "lacks a functional Early Intervention System" (ibid.: 82) may have particular pertinence to the Floyd killing. An early intervention system is a common software-based tool used by police management to flag officers who show performance patterns, such as frequent use of force, that require supervisory attention. The DOJ, in a 2015 review, had warned the MPD that its early intervention system, originally set up in 2009, was not operating properly (Jany 2015). Had the MPD followed the DOJ's earlier recommendation to correct this system, it is possible that Chauvin's use-of-force patterns would have been detected and addressed before the Floyd tragedy. Chauvin, a nineteen-year MPD veteran, had had a long record of civilian complaints. He also had restrained people by kneeling on their neck or upper back on eight occasions, according to prosecutorial evidence (Alfonseca 2021).

The Floyd event, in short, signaled that there was something fundamentally wrong with the MPD, including how it pursued reforms. The state human rights department and the DOJ both proposed a series of new reforms to correct matters and indicated that there would be greater oversight and monitoring. But neither agency's report tells us *why* the MPD's past reforms—including a three-year police-community dialogue process carried out in collaboration with the National Initiative for Building Community Trust and Justice (Jannetta et al. 2019)—had failed. And herein lies a pivotal debate: Would the new reforms produce better outcomes?

The state and federal agencies, and city officials such as Minneapolis mayor Jacob Frey, clearly believed that new reforms and with greater oversight would make a difference. A 22-member Community Safety Work Group appointed by the mayor rolled out a series of reforms in June 2022 (Mannix 2022). The next year, the city and the state human rights department settled a court-approved consent decree to "address race-based policing" in the MPD and strengthen public safety (Minnesota 2023). (As of May 2024, the city was in negotiations with the DOJ regarding that agency's separate investigation and findings.) For the abolition movement in Minneapolis and elsewhere, on the other hand, the solution was not to devise better reforms but rather to question policing as an institution, and to build social justice and economic remedies that lay foundation for true public safety.

Further Reading

Alfonseca, Klara. 2021. "Derek Chauvin Pleads Not Guilty in 2017 Excessive Force Case Involving 14-Year-Old Black Boy." ABC News. September 16.

Associated Press. 2020. "Fear, Police Culture Prevented Officers from Stopping Veteran Cop Kneeling on George Floyd, Observers Say." *Oregonian*, June 7. Accessed January 8, 2025. https://www.oregonlive.com.

Jannetta, Jesse, Sino Esthappan, Jocelyn Fontaine, Mathew Lynch, and Nancy G. La Vigne. 2019. *Learning to Build Police-Community Trust.* Washington, DC: Urban Institute. Accessed January 8, 2025. https://www.urban.org/research/publication/learning-build-police-community-trust.

Jany, Libor. 2015. "Justice Department Releases Report on MPD 'Early Intervention System.'" *Star Tribune*, January 28.

Mannix, Andy. 2022. "Minneapolis Mayor Frey's Community Safety Group Rolls Out Proposals to Reform Police Department." *Star Tribune*, June 27.

Minnesota Department of Human Rights. 2022. *Investigation into the City of Minneapolis and the Minneapolis Police Department*, April 27. Accessed January 8, 2025. https://mn.gov/mdhr/mpd/findings.

Minnesota Department of Human Rights. 2023. "Minnesota Department of Human Rights Reaches Court Enforceable Agreement with City of Minneapolis to Address Race-Based Policing and Strengthen Public Safety." Accessed January 8, 2025. https://mn.gov/mdhr/mpd/agreement/terms.jsp.

Tarm, Michael. 2021. "Explainer: Was Officer's Knee on Floyd's Neck Authorized?" Associated Press, April 5. Accessed January 8, 2025. https://apnews.com.

US Department of Justice. 2023. *Investigation of the City of Minneapolis and the Minneapolis Police Department.* Washington, DC, June 16. Accessed January 8, 2025. https://www.justice.gov/opa/press-release/file/1587661/download.

Vitale, Alex S. 2020. "The Answer to Police Violence Is Not 'Reform.' It's Defunding. Here's Why." *Guardian*, May 31.

Q26: What do the police abolitionists want?

Answer: Police abolitionists (Correia and Wall 2021; Kaba and Ritchie 2022; Purnell 2021; Vitale 2021) are guided by a broad-scope, radical, and rather amorphous political philosophy known as abolition. This centrally includes abolishing police and prisons, while investing in "housing, employment and healthcare in ways that directly target the problems of public safety" (Vitale 2020). Crime, or "harm between persons," would be addressed by "a justice system based on reparation and reconciliation rather than retribution and vengeance" (Davis 2003: 107). Communities would further enhance safety through networks of mutual aid under models known as "transformative justice" and "reciprocal care" (Hayes and Kaba 2023).

Police abolition is an outgrowth of the prison abolition movement, which had its major US launch with "Critical Resistance: Beyond the Prison-Industrial

Complex," a 1998 conference in Berkeley, California. Lead movement thinker Angela Davis, in *Abolition Democracy* (2005), influentially described prison abolition as a continuation of the struggle against slavery, drawing on the work of black sociologist W. E. B. Du Bois. To this, the movement adds a host of aims linked to identity politics—black, queer, feminist (Carruthers 2018; Davis et al. 2022). On an economic and systemic level, abolitionists want to end "racial capitalism" and build an egalitarian alternative. Davis (2005: 103) identifies the systemic goal as socialism. Another movement pioneer, Ruth Wilson Gilmore, describes the goal in more poetic terms: "Abolition is about presence, not absence. It's about building life-affirming institutions" (qtd. in MPD150 n.d.).

The Facts: The post-Floyd activism is often called the police *defunding* movement rather than police *abolition* movement, given that "defund the police" has become the central movement demand (Levin 2020). A pertinent question then becomes: Does the movement seek to defund the police—that is, by redirecting some portion of budgets to social programs while still keeping police—or to ultimately abolish policing? The aims of police and prison abolition, and the broader abolitionist vision advanced by Davis and Gilmore, more centrally and accurately define today's movement. Police defunding is a demand developed specifically by abolitionists. The call to move part of a police budget into social programs is clearly more winnable than is a call to abolish police; the former then becomes a strategic pathway to the latter.

Some argue that defunding and abolition should be viewed as separate projects (Henderson and Yisrael 2021). But such is not the predominant view within the movement itself. As the national group, Critical Resistance, puts it in their *Abolish Policing* organizer's toolkit, "We work to defund policing as a way to abolish it. … As abolitionists, when we say defund, we mean boldly taking chunks out of the policing apparatus" (2020: 15). The connection between defund and abolition is further underscored by respected organizers Mariame Kaba and Andrea Ritchie in their comprehensive work, *No More Police: A Case for Abolition* (2022: 9). The authors describe how they collaborated to advance both abolitionism and defund organizing nationally. In June 2020, as the Floyd protests were in full bloom, Kaba published her widely read *New York Times* op-ed entitled, "Yes, We Mean Literally Abolish the Police" (2020). At the same time, Ritchie "was hosting weekly calls with defund organizers" (Kaba and Ritchie 2022: 9). The two gathered demands and strategies into a toolkit entitled *Defund Police, Fund the People, Defend Black Lives*. Ritchie "also coordinated the development of defundpolice.org and supported defund fellows in over a dozen cities across the country through the Community Resource Hub" (ibid.).

A contrary account of these issues is offered by Howard Henderson and Ben Yisrael (2021) of the Washington-based Brookings Institution. Opponents of police defunding have promoted a myth that "defund means abolish," according to these authors.

> Opposers claim the movement undermines public safety through its efforts to end policing. The truth: the movement seeks to demilitarize police departments and reallocate funding to trained mental health workers and social workers to reduce unnecessary violent encounters between police and citizens.

Henderson and Yisrael do have a legitimate point: defunding and abolition are not the same. A number of cities have piloted initiatives that reroute police funds or duties to other agencies, such as for 911 calls involving mental health crises, without undermining public safety (Akinnibi 2020). Still, disconnecting defund from abolition does not help us understand today's movement, its goals, or its philosophy.

Though it is true that some cities have productively shifted some police duties to other agencies, and indeed that many police services could be better handled by social workers or other specialists, police defunding or service reallocation does get enormously complicated. Some cities such as Los Angeles (Arango 2021) trimmed their police budgets in response to fierce Floyd protests, but then restored police to full funding the next year in the face of rising gun violence. As criminologists Cynthia Lum, Christopher Koper, and Xiaoyun Wu (2022) point out, adequate social services within a city would cost far more than a redirected police budget could provide.

Police defunding also encounters specific challenges as a strategy for reducing police abuse. Many people do believe that police can be reformed; some experiences with DOJ-led reforms in Ferguson, Los Angeles, and other locales have been positive (see Chapters 6 and 7; and Rushin 2017). But reform itself often requires funding such as for training, police-community relations work, civilian oversight, or consultants. If police defunding means there are less funds available for reform, might this not leave police abuse uncorrected and unaddressed?

In an important sense, police defunding builds on abolitionist assumptions that themselves deserve scrutiny. Notably, abolitionists believe that the police cannot be reformed. "The violence of policing cannot be reformed—because violence is inherent to the institution itself," say Kaba and Ritchie (2022: 18).

Abolitionists also contend, when reforms fail, that it is because the purpose of the police is not really about public safety. Kaba and Ritchie theorize, "The role of the police is not to create safety but to establish and maintain a violent social order rooted in white supremacy, patriarchy, wealth accumulation, and the protection of private property over public good" (17). Their thesis is echoed by others: "Policing was not designed for public safety but as a tool to exploit, punish, and control Black and other racially and class marginalized communities" (McHarris 2021: 50). Discussions, then, about police defunding are best situated within full debates about abolition, the purpose of police, the viability of reform, as well the big-picture questions about economic and social justice and the roots of crime.

Further Reading

Akinnibi, Fola. 2020. "NYC Pilot Tries Mental Health Responders in Place of Police." Bloomberg News, November 13. Accessed January 9, 2025. https://www.bloomberg.com/news/articles/2020-11-13/nyc-pilot-sends-health-workers-in-place-of-police.

Arango, Tim. 2021. "A Year after George Floyd: Pressure to Add Police amid Rising Crime." *New York Times*, May 23.

Carruthers, Charlene A. 2018. *Unapologetic: A Black, Queer, and Feminist Mandate for Radical Movements*. Boston: Beacon Press.

Correia, David, and Tyler Wall, eds. 2021. *Violent Order: Essays on the Nature of the Police*. Chicago: Haymarket.

Critical Resistance. 2020. *Our Communities, Our Solutions: An Organizer's Toolkit for Developing Campaigns to Abolish Policing*. Oakland, CA, October. Accessed January 9, 2025. https://criticalresistance.org/resources/our-communities-our-solutions-an-organizers-toolkit-for-developing-campaigns-to-abolish-policing/.

Davis, Angela Y. 2003. *Are Prisons Obsolete?* New York: Seven Stories Press.

Davis, Angela Y. 2005. *Abolition Democracy: Beyond Empire, Prisons, and Torture*. New York: Seven Stories Press.

Davis, Angela Y., Gina Dent, Erica R. Meiners, and Beth E. Richie. 2022. *Abolition. Feminism. Now*. Chicago: Haymarket.

Hayes, Kelly, and Mariame Kaba. 2023. *Let This Radicalize You: Organizing and the Revolution of Reciprocal Care*. Chicago: Haymarket.

Henderson, Howard, and Ben Yisreal. 2021. "7 Myths about 'Defunding the Police' Debunked." Washington, DC: Brookings Institution, May 19. Accessed January 9, 2025. https://www.brookings.edu/articles/7-myths-about-defunding-the-police-debunked.

Kaba, Mariame. 2020. "Yes, We Mean Literally Abolish the Police." *New York Times*, June 12.

Kaba, Mariame, and Andrea J. Ritchie. 2022. *No More Police: A Case for Abolition*. New York: New Press.

Levin, Sam. 2020. "Movement to Defund Police Gains 'Unprecedented' Support across the US." *Guardian*, June 4.

Lum, Cynthia, Christopher S. Koper, and Xiaoyun Wu. 2022. "Can We Really Defund the Police? A Nine-Agency Study of Police Response to Calls for Service." *Police Quarterly* 25, no. 3: 255–80.

McHarris, Philip V. 2021. "Disrupting Order: Race, Class, and the Roots of Policing." In David Correia and Tyler Wall, eds., *Violent Order: Essays on the Nature of the Police*, 31–52. Chicago: Haymarket.

MPD150. n. d. "What Are We Talking about When We Talk about a 'Police-Free Future?'" Accessed January 9, 2025. https://www.mpd150.com/what-are-we-talking-about-when-we-talk-about-a-police-free-future. (MPD150 is an abolitionist group in Minneapolis.)

Purnell, Derecka. 2021. *Becoming Abolitionists: Police, Protests, and the Pursuit of Freedom*. New York: Astra House.

Rushin, Stephen. 2017. *Federal Intervention in American Police Departments*. New York: Cambridge University Press.

Vitale, Alex S. 2020. "The Answer to Police Violence Is Not 'Reform.' It's Defunding. Here's Why." *Guardian*, May 31.

Vitale, Alex S. 2021. *The End of Policing*, 2nd ed. New York: Verso.

Q27: How did the abolition movement fare in Minneapolis post-Floyd?

Answer: The movement has not had its way, either in Minneapolis or nationally. Whereas the general public recognized the need for change in policing, the movement's defunding and abolitionist remedies did not find deep support outside of movement and radical-left milieus. In the Minneapolis case, where general trust of the police fell to new lows after Floyd's murder, a ballot measure (Question 2) to dismantle and replace the MPD did attract sizeable support with 44 percent voting in favor. But a 56 percent majority were unconvinced, including most of the city's black voters (Shortal 2021). That Jacob Frey also won reelection in the November 2021 vote, the mayor being a vocal opponent of Question 2 and strong supporter of police reform, was a further signal that the abolition movement had not prevailed (Karnowski 2021). The abolitionists may still regard reform efforts as "phony" (Phelps, Ward, and Frazier 2021: 429); but the reform path, now under a consent decree with the Minnesota human rights department, is where the city was moving. Any good that may accrue from the forthcoming reforms should be credited, at least in part, to the abolitionists, whose years-long local work against police abuse helped build the momentum for change. Nonetheless, it is also true that the city remains much divided over its policing and public safety direction.

The Facts: Without minimizing the abolition movement's constructive role in pressing for change in Minneapolis and elsewhere, the movement could not lead or unite Minneapolis in a manner equal to its potential in this liberal city. The movement's ideology itself—with its surefooted assumptions about the nature of the police (see Correia and Wall 2021)—has discouraged the movement's full investigation of the issues and also discouraged activists from listening to people's views outside of the movement. Divisions emerged between the movement and Minneapolis's black community, notably in the city's predominantly black North Side, where gun violence was on the rise in summer 2020 and beyond and where the movement's defund-the-police messaging did not resonate well (Rao 2020). "This city is bleeding," said Cathy Spann, a resident in the North Side's Jordan neighborhood and who was part of a group that was suing the city to provide more police coverage. "We are asking for transformation of the police department, the culture of the police department. But right now, today, with communities such as Jordan that are under siege with gun violence, what we are asking is that we need public safety while transformation is occurring" (qtd. in Chapman 2020). That the abolitionists had not listened well to the city's black community is suggested by Minneapolis civil rights lawyer Nekima Levy Armstrong (2021) in an op-ed published after the defeat of Question 2. The measure, she wrote,

> would have almost certainly created a cascade of unintended consequences that would have harmed Black residents by reducing the number of police officers and the quality of oversight without creating an effective alternative.
>
> Supporters of the measure held no public hearings about it and made little effort to listen to Black residents' concerns or the opinions of experts. The main issue that many Black people were worried about—the significant increase in gun violence, carjackings and homicides here in the past year or so—was largely ignored.

A disinclination to fully hear community concerns about public safety, or to entertain diverse views about how to deal with the MPD and its abuses, limited the abolition movement's leadership potentials in Minneapolis. Though the movement did, through Question 2, develop and put before the people an innovative public safety solution, developing solutions through deeper collaboration with community—including with the majority who believe in policing—may have produced alternatives that have not yet been imagined and that could unite the community as well.

Further Reading

Armstrong, Nekima Levy. 2021. "Black Voters Want Better Policing, Not Posturing by Progressives." *New York Times*, November 9.

Chapman, Reg. 2020. "'This City Is Bleeding': Judge Allows 'Minneapolis8' Lawsuit to Move Forward." CBS News Minnesota, November 23. Accessed January 9, 2025. https://www.cbsnews.com.

Correia, David, and Tyler Wall, eds. 2021. *Violent Order: Essays on the Nature of the Police*. Chicago: Haymarket.

KARE11, November 3. Accessed January 9, 2025. https://www.kare11.com.

Karnowski, Steve. 2021. "Jacob Frey Wins 2nd Term as Minneapolis Mayor after Bitter Race." PBS, November 3. Accessed January 9, 2025. https://www.pbs.org/newshour/politics/jacob-frey-wins-2nd-term-as-minneapolis-mayor-after-bitter-race.

Phelps, Michelle S., Anneliese Ward, and Dwjuan Frazier. 2021. "From Police Reform to Police Abolition? How Minneapolis Activists Fought to Make Black Lives Matter." *Mobilization* 26, no. 4: 421–41.

Rao, Maya. 2020. "On Minneapolis' North Side, Residents Question Calls to Defund Police." *Star Tribune*, June 24.

Shortal, Jana. 2021. "Breaking Down Voting Data on Minneapolis Ballot Question."

Q28: How did the abolition movement fare in Congress post-Floyd?

Answer: Nationally speaking, the abolition movement's most significant post-Floyd achievement may have been simply to build a wide public recognition of the need for "major changes" in policing, as found in a July 2020 Gallup poll (Crabtree 2020). Over thirty states passed police reform legislation in the year after the Floyd killing (Eder, Keller, and Migliozzi 2021). Yet, no national remedy was passed by Congress. Two competing proposals on policing did appear on the national stage. One was a comprehensive reform bill, the George Floyd Justice in Policing Act (hereinafter, the Floyd Act; US Congress 2021). Though supported by Congress Democrats and President Biden, the bill wound up getting blocked by Senate Republicans. The other proposal was the BREATHE Act, an abolition-inspired plan developed by the Movement for Black Lives (M4BL). BREATHE gained many endorsements from progressive organizations but few endorsements from Congress members, and it was never formally introduced in Congress. Both initiatives nevertheless deserve study and can contribute much to debates around police reform and abolition.

The Facts: The Floyd Act was introduced by Congresswoman—and now Los Angeles mayor—Karen Bass (D-CA) on June 8, 2020. The first-ever congressional bill of its kind, it included provisions on racial profiling, use of force, demilitarization of police, data collection, and the setting of national standards. It was backed by major civil rights groups as well as by the Floyd family (Leadership Conference 2021; Shear and Fandos 2021). The bill's reception was heavily along party lines, with Democrats in support and Republicans opposed. Though it had no prospect of passing under President Trump, it did have potential after Biden's election in November 2020, and was reintroduced into Congress the following February. The Floyd Act easily passed the majority-Democratic House; it then stalled and later died, however, in the Senate owing to Republican opposition (Fram 2021).

The Floyd Act may have prevailed had it been accompanied by a grassroots national campaign. But there was no such campaign to speak of. And this absence itself is striking, given that an estimated 15 to 26 million Americans had joined the summer 2020 Floyd protests, this being the largest single protest wave in US history (Buchanan, Bui, and Patel 2020). Civil rights groups such as the NAACP did urge members to write to Congress in support of the bill, while Biden pressed for passage by May 25, 2021—the anniversary date of the Floyd killing (Cox 2021). But such activity becomes far more impactful when joined with mass marches and other forms of public presence that help drive social change.

The lack of grassroots mobilization around the Floyd Act does make sense in view of the rise of abolitionism and its general skepticism toward police reform, which included abolition leaders publicly *opposing* the Floyd Act. In fact, M4BL sent a March 2021 letter to Congress (Movement 2021; Letter of opposition to the George Floyd Justice in Policing Act," was accessed by coauthor Howard Ryan from the BREATHE website at breatheact.org in 2022. The website has since been shut down. The letter remains in Ryan's possession.) opposing the Floyd Act and urging instead support for BREATHE. M4BL objected to the Floyd Act primarily because it would devote further federal dollars to policing.

Derecka Purnell, author of *Becoming Abolitionists* (2021a), joined M4BL in opposing the bill, claiming that it would not have saved Floyd's life and that "police will still kill more than 1,000 people every year" (2021b). Organizers Mariame Kaba and Andrea Ritchie later elaborated in an article entitled, "Why We Don't Say 'Reform the Police'" (2022):

> Nothing in the legislation named for him would have prevented George Floyd's murder, nor changed the conditions that brought him into contact with the cops who killed him. Millions watched Derek Chauvin, a cop trained in "implicit bias," de-escalation, and the dangers of putting pressure on a person's neck ... snuff out the life of a Black man over a $20 bill.

Abolition leaders may be correct that the Floyd Act, by itself, would not have saved Floyd's life. But as coauthor Howard Ryan (2022: 39) comments,

> Police reform has too often been framed as a top-down endeavor entailing the passing of laws or the hiring of the right police chief. It has too rarely been imagined as a bottom-up democratic intervention by mobilized communities. Under the latter model, the provisions of the Floyd Act could provide rich tools for change by community activists. At minimum, the bill deserved vigorous debate on the left and with a wide-ranging assessment of reform, how it is practiced and could be practiced.

In July 2020, in a direct challenge to the Floyd Act, M4BL rolled out its own legislative plan, the BREATHE Act. BREATHE draws inspiration from the final words of Floyd and of New York City police chokehold victim Eric Garner: "I can't breathe." The plan forefronts provisions consistent with police abolition—cutting most federal aid for local and state police agencies, cutting federal prison spending, and shuttering certain federal law enforcement agencies such as Immigration and Customs Enforcement and the Drug Enforcement Administration. At the same time, BREATHE would provide a progressive wish list of economic safety through health, housing, and job guarantees, funded by restructured taxes targeting the wealthy and major cuts in military spending. Other provisions include voting justice, climate justice, and various forms of reparation.

Beyond progressive endorsements, BREATHE did not include a national organizing plan; its public face—a website urging visitors to email their Congress member, host a house party, and spread the word on social media—does not match the ambitious character of BREATHE's demands. Despite that limitation, the proposal does offer much to reflect upon, as equally does its ill-fated competitor, the Floyd Act. Because the bulk of police funding in the United

States is locally generated—86 percent in 2017, according to the Urban Institute (Auxier 2020)—BREATHE is only modestly a police defunding proposal. But it does fill an important gap within police defunding strategy, as discussed in Q27, which is that rerouted police budgets could not come close to providing an economic and social safety net. BREATHE, on the other hand, takes seriously the costs of a robust safety net and, by implication, acknowledges too that federal action would be pivotal for any viable path to economic justice.

Important limitations in BREATHE should be noted, however, beyond the obvious one of lacking an organizing plan. First, the measure's most ambitious and far-reaching provisions are those involving economic and health security; it is, in essence, a comprehensive anti-poverty initiative. Its frontal message, however, is about policing and police chokeholds, in the spirit of police defunding and abolition. Indeed, in the abolition movement more generally, the largest demands are economic ones, whereas the focal point is on policing, or what is often called "reducing the police footprint." We might then say that abolitionists—both through BREATHE and through the local defund campaigns—have made police defunding and abolition the doorway through which to achieve economic justice. And one reasonable question to ask is, why not simply build a movement for economic justice? Is that not a sufficiently grand challenge on its own? The implication of BREATHE, and of abolition's local campaigns, is that people must accept the movement's abolitionist ideas about police in order for them to win the economic programs. And since Americans overwhelmingly want policing—as seen in polls and post-Floyd electoral politics (Blake 2021, Craig 2021)—the front-dooring of police abolitionism does not quite assist the building of an economic justice movement.

The foregoing does not intend to suggest that the policing struggle be set aside in favor of the economic struggle. Because the major economic policies would require federal action, whereas policing is governed locally and with many gains possible locally, a policing focus may actually prove more productive in the short term. The purpose here, rather, is to begin generating questions and discussions of a strategic nature, where policing issues and economic issues—as well as a host of race, gender, and other issues—are explored as part of the same whole.

Abolition clearly does seek to approach the world in a connected way. "Our people are safe when their needs are met. We need guaranteed housing, quality healthcare including mental health services, jobs that pay a living wage, food, education, and childcare" (Critical Resistance 2020: 17). It urges that we allow full space for the imagination. "While reform requires us to affirm the current system and surrender our imagination to the carceral state, abolition encourages us to dream new worlds and challenges us to use our best thinking to build a better society" (Kaba and Ritchie 2022). What the social change agent must not forget, however, is that we all like to imagine, and that what one person imagines may conflict with what another imagines. Engaging with communities and then developing visions in a truly collaborative way may be a better way forward.

Further Reading

Auxier, Richard C. 2020. "What Police Spending Data Can (and Cannot) Explain amid Calls to Defund the Police." Washington, DC: Urban Institute, June 9. Accessed January 9, 2025. https://www.urban.org/urban-wire/what-police-spending-data-can-and-cannot-explain-amid-calls-defund-police.

Blake, Aaron. 2021. "The Electoral Demise of 'Defund the Police.'" *Washington Post*, November 5.

Buchanan, Larry, Quoctrung Bui, and Jugal K. Patel. 2020. "Black Lives Matter May Be the Largest Movement in U.S. History." *New York Times*, July 3.

Cox, Chelsey. 2021. "'Our Opportunity to Make Some Real Progress': Biden Urges Congress to Pass Police Reform by the Anniversary of George Floyd's Death." *USA Today*, April 28.

Crabtree, Steve. 2020. "Most Americans Say Policing Needs 'Major Changes.'" Gallup. July 22. Accessed January 9, 2025. https://news.gallup.com/poll/315962/americans-say-policing-needs-major-changes.aspx.

Craig, Tim. 2021. "In a Setback for Black Lives Matter, Mayoral Campaigns Shift to 'Law and Order.'" *Washington Post*, October 30.

Critical Resistance. 2020. *Our Communities, Our Solutions: An Organizer's Toolkit for Developing Campaigns to Abolish Policing*. Oakland, CA, October. Accessed January 9, 2025. https://criticalresistance.org/resources/our-communities-our-solutions-an-organizers-toolkit-for-developing-campaigns-to-abolish-policing/.

Eder, Steve, Michael H. Keller, and Blacki Migliozzi. 2021. "As New Police Reform Laws Sweep across the U.S., Some Ask: Are They Enough?" *New York Times*, April 18.

Fram, Alan. 2021. "U.S. Lawmakers End Bipartisan Police Overhaul Talks with No Deal." *Los Angeles Times*, September 22.

Kaba, Mariame, and Andrea J. Ritchie. 2022. "Why We Don't Say 'Reform the Police." *Nation*, September 2.

Leadership Conference on Civil and Human Rights. 2021. Civil Rights Leaders Call on Congress to Pass George Floyd Justice in Policing Act. Press release, February 24. Washington, DC. Accessed January 9, 2025. https://nul.org/news/civil-rights-leaders-call-congress-pass-george-floyd-justice-policing-act.

Movement for Black Lives. 2021. Letter of opposition to the George Floyd Justice in Policing Act. March. Accessed November 2022. https://breatheact.org.

Purnell, Derecka. 2021a. *Becoming Abolitionists: Police, Protests, and the Pursuit of Freedom*. New York: Astra House.

Purnell, Derecka. 2021b. "The George Floyd Act Wouldn't Have Saved George Floyd's Life. That Says It All." *Guardian*, March 4.

Ryan, Howard. 2022. "Police Abolitionism: A Marxist Critique." *Social Justice: A Journal of Crime, Conflict, and World Order* 49, no. 1/2: 25–54.

Shear, Michael D., and Nicholas Fandos. 2021. "George Floyd's Family Meets with Biden amid Push for Police Reform." *New York Times*, May 25.

US Congress, House. 2021. *George Floyd Justice in Policing Act of 2021*. HR 1280, 117th Congress. Introduced February 24. Accessed January 9, 2025. https://www.congress.gov/bill/117th-congress/house-bill/1280.

9

Conventional Police Reform and Potential Alternatives

The vast body of today's police reform in America is herein identified as *conventional police reform*. Conventional reform, at the federal level, finds major expression in the landmark report of President Obama's 21st Century Policing Task Force (President's Task Force 2015) and in the Department of Justice consent decrees aimed at ending unconstitutional patterns in local police agencies (Rushin 2017). At the local level, it finds expression in new police department policies and trainings; in civilian police review boards; and in the legal interventions of the ACLU and other civil rights groups, which often lead to court decisions (as in *Floyd v. New York City* 2013) requiring that police conduct complies with the Constitution.

The central limitation of conventional reform—its assumption of the law enforcement model of policing—is addressed in Chapter 1 of this book. Such does not argue, however, that progress is never achieved under that model. By what measure might conventional reform reasonably be assessed? Two potential criteria are (1) Has reform reduced police abuse in terms of the triad discussed in Chapter 2: over-enforcement, excessive force, and discrimination? and (2) Has reform made communities safer? A third criterion could well be added that asks to what extent reform has been nationally effective. Thus, we might ask about America's decentralized policing system and whether effective reform should include borrowing from the centralized police governance models that are more typical in Europe (see Hirschfield 2020). But for discussion purposes here, we pose the narrower question of whether conventional reform has been effective in the local context and within our highly decentralized system. In Q30, we look at potential alternative approaches for reform.

Further Reading

Floyd v. City of New York, 2013. 959 F. Supp. 2d 540, S.D.N.Y.
Hirschfield, Paul. 2020. "Policing the Police: U.S. and European Models." *Journal of Democracy* 31, no. 4: 166–81.
President's Task Force on 21st Century Policing. 2015. *Final Report of the President's Task Force on 21st Century Policing.* Washington, DC: Community Oriented Policing Services.
Rushin, Stephen. 2017. *Federal Intervention in American Police Departments.* New York: Cambridge University Press.

Q29: Has conventional police reform worked?

Answer: Conventional reform has sometimes worked and sometimes not, but even its successes have been mixed. The Department of Justice consent decree in Baltimore (detailed in Q21 in Chapter 6) succeeded in reducing over-enforcement but does not seem to have made the community safer. In New York City, a 1993 ban on police chokeholds has not been very effective, although civilian complaints involving chokeholds did decline in the years following the widely publicized police chokehold killing of Eric Garner in 2014. While the influence of the Obama task force recommendations on police reform today has been considerable, it is restrained by the limits of the existing police mandate, as described in Chapter 1. Thus, the ultimate effectiveness of the reforms is likely to be tempered with mixed results.

The Facts: Baltimore has been the site of one our country's largest police reform projects, conducted under DOJ and court supervision since a consent decree was issued by a US District Court in January 2017 (*United States of America* 2017). The consent decree, in turn, was the culmination of several events. The unarmed Freddie Gray was killed in April 2015 while being transported in a police van; protests and riots came in response; a DOJ investigation then found systemic problems in the Baltimore Police Department (BPD), recommending a host of reforms; finally, the City of Baltimore agreed to abide by the reforms as stipulated in the consent decree. The decree's reforms have now been in progress since 2017 and have yet to be completed.

The Baltimore decree includes provisions pertinent to all three components of the police abuse triad (over-enforcement, excessive force, and discrimination) discussed in Chapter 2. It also includes provisions toward making Baltimore safer. As we described in Chapter 6, BPD's progress toward these reforms has been mixed. When we compare the five-year period before the killing of Freddie Gray in 2015 to a five-year period following the consent decree, BPD cut arrests by nearly 80 percent. This is indicative of a reduction in over-enforcement. In addition to making fewer arrests, BPD reports a decrease in the use of force in the period following the consent decree. However, with regard to the third leg of the police abuse triad—discrimination—racial disparities in arrests have *increased* since the consent decree and monitoring began. Finally, with regard to making Baltimore communities safer, violent crime remains very high and has actually trended toward higher levels than before the Freddie Gray killing. What further complicates our assessment of the efficacy of the DOJ intervention is the fact that clearance rates for homicide and other violent crimes have gotten worse since 2018. Before 2015, 58 percent of homicides and 60 percent of violent crimes went unsolved. Since 2018, these numbers have grown to 68 percent and 77 percent, respectively.

The police killing of Freddie Gray in Baltimore had its corollary tragedy in New York City, where, in July 2014, police fatally choked Eric Garner, undeterred by Garner's complaint, "I can't breathe" (Goldstein and Schweber 2014). The attendant New York City protests, joined by other police-triggered protests nationally, led President Obama to announce a blue-ribbon policing task force that December. Amid the post-Garner inquiries, the city's Civilian Complaint Review Board (CCRB) issued a report on how the New York Police Department (NYPD) had, for two decades, hardly enforced its own policy (New York City 2014). Former NYPD police commissioner Raymond Kelly had issued a chokehold ban in 1993 (ibid.: 13). Yet, in the year before the Garner killing alone, the CCRB had received 219 civilian complaints about police chokeholds (ibid.: ix).

One takeaway from the CCRB report would be that the NYPD's own departmental initiative was not successful in reducing excessive force as manifested in the chokeholds. Over the prior decade, according to the CCRB, chokehold complaints had ranged between 140 to 240 annually (ibid.: 21). Another takeaway, however, could raise questions about the efficacy of the CCRB—or of civilian review boards generally (see Perry 2006)—in holding police to high reform standards. The CCRB had, after all, been created in 1993, the same year as Commissioner Kelly had announced the chokehold prohibition. Clearly, and despite hundreds of relevant complaints, the agency's oversight had not borne much impact on police practice in this area.

A more recent report sheds further interesting light on New York City's police chokehold story. Ostadan and Quigley (2024), in a July 2024 report published in the *Gothamist*, a news service operated by New York Public Radio, analyzed CCRB data on chokehold complaints over the prior two decades. The numbers were lower from 2015 to 2022, when the CCRB received, on average, 133 chokehold allegations annually—compared to an annual average of 207 from 2005 to 2014. The reduced complaints may well reflect the heightened public scrutiny over NYPD chokeholds in the post-Garner years. They may equally reflect impact of the 2013 court decision in *Floyd v. New York City*, which found the NYPD's long-standing stop-and-frisk practices to be in violation of the Fourth and Fourteenth Amendments to the Constitution. In the years following the *Floyd* decision, the NYPD's stop-and-frisk annual numbers declined by over 95 percent (NYCLU 2019), no doubt bearing a positive impact on the department's reduced chokehold complaints. On the other hand, Ostadan and Quigley (2024) also report that, in 2023, the chokehold complaints received by the CCRB jumped to 230—that is, close to the levels seen prior to Garner. One potential explanation for the increase would link to the well-known law-and-order politics of Eric Adams, the former police officer who was elected New York City mayor in November 2021, and who is alleged to be overseeing an increase in illegal police stops (Meko and Fitzsimmons 2024).

What we can conclude from the New York City record of police chokeholds and pertinent civilian complaints is that locally generated conventional reforms produce mixed results as a strategy for addressing excessive force. Even the quite promising results emanating from the Garner protests and the *Floyd* decision could be reversed by political and social trends, such as rise in violent crime joined with attendant law-and-order political campaigns.

While conventional reform has often fallen short locally, as in Baltimore and New York City, we can also identify problems in how police reform has been conceptualized at the national level. President Obama's policing task force was composed of distinguished police leaders, social activists, law professors, labor organizers, and an assortment of other stakeholders. It was convened in response to the killing of Michael Brown in Ferguson and the civil unrest that followed. It was also fueled by the police killings of Eric Garner in New York and twelve-year-old Tamir Rice in Cleveland, as well as the 2012 killing of Trayvon Martin by an armed member of a Neighborhood Watch. It was the Martin homicide that gave rise to the Black Lives Matter (BLM) Movement, which also pressured the White House to do something more to stop the racialized police violence.

There is perhaps no single document that has borne larger influence on American police reform today than has the Obama report. In many police organizations, the report has become a playbook of sorts. As we explain in Chapter 6, the report was well received by the International Association of Chiefs of Police, the Police Executive Research Forum, Major Cities Chiefs Association, and the National Association of Black Law Enforcement Executives. The task force tried to address specific problems such as new technologies, accountability structures, and increased transparency, but all while maintaining the status quo on the law enforcement mandate. Instead of questioning the purpose of policing in contemporary American society, the task force fully embraced the concept of procedural justice and evidence-based methods to find ways to do law enforcement more effectively and fairly. Therefore, the Obama report and its various recommendations may be limited as a guide for local police leaders.

Three themes prominent in the Obama report are procedural justice, trust of the police, and the idea of "guardian" policing. Procedural justice is based on four basic principles: treat people with dignity and respect, give individuals voice during encounters, remain neutral and transparent in decision making, and convey trustworthy motives (President's Task Force 2015: 10). These are *superficially* just and productive principles, but they do run into conflict when situated within the law enforcement game and mandate (see Chapter 1). How can police officers who must meet scorecard demands—say, for arrests and summonses—and who are consequently trained to view communities as targets for such departmental priorities, be expected at the same time to "treat people with dignity and respect?" By the same token, how can community members who are so targeted be expected to regard police as partners deserving trust? If the police are freed from the law enforcement game, and embrace new approaches involving authentic collaboration, with a frank willingness to reverse policing's historic patterns of systemic violence and discrimination, perhaps models of procedural justice can become more genuine and practicable.

The task force points to lack of trust as a central issue in American policing:

> Trust between law enforcement agencies and the people they protect and serve is essential in a democracy. It is key to the stability of our communities, the integrity of our criminal justice system, and the safe and effective delivery of policing services. (President's Task Force 2015: 1)

Trust must be earned. However, the police as law enforcement cannot—and perhaps should not—be trusted. If the role of the police in society is crime control and social order via law enforcement, gaining the trust of communities that bear the brunt of the law enforcement activity is virtually impossible—even if the officers are respectful, give citizens a voice, remain neutral and transparent, and convey trustworthy motives.

The suggestion to shift from a warrior to guardian mindset is also problematic. Task force member Susan Rahr, the executive director of the Washington State Criminal Justice Commission, wrote the following for the task force:

> How officers define their role will set the tone for the community. As Plato wrote, "In a republic that honors the core of democracy—the greatest amount of power is given to those called Guardians. Only those with the most impeccable character are chosen to bear the responsibility of protecting the democracy." (ibid.: 11)

It is interesting that Rahr highlights Plato's use of the term "guardians" in this way. In his book *Republic*, Plato referred to justice as that which is in the best interest of the state. He argued for rigid class divisions with no class mixing. "When each class in the city minds its own business, the money-earning class, as well as the auxiliaries and guardians, then this will be justice" (Plato cited in Popper 1966: 90). In other words, Plato refers to class privilege as justice.

Although the Obama report claims the guardian model as an advance over traditional warrior policing, both models actually share underlying assumptions of the law enforcement mandate, that is, that the police can maintain order, root out evil, and protect the public. The thin-blue-line symbol and "protect and serve" slogan capture this sentiment effectively. Whether the police are viewed as guardians or warriors is less important than the fact that police work is viewed as a war of good versus evil. The Obama task force did not acknowledge the fact that the American policing system—organized for crime control and social order through law enforcement—is an integral part of a larger social system that maintains racial and class divisions much like the role of Plato's guardians. Instead, it recommended evidence-based practices for crime control and better police-community relations, thereby avoiding the more difficult task of restructuring the police in American society.

The task force reforms did not address the roots of police abuse in the law enforcement mandate. Since the report was released in 2015, the problems of over-enforcement, excessive force, and discrimination in the practice of American policing have continued unimpeded (Chapter 2). Thus, it seems that the task force recommendations either have not been implemented with fidelity or they simply do not work as expected.

Further Reading

Baltimore Police Department (BPD) Consent Decree Monitoring Team. 2023. *The Community's Experiences and Perceptions of the Baltimore City Police Department Survey Draft Report.* https://www.morgan.edu/Documents/ADMINISTRATION/CENTERS/IUR/Research/DOJPoliceReport.pdf.

Floyd v. City of New York. 2013. 959 F. Supp. 2d 540, S.D.N.Y.

Goldstein, Joseph, and Nate Schweber. 2014. "Man's Death after Chokehold Raises Old Issue for the Police." *New York Times*, July 18.

Meko, Hurubie, and Emma G. Fitzsimmons. 2024. "Illegal Police Stops Have Risen Under Mayor Adams, Despite Court Mandate." *New York Times*, September 5.

New York City Civilian Complaint Review Board. 2014. *A Mutated Rule: Lack of Enforcement in the Face of Persistent Chokehold Complaints in New York City.* New York. https://www.nyc.gov/html/ccrb/downloads/pdf/Chokehold%20Study_20141007.pdf.

New York Civil Liberties Union (NYCLU). 2019. Stop-and-Frisk Data. New York. March 14. https://www.nyclu.org/data/stop-and-frisk-data.

Ostadan, Bahar, and Lia Quigley. 2024. "Has Policing Changed since Eric Garner Was Killed? Here's What a Decade of Data Shows." *Gothamist*, July 17. https://gothamist.com/news/has-policing-changed-since-eric-garner-was-killed-heres-what-a-decade-of-data-shows.

Perry, Robert A. 2006. *Mission Failure: Civilian Review of Policing in New York City.* New York: New York Civil Liberties Union. https://www.nyclu.org/sites/default/files/publications/nyclu_pub_mission_failure.pdf.

Popper, Karl R. 1966. *The Open Society and Its Enemies: Plato*. Princeton, NJ: Princeton University Press.

President's Task Force on 21st Century Policing. 2015. *Final Report of the President's Task Force on 21st Century Policing*. Washington, DC: Community Oriented Policing Services.

United States of America v. Police Department of Baltimore City, et al. 2017. Consent Decree. https://www.justice.gov/opa/file/925056/dl.

Q30: Are there alternatives for reform that could reduce police abuse and make communities safer for both residents and the police?

Answer: Yes. It is possible to restructure the American police institution to reduce abuse and make communities safer, but this deeper level of reform is not typically part of the American police reform agenda. The most progressive reform initiatives in our era, including the Obama Task Force for 21st Century Policing (President's Task Force 2015), hold tightly to the law enforcement approach to policing. The current crisis in American policing can be attributed to the ineffectiveness of conventional reforms to adequately reduce police abuse and improve public safety. The good news is that creative alternatives arise only out of crisis. Now more people are speculating about better ways to make communities safe. This includes proposals to defund or abolish the police, while replacing them with grassroots and social service alternatives. The proposed alternatives also include situational policing, which reimagines the American police mandate. By replacing crime control and social order through law enforcement with building strong and safe neighborhoods, a new game is formed. This new game would require new scorecards with metrics that include cohesion and trust among residents and with police. It would also include new playbooks tailored to community needs and developed by both residents and the police. At the time of this book's publication, however, conventional reform based on a law enforcement mandate remains the field's predominant remedy to police abuse.

The Facts: The institution of American policing is in crisis. This may seem obvious, particularly considering the heightened awareness and public discontent about police abuse today. However, the word "crisis" is used here in the way Thomas Kuhn used it in his book *Structure of Scientific Revolutions* (1970). Specifically, Kuhn described *crisis* as a stage in the historical development of a mature science. And this development, he wrote, has parallels in the development of a mature institutional practice (ibid.: 92). To make this point clearer, and to highlight the distinction between conventional and alternative police reforms, we must first describe this developmental sequence—or in Kuhn's term, its *structure*.

A mature science—or institution (e.g., American policing)—experiences alternating phases of *normal practice* and *revolution*. Normal practice refers to problem- and puzzle-solving activity within a community of practitioners who share a particular viewpoint and exemplars of practice. Kuhn calls this a paradigm. The American police mandate for crime and social order through law enforcement is a good example of a paradigm. Within this paradigm, police practice is a *game* (i.e., law enforcement). The logic of the game is operationalized in its *scorecard*, which prioritizes arrests, citations, and the seizure of illegal guns and drugs as measures of good police work. The law enforcement game also requires *playbooks* that routinize procedures for solving problems and puzzles. The contemporary police institution was organized for public safety, but its professional practice is puzzle-solving. Puzzles, according to Kuhn, are special categories of problems that test the ingenuity of practitioners. In the field of policing, puzzles include rising crime rates, low crime clearance rates, gang violence, shootings, homicides, burglaries, motor vehicle thefts, and other complicated public safety concerns. To solve these puzzles, the American police rely on exemplars in the field, many of which are "evidence-based" practices or model policies endorsed by professional law enforcement groups. Over many decades, a body of knowledge has accumulated about methods for crime control and social-order puzzle-solving via normal law enforcement practice.

Since the law enforcement paradigm predicts successful public safety outcomes, police officials expect success and fail to see anomalies, that is, the unexpected or unanticipated outcomes of the law enforcement approach. These anomalies include stable rates of crime and violence, reduced trust in police, increased police abuse, and low crime clearance rates. Kuhn explained the psychological nature of this by describing an experiment in which subjects were asked to identify a series of playing cards, some of which were anomalous—for example, a red six of spades and a black four of hearts (ibid.: 63). These anomalous cards were almost always characterized as normal by the subjects in the experiment. Kuhn said this occurs because of the tendency to make our observations fit the conceptual categories we expect based on prior experiences. It simply takes a long time to notice anomalies, and when we do, it can be extremely disorienting. Kuhn said the awareness of anomalies "opens a period in which conceptual categories are adjusted until the initially anomalous has become the anticipated" (ibid.: 64). In American policing, the anomalous (i.e., stable rates of crime, poor police-community relations, low crime clearance rates, and police abuse) has become the expected. Still, a paradigm change is resisted by the profession.

The practice of professional law enforcement produces anomalies that were probably first unrecognized but are now accepted as normal. For example, it is difficult from within the police profession to see—or care about—the harm resulting from over-enforcement, excessive force, and discrimination (as discussed in Chapter 2). It is also difficult to recognize when exemplars of effective policing do not really work in the way they promise, such as the DOJ example provided in Q29. There are many other examples of evidence-based exemplars for crime control puzzle-solving that seem to work experimentally, but probably only mask the structural limitations in the law enforcement paradigm itself. For example, consider two popular evidence-based law enforcement exemplars for solving the puzzle of urban gun violence and homicide, Project Safe Neighborhoods (PSN) and a strategy known as "pulling levers."

PSN is a focused law enforcement approach that targets violent offenders deemed most likely to commit future acts of violence. Once these specific people are identified by the police, a team of criminal justice practitioners and social service providers work to deter or incapacitate them. It is a carrot-and-stick approach. The police build criminal cases against the potential violent offenders, thereby increasing the certainty and severity of punishment if they are prosecuted. The offenders are then offered opportunities to change their lives by connecting with the social service providers.

In a random controlled trial of PSN in Tampa, Florida, between 2013 and 2018, researchers found statistically significant reductions in violence and gun crime and called the program a great success. Although there is little reason to doubt that this evaluation did show positive results in Tampa (Fox, Allen, and Toth 2022), the lasting impact is doubtful. Figure 9.1 shows homicide rates in Tampa from 1990 to 2023. The PSN evaluation period is identified to highlight how an evidence-based law enforcement puzzle-solving exemplar can be successful yet conceal the limitations of the law enforcement paradigm. Although the focus of the PSN research was gun violence, homicides in Tampa still appear to be rising.

Similarly, the law enforcement exemplar, "pulling levers," was evaluated as successful in Stockton, California (Braga 2008). The pulling levers strategy has officers select a particularly troubling crime in their jurisdiction as their focus. Then, the strategy calls for the convening of an interagency working group of

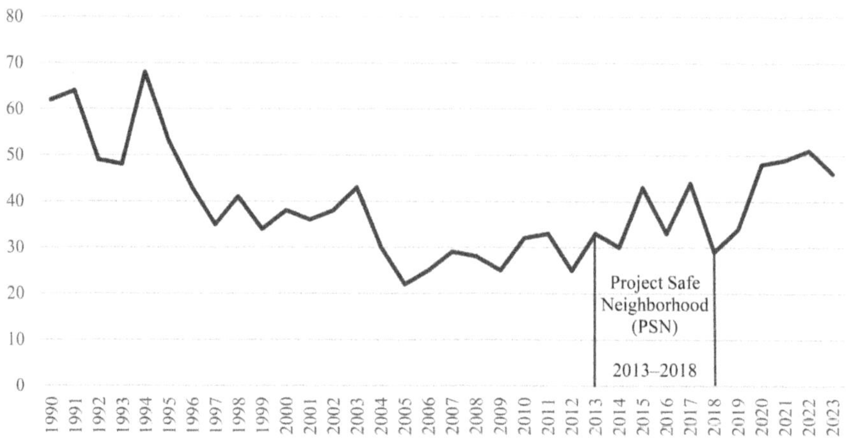

Figure 9.1 Homicides in Tampa, Florida, 1990–2023.
Source: Data from FBI Crime Data Explorer, https://cde.ucr.cjis.gov.

law enforcement practitioners. This group conducts research to learn all it can about the offenders and the crimes and to pull every lever possible to stop the violent behavior.

In Stockton, California, the police selected gun homicide as a problem and—as a first step in solving it—convened a Gang Street Enforcement Team (GSET). The GSET started by targeting *any* illegal behavior by active gang members. This included minor infractions, such as for motor vehicle violations or drinking alcohol in public. The police then sent messages to gang members that gun violence would "no longer be tolerated." If gang members did not stop the violence, then all manner of law enforcement (i.e., pulling every lever) would be applied to back up the threat (ibid.: 335). Following the intervention, the evaluation of the strategy was deemed "highly proactive and effective" by the Center for Evidence-Based Crime Policy at George Mason University. However, as shown in Figure 9.2, the real impact of this approach is questionable. Prior to the pulling levers strategy, homicides in Stockton were in decline. Homicides also declined during the research period. However, as of the end of 2023, homicide trends still appear to be rising. This is not to disparage the evidence-based research that is, no doubt, methodologically sound. It is just to show the disconnect between what is accepted as an exemplar of evidence-based puzzle-solving in the law enforcement paradigm and the anomalous results.

Like the anomalies Kuhn described in the card experiment, the observations of rising homicides in Tampa and Stockton seem to be unrecognized by the researchers and the evidence-based criminal justice community. This is likely to occur for four reasons. First, the observations do not fit the expectations

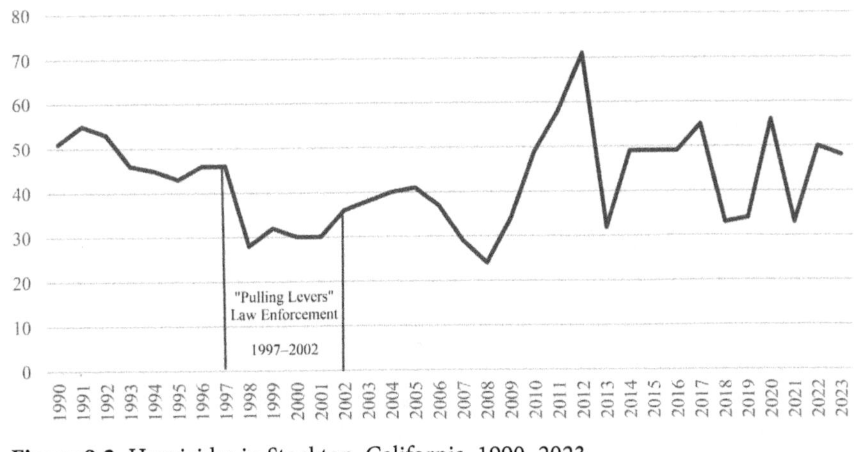

Figure 9.2 Homicides in Stockton, California, 1990–2023.
Source: Data from FBI Crime Data Explorer, https://cde.ucr.cjis.gov.

of the law enforcement paradigm—that is, that serious enforcement will have a deterrent effect on potential offenders. Second, results are examined via a scientific standard that prioritizes statistical significance over more practical assessments of police puzzle-solving. Third, there are political interests in keeping the law enforcement paradigm in spite of anomalies. And fourth, the professional law enforcement community—and all its supporters—fully believe that complicated puzzles like gun violence can be solved by the law enforcement approach despite anomalous results that might sometimes occur.

According to Kuhn, revolutions occur when serious and recurring anomalies create a crisis in a field. When this occurs, the affected community first tries to find ways forward without abandoning the paradigm. This is why conventional reforms have been the primary approach and why criminologists have described police reform since the 1960s as the "era of conflicting pressures" (Walker and Katz 2011). This dubious title reflects the increasing pressure from outside the profession to diversify the police, control police discretion, increase transparency and accountability, implement citizen oversight and community policing, end racial profiling, and respond to federal litigation and comply with court settlements, all while keeping the law enforcement paradigm intact.

Criminologists in the 1970s predicted the current crisis. Peter Manning (1978), for example, argued that the mandate for crime control and social order through law enforcement is impossible. He said it was impossible because the police have little control over structural conditions leading to crime and violence. Therefore, he argued that, to retain legitimacy the police must resort to theatrics—that is, manipulating appearances to portray they are successful. In this regard, Manning wrote:

> The police have trouble. Among the many occupations now in crisis, they best symbolize the shifts and strains in our changing socio-political order. They have been assigned the task of crime prevention, crime detection and the apprehension of criminals. Based on their legal monopoly of violence, they have staked out a mandate that claims to include the efficient, apolitical, and professional enforcement of the law. … The police have staked out a vast and unmanageable social domain. And what has happened as a result of their inability to accomplish their self-proclaimed mandate is that the police have resorted to manipulation of appearances. (ibid.: 8)

Since the police are expected to manage complex social problems that are outside of their control, most of their efforts are devoted to giving the impression that they are, in fact, successful. This is partly how the institution retains legitimacy in the eyes of the public. To the public, police officials promise to "protect and serve" and use evidence-based practices in doing so. But backstage, officers prepare for the battle of good versus evil, with a mindset of catching criminals to make communities safer. Despite policies and practices that may be ineffective, or even counterproductive and abusive, the police themselves—under their self-styled image as a thin blue line between order and chaos—cannot imagine why the community would be less than fully supportive of their efforts.

The police are frustrated and so is the community. When people "call the cops," they are moving outside everyday community life and surrendering to a higher authority, one that can use violence to ensure compliance (Bittner 1970). As discussed earlier, when formal social control by the police increases, informal social control mechanisms within a community may decrease. In other words, it may be easier to just call the cops than to mobilize a community response. However, when the community can no longer trust the police, alternative forms of social control may emerge, such as private security, Neighborhood Watch, or street gangs.

When the crisis cannot be resolved by the professional community of practitioners through conventional methods, new candidate theories emerge in a what might be called a "post-paradigm period of speculation." The conventional approaches to police reform discussed in Chapters 5 through 8—as well as the evidence-based exemplars of law enforcement practice in places like Tampa and Stockton—are attempts within the paradigm to deal with anomalies and seemingly unsolvable puzzles. The fact that these conventional reforms have yet to reduce police abuse or improve public safety is the reason why post-paradigm speculation in recent years has begun. This speculation includes calls to defund or abolish the police as we know it (see Chapter 8).

Another example of this post-paradigm speculation can be found in a report on police reform by the Brookings Institution, a liberal Washington-based think tank (Ray and Neily 2021). In chapter 1 of the report, the researchers recommend a new and different role for the American police, one that incentivizes positive outcomes rather than rewarding law enforcement outputs, such as arrests, citations, and the use of force. They describe it as cultural change in the following excerpt from the report:

> [There] must be a change to police culture regarding how police officers view themselves and view others. Part of changing culture deals with transforming how productivity and awards are allocated. Police officers overwhelmingly need to make forfeitures in the form of arrests, citations, and tickets to demonstrate

> leadership and productivity. Police officers rarely get credit for the everyday, mundane things they do to make their communities safe and protect and serve. We believe there must be a fundamental reconceptualization of both the mission of police and the culture in which that mission is carried out. Policing can be about respecting individuals and not using force. It is an ethical approach to policing that requires incentives for positive outcomes rather than deficits that rewards citations and force. (ibid.: 12)

This statement by Ray and Neily reflects a growing sentiment among police practitioners and policing scholars that there may be no way to reduce the harms and shortcomings of the law enforcement paradigm other than by changing it. What they describe as police *culture* is actually internalized police *structure*. By this we mean the game of crime control and social order through law enforcement. Normal behaviors described as problematic are not simply cultural habits passed down from one generation to the next that can be corrected via changes in playbooks or education, training, and oversight. Instead, they are the result of internalization of the rules and logic of the law enforcement game (i.e., its structure). In this case, cultural change requires structural change. Structural change means changing the law enforcement mandate.

According to Kuhn (1970), if the crisis in the field cannot be resolved via conventional reforms, new theories emerge, along with a battle within the community of practitioners for its acceptance. These new theories are often informed by new scientific findings and perspectives in related fields, such as those published by University of Chicago sociologists at the dawn of the twenty-first century (Sampson and Raudenbush 1999). They argued that both crime and community disorder arise from weakened informal social controls that have structural antecedents. This means that things like concentrated disadvantage, racial and economic inequality, and the practices of institutions—such as the police and criminal justice system—serve to weaken a community's informal social controls making it more vulnerable to crime and violence. They used the concept "collective efficacy" in their evaluation of neighborhood-level social control. Collective efficacy means "cohesion among residents combined with shared expectations for social control in public space" (ibid.: 603). In a practical sense, this means neighbors know and trust each other and they are willing to pitch in to help keep the community safe.

In a survey of 196 Chicago neighborhoods, Sampson and Raudenbush found that low collective efficacy was the most significant predictor of disorder and crime. These findings give us a new way to think about policing and police reform. The roots of crime are linked both to the social structure (see Chapter 5) and to social processes like collective efficacy. Although the police have little power to change the social structure, the police *can*—if reimagined—help communities develop greater collective efficacy and neighborhood strength. Aligning police reform with a larger, and arguably more effective, public safety agenda that targets the roots of crime would include ensuring basic human needs such as jobs, housing, and economic and social justice. Situational policing, as proposed by researchers James Nolan and Joshua Hinkle (2021; see also Markovic 2009), is a model through which the American policing system could build a new game and scorecard that focuses on the social process roots of neighborhood crime.

Situational policing is a way to think anew about the role of the police in American society. It is a new game in which the police and residents work together to create safe, strong neighborhoods and communities. In other words, the police are not in communities primarily to enforce laws, but to build strong relationships so they—the police and community—can make the neighborhood safer together. This is not to say the police would not enforce laws, but such would become a tool of last resort to be used in furtherance of building a strong, safe neighborhood. In this model, the strong neighborhood ideal becomes the desired end of all police practice.

A strong community is one where relationships are strong (high levels of collective efficacy) and crime is low. The situational policing scorecard shifts from focusing on police outputs, such as arrests and citations, to community outcomes, that is, progress toward the strong neighborhood ideal. In addition, new playbooks are developed by the police and community together. These specify the ways the police and community will work together collaboratively to make local neighborhoods safer and stronger (Nolan, Conti, and McDevitt 2004; Nolan, DeKeseredy, and Brownstein 2022).

Here is how it might work. Police officers are assigned to local neighborhood places. First, they work with residents to collect baseline data regarding levels of crime and strength of neighborhood-level collective efficacy. Next, the officers work with residents to summarize the findings and present them to a larger segment of the community and neighborhood. The officers and residents then engage in dialogue to develop neighborhood goals and strategies (or playbooks) for increasing collective efficacy and decreasing crime. Finally, the police and residents engage in continuous discussion and evaluation of progress toward the strong neighborhood ideal. The following paragraphs provide more detail about each part of the process.

On a scale of 1 to 5, please indicate your level of agreement to the following survey items.

1.................2............3...............4...............5				
Strongly Disagree	Disagree	Neutral	Agree	Strongly Agree

Generally speaking, the people in my neighborhood...

- Know how to work together to prevent crime.	1......2.......3.......4........5
- Are willing to help one another.	1......2.......3.......4........5
- Watch out for each other.	1......2.......3.......4........5
- Trust each other.	1......2.......3.......4........5
- Trust the police.	1......2........3.......4........5

Figure 9.3 Sample survey for neighborhood-level collective efficacy.
Source: Nolan and Hinkle 2021.

Collecting baseline data. To begin their work together, the police with residents collect baseline information on the neighborhood-level collective efficacy—which refers to the strength of cohesion and trust in the neighborhood and the willingness of residents to help each other. This is typically accomplished by way of a survey, such as the sample provided in Figure 9.3. In addition to information about collective efficacy, the baseline data collection should include information about neighborhood crime. One way to obtain this information is to ask residents whether crime in their neighborhood is higher, lower, or the about the same as the city or town average. The residents' subjective evaluation of crime in their neighborhood can be verified by official police data. By establishing both the level of crime and the strength of collective efficacy, the police and community are better able to develop specific strategies (i.e., playbooks) for making improvements in both measures.

Summarizing findings and establishing a starting point for collaborative work. The police work with members of the community to summarize the baseline data to establish a starting point for their work together. The starting point refers specifically to the level of crime and collective efficacy, as shown in Figure 9.4. The figure provides an example of how residents and police can use the baseline data to establish a starting point for collaborative work. In this example, the neighborhood is experiencing high rates of crime and low levels of collective efficacy. However, the starting point could be any place along this grid.

Developing playbooks for increasing collective efficacy and reducing crime. Police-community playbooks tailor strategies in accord with their

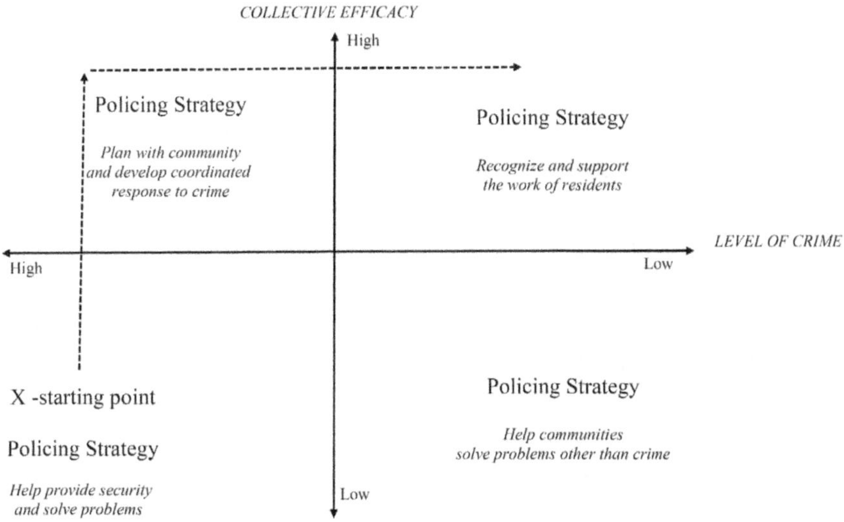

Figure 9.4 Situational policing framework.
Source: Figure created by James Nolan.

location on the situational policing scorecard. For example, in Figure 9.4, the starting point is high crime rate and low collective efficacy. In this neighborhood playbook, the police might agree to step up enforcement of public order offenses, such as open-air drug markets, while also working to get more people and resources involved in solving crime-related problems.

In this way, law enforcement for social order, which has historically been problematic, may be appropriate in a situational policing approach as a first step toward building a strong, safe neighborhood. But it is accompanied by a commitment from the community to work with the police to solve problems related to crime and to get more people and resources involved. If the starting point is high crime and strong collective efficacy, a playbook might have the police involved in collaborative planning and coordinating a system-wide response to crime. In neighborhoods with low levels of crime and low levels of collective efficacy, a police-community playbook might include the police working on issues not directly related to crime, such as helping residents establish after-school programs for kids or building playgrounds in underserved areas (Stokes and Gill 2020).

This type of activity is usually not considered "real" police work, because it is not law enforcement. However, in the situational policing game, this kind of practice is the real work of the police. Finally, in neighborhoods that have low crime and high collective efficacy, a police-community playbook might have the police joining forces to support the community's good efforts in a variety of non-law-enforcement ways. This is important because the role of the police is changed in this new game. Law enforcement is not eliminated, but it is one of many strategies that can be used in police-community playbooks to make neighborhoods and communities stronger and safer.

Ongoing discussion and evaluation of progress. The situational policing scorecard enables officers and residents to continually monitor progress along the two dimensions—crime and collective efficacy. The playbooks that are developed for each of four neighborhood types—high crime/low collective efficacy, high crime/high collective efficacy, low crime/low collective efficacy, and low crime/high collective efficacy—are easily adaptable to changing conditions. What is most important in this new policing game, and what should be recognized and rewarded in the police organization, is what the officers achieve by working in collaboration *with* the community. This is far different from the focus on police-officer outputs such as number of stops, searches, arrests, and gun and drug seizures that are important in the law enforcement game. To succeed in the situational policing game, a new police officer disposition and worldview must develop, one that helps officers succeed in their collaborative work in communities to solve problems and build relationships so that crime and other social problems cannot thrive. This type of deep, structural reform would have police focused on root causes of crime (social processes and informal social control) rather than simply seeking people to arrest or control. For more information on the situational policing approach, see "Tools for a New Situational Policing" (Nolan and Hinkle 2021).

The transition to a new paradigm is a revolution. However, in this period of speculation, no new paradigm in American policing has emerged as a front-runner. Situational policing is just one speculation at this point, and it is still being tested. Therefore, the crisis in American policing is ongoing, and more post-paradigm speculation is anticipated.

Many of the conventional reforms in American policing, especially those since the 1960s, have made significant improvements to normal police practice. However, the problem- and puzzle-solving ability of the police via the law enforcement paradigm falls far short of public expectations, especially when dealing with more systemic issues, such as gun violence, drug abuse, school safety, sexual assault, domestic violence, and all forms of police abuse. Enforcement-driven policing has produced harm for large segments of society and has fueled movements to defund or abolish the police. It has also created a crisis in the recruiting of qualified candidates for the police profession. However, it is against this bleak backdrop that encouraging speculations about a new and different role for the police in American society have begun to emerge (Markovic 2009). Based on historical patterns of progress through periods of normal practice and revolution, we anticipate this trend will continue until a new paradigm is found. This will bring forth a new game, scorecard, and playbook, providing solutions to public safety problems and puzzles that may make communities safer for both residents and the police.

We want to close this chapter—and book—with a quote from sociologists Pierre Bourdieu and Loïc Wacquant (1992) that we think is apropos to this period in the history of American policing:

> The task [of reform] is to produce … a "new gaze," a sociological eye. And this cannot be done without a genuine conversion, a metanoia, a mental revolution, a transformation of one's whole vision of the social world. (ibid.: 251)

With a new police paradigm (i.e., mandate and exemplars of practice), police officials would develop new types of strategies and instruments for their work. More importantly, as Kuhn suggests, they would see new and different things even when they are looking at the same problems and instrumentation as before (ibid.: 111). With a new worldview, perhaps alternatives to conventional reforms would show a better way to make communities safer for both residents and the police.

Further Reading

Bittner, Egon. 1970. *The Functions of Police in Modern Society: A Review of Background Factors, Current Practices, and Possible Role Models*. Washington, DC: National Institute of Mental Health, Center for Studies in Crime and Delinquency.

Bourdieu, Pierre, and Loïc J. D. Wacquant. 1992. *An Invitation to Reflexive Sociology*. Chicago, IL: University of Chicago Press.

Braga, Anthony A. 2008. "Pulling Levers Focused Deterrence Strategies and the Prevention of Gun Homicide." *Journal of Criminal Justice* 36: 332–43.

Fox, Bryanna, Scott F. Allen, and Alexander Toth. 2022. "Evaluating the Impact of Project Safe Neighborhoods (PSN) Initiative on Violence and Gun Crime in Tampa: Does It Work and Does It Last?" *Journal of Experimental Criminology* 18: 543–67.

Kuhn, Thomas, S. 1970. *The Structure of Scientific Revolutions*. Chicago: University of Chicago Press.

Manning, Peter K. 1978. "The Police: Mandate, Strategies, and Appearances." In Peter K. Manning and John Van Maanen, eds., *Policing: A View from the Street*, 7–31. Santa Monica, CA: Goodyear Publishing.

Markovic, John. 2009. "Neighborhoods Matter: A Situational Policing Perspective." *Geography & Public Safety* 2, no. 2 (December). https://www.ojp.gov/pdffiles1/nij/229228.pdf.

Nolan, James J., and Joshua C. Hinkle. 2021. "Tools for a New Situational Policing." In James J. Nolan, Frank Crispino, and Timothy Parsons, eds., *Policing in an Age of Reform: An Agenda for Research and Practice*, 193–212. London: Palgrave Macmillan.

Nolan, James J., Norman Conti, and Jack McDevitt. 2004. "Situational Policing: Neighbourhood Development and Crime Control." *Policing & Society* 14, no. 2: 99–117.

Nolan, James J., Walter S. DeKeseredy, and Henry H. Brownstein. 2021. "Police Ethics in Rural Contexts: A Left Realist Consequentialist View." *International Journal of Rural Criminology* 7, no. 1: 2–21.

President's Task Force on 21st Century Policing. 2015. *Final Report of the President's Task Force on 21st Century Policing.* Washington, DC: Community Oriented Policing Services.

Ray, Rayshawn,and Clark Neily. 2021. "Police Reform." In Rayshawn Ray and Brent Orrell, eds., *A Better Path Forward for Criminal Justice: A Report by the Brookings-AEI Working Group on Criminal Justice Reform*, April. https://www.brookings.edu/wp-content/uploads/2021/04/Better-Path-Forward_Brookings-AEI-report.pdf.

Sampson, Robert J., and Stephen W. Raudenbush. 1999. "Systematic Social Observation of Public Spaces: A New Look at Disorder in Urban Neighborhoods." *American Journal of Sociology* 105, no. 3: 603–51.

Stokes, Robert J., and Charlotte Gill, eds. 2020. *Innovations in Community-Based Crime Prevention: Case Studies and Lessons Learned.* Princeton, NJ: Springer.

Walker, Samuel, and Charles Katz. 2011. *The Police in America: An Introduction*, 7th ed. New York: McGraw Hill.

Index